Hong Kong Crime Films

Hong Kong Crime Films
Criminal Realism, Censorship and Society, 1947–1986

Kristof Van den Troost

EDINBURGH
University Press

Edinburgh University Press is one of the leading university presses in the UK. We publish academic books and journals in our selected subject areas across the humanities and social sciences, combining cutting-edge scholarship with high editorial and production values to produce academic works of lasting importance. For more information visit our website: edinburghuniversitypress.com

© Kristof Van den Troost, 2024

Grateful acknowledgement is made to the sources listed in the List of Illustrations for permission to reproduce material previously published elsewhere. Every effort has been made to trace the copyright holders, but if any have been inadvertently overlooked, the publisher will be pleased to make the necessary arrangements at the first opportunity.

Edinburgh University Press Ltd
13 Infirmary Street, Edinburgh, EH1 1LT

Typeset in 10/14 Ehrhardt by
by Cheshire Typesetting Ltd, Cuddington, Cheshire

A CIP record for this book is available from the British Library

ISBN 978 1 3995 2176 5 (hardback)
ISBN 978 1 3995 2177 2 (paperback)
ISBN 978 1 3995 2178 9 (webready PDF)
ISBN 978 1 3995 2179 6 (epub)

The right of Kristof Van den Troost to be identified as the author of this work has been asserted in accordance with the Copyright, Designs and Patents Act 1988, and the Copyright and Related Rights Regulations 2003 (SI No. 2498).

Contents

List of Illustrations   vii
Acknowledgements   ix
Notes on Transliteration   xii

Introduction: Criminal Realism   1

Part I: The Generic Landscape of the Post-War Hong Kong Crime Film, 1947–1969

1. Gangsters and Unofficial Justice Fighters: Realist *Lunlipian* versus Action-Adventure Films   27
2. Detectives and Suspense Thrillers: Remaking Hitchcock in Hong Kong   55

Intermezzo: Censorship of Cinematic Crime and Violence in Colonial Hong Kong   82

Part II: The Modern Hong Kong Crime Film, Criminal Realism and Hong Kong Identity, 1969–1986

3. A New Form of Criminal Realism   113
4. Crime Films and Hong Kong Identity   141
5. The New Wave, Critical Discourse and Deepening Localisation   164

Afterword: The Uncertain Present and Future of Criminal Realism in Hong Kong   190

Glossary	198
Filmography	206
Bibliography	218
Index	236

Illustrations

Figures

1.1	Newspaper ad for *Hot-Tempered Leung's Adventure in Hong Kong* (1947)	34
1.2	Shots from the interrogation scene in *We Want to Live* (1960)	40
1.3	Publicity picture for *How Wong Ang the Heroine Solved the Case of the Three Bodies* (1959)	46
1.4	Medium close-up of a masked heroine in *Black Rose* (1965)	52
2.1	Publicity picture showing Ng Cho-fan as detective Chong Chung-yan in *Murderer in Town* (1958)	59
2.2	Chui San-yuen as Detective Charlie Chan in *The Net of Divine Retribution* (1947)	62
2.3	'Detective Tso' (centre) investigates in *The Mystery of the Human Head* (1955)	66
2.4	The signature shot of the '999' series: a hand dialling the new emergency number in *Dragnet* (1956)	70
2.5	The male and female gazes in *Backyard Adventures* (1955)	78
IM.1	Nigel Watt (third from left), Commissioner for Television and Films, attending a switching-on ceremony at Salon Films, 16 June 1978	89
IM.2	Still from *Death Valley* (1968)	95
IM.3	Poster of *Back Street*, also known as *The Bodyguards* (1973)	100
IM.4	Subtly subverting the 1973 Fight Crime Campaign: *Payment in Blood* (1973)	102
3.1	Director Chor Yuen addresses the camera at the beginning of *The Joys and Sorrows of Youth* (1969)	123

3.2	Newspaper ad for *Teddy Girls* (1969)	125
3.3	Location shooting in a working-class neighbourhood in *The Delinquent* (1973), with onlookers visible in the background	129
3.4	Poster for *Police Force* (1973)	131
3.5	Poster for *Big Brother Cheng* (1975), showing the eponymous protagonist in front of a giant *yi* 義, indicating the values of righteousness, brotherhood, loyalty	134
4.1	Hung Ying (Alan Tang) accepts the dragon baton in *Law Don* (1977)	149
4.2	Still from *Bank Busters* (1978)	155
4.3	A Vietnamese refugee compares Hong Kong and Vietnam in *The Story of Woo Viet* (1981)	158
4.4	A cop surnamed Mao shows his identification, and a picture of himself with Chinese leader Deng Xiaoping in *Long Arm of the Law III* (1989)	162
5.1	Youngsters preparing Molotov cocktails in *Dangerous Encounter of the First Kind* (1980)	176
5.2	In the midst of a vicious gunfight in *The Servants* (1979), Inspector Chow (Chu Kong) insists on doing things by the book	180
5.3	Posters for an anti-drug campaign and the movie *Superman* (1978) are contrasted with the reality of the frail beggars in front of them in *The System* (1979)	183
5.4	Death of an undercover: the pietà scene concluding *Man on the Brink* (1981)	187
AW.1	Cops intimidate and harass protesters in *May You Stay Forever Young* (2021)	195

Table

| 2.1 | Hitchcock remakes in Hong Kong (1947–1970) | 73 |

Acknowledgements

This book has grown out of my dissertation, finished now well over a decade ago. As such it remains indebted to my PhD supervisor, Ann Huss, and I am endlessly grateful for her continued support and advice over the years, as well as for the inspiring example she sets through her work with and for students at the Chinese University of Hong Kong (CUHK).

Many friends have read early drafts of chapters or assisted by pointing me towards useful primary sources. I am particularly grateful to Jing Jing Chang, Tom Cunliffe, Victor Fan, Scott McKay and Sebastian Veg, who made time to read and thoughtfully comment on early drafts of some of the chapters in this book. Aki Kung offered significant help at a very early stage by pointing me towards resources I ended up using a lot. Jessica Yeung kindly shared some of her own writings, research materials and thoughts during the final phases of writing this book. All remaining errors and shortcomings are of course my own.

Other friends, many of them cinephiles and film scholars, have provided intellectual and emotional support over the years. Timmy Chen deserves special mention, for advice he gave early on that ended up significantly shaping this book, but also for the many interactions we had as co-teachers of a Taiwanese cinema field trip course, and later, due to the COVID-19 pandemic, its Hong Kong cinema variant. I am also grateful to the other friends who participated in the 'film salons' I hosted at my Kowloon apartment and that make up some of my fondest memories of the past decade: Celia Carracedo, Estela Ibáñez García, Nis Grøn, Lin Yiping, Benny Lu and Wei Ping. My gratitude further goes to Gary Bettinson, Belinda He, Calvin Hui, Karen Fang, Jennifer Feeley, Ben Scent, Yang Wei and Zhao Xinyi.

At CUHK, I thank my colleagues at the Centre for China Studies, both past and present. David Faure, Jan Kiely and John Lagerwey deserve a special mention here for their support for my work over the years, and for making the Centre such a welcoming space for research and intellectual inquiry. Many of the Centre's students have assisted with my research at various stages. I gladly acknowledge the hard work of Chan Yee Ting, Ophelia Chen, Janet Lau, Li Siyi, Shang Lisha, Tang Lin and Wu Yueqian – without them, this book might never have gotten written.

Several grants from CUHK's Faculty of Arts and an Early Career Scheme grant (No. 24604619) from the Research Grants Council of Hong Kong allowed me the time to focus on writing and share my research at conferences. The Faculty of Arts' Direct Grant also enabled me to hire a research assistant: Carolyn Lau helped me tremendously by organising some of the huge quantities of documents related to censorship I had found at various archives. I am grateful to Celestial Pictures Ltd, Eng Wah & Company, Getty Images, Kong Chiao Film Company, Media Asia Film Distribution (HK) Ltd and Television Broadcasts Ltd for granting me the right to use some of the images included in this book, and to the Faculty of Arts for awarding me a Publication Support Grant that helped to cover copyright fees and other expenses.

I thank Kenny Ng for pointing me towards the Government Records Service (Hong Kong) when I first started to get interested in researching the history of film censorship, as well as the staff at the Government Records Service, the Hong Kong Film Archive and the National Archives in London. I owe a debt of gratitude especially to May Ng and Po Fung, (formerly) at the Hong Kong Film Archive, as they were very helpful in giving me access to films and other research materials. Po Fung's writing on Hong Kong crime films has also been a very useful resource for my own work. At Edinburgh University Press, I salute Grace Balfour-Harle, Sam Johnson and Gillian Leslie for their patience and professionalism. My gratitude further goes to the anonymous reviewers who offered constructive feedback and suggestions.

Finally, I thank my parents, Guido Van den Troost and Danny Van Elewijck, and my brother Pieter-Jan, for their support from afar. I dedicate this book to my wife, Tinky Wong, and our two children, Karel and Tess, both born as this book was being written.

The Intermezzo incorporates excerpts adapted from three of my earlier publications:

- 'Born in an Age of Turbulence: Emergence of the Modern Hong Kong Crime Film', originally published in *Always in the Dark: A Study of Hong Kong Gangster Films* (English edition), edited by Po Fung (Hong Kong Film Archive, 2014)

- 'Under Western Eyes? Colonial Bureaucracy, Surveillance and the Birth of the Hong Kong Crime Film', originally published in *Surveillance in Asian Cinema: Under Eastern Eyes*, edited by Karen Fang (Routledge, 2017)
- 'Genre and Censorship: The Crime Film in Late Colonial Hong Kong', originally published in *Renegotiating Film Genres: East Asian Cinemas and Beyond*, edited by Lin Feng and James Aston (Palgrave Macmillan, 2020)

Notes on Transliteration

As the great majority of films discussed in this book use the Cantonese language (or some say, topolect/regiolect), I have for the sake of consistency opted to use a Cantonese transliteration system (Jyutping) for all Chinese-language film and book titles. For the names of individuals, companies and geographical locations, I have aimed to use the most common name under which they are known in English. For this I have drawn on the Hong Kong Movie Database (hkmdb.com) and the Hong Kong Film Archive catalogue. I have used Jyutping only where no such English name could be found.

The one major exception to the preference given to Jyutping in this book is where specific Chinese terms (such as *jianghu*, *lunlipian*, and so on) are used or Chinese literary classics (such as the *Shuihuzhuan*) are mentioned. As many of these terms and titles are commonly used in English-language writing on China and Hong Kong, I have followed the convention to write these terms and titles in pinyin, with the pronunciation in Jyutping added when they are first used.

For further clarity, I have also included the names of individuals and the titles of books and films in traditional Chinese characters when they first appear.

Introduction: Criminal Realism

UNBELIEVABLE AS IT may seem, this book is the first academic monograph on the history of the Hong Kong crime film. Indeed, although individual Hong Kong crime films have been the subject of books and articles, they have never been placed together and substantially analysed as crime films. When genre is a point of interest in the analysis of these films, the focus has mostly been on martial arts or action (for example, Hunt 2003; Morris, Li and Chan 2005; Teo 2009; Suo 2010; Yip 2017). The basic intervention of this monograph is to de-emphasise action, and instead to pay more attention to crime films' storylines, stock characters, narrative patterns and their real-life inspirations. Something similar has previously been done in studies on related but narrower categories, such as Hong Kong gangster films (for example, Lo K. 2007; Nochimson 2007; Desser 2009; Po 2014a) and Hong Kong noir (for example, Shin and Gallagher 2015; Yau and Williams 2017). The crime film encompasses both these genres and more, and while this makes it a terrifyingly broad category, this book asserts that it is the most appropriate scale to assess crime films' relationship to the sociopolitical environment in which they were produced. It forces one, for example, to confront the often-contradictory visions on the social status quo found in gangster films and police thrillers, and makes it more obvious that the boundaries between these two stock figures are frequently blurred – a feature of crime films anywhere, but one particularly prominent and significant in the Hong Kong context. Sketching out the development of the crime film over several decades also allows one to more clearly see the longer-term shifts in crime films' representations of, say, the colonial police force, or the principle of the rule of law.

Hong Kong Crime Films covers the history of the genre until around 1986, the year when *A Better Tomorrow* (本　 *Jinghung bunsik*) became a massive hit and brought the Hong Kong crime film to greater global attention. The films of its director, John Woo 吳宇森, and the many others that followed have already received ample coverage in the academic literature on Hong Kong cinema. Less well understood, however, is the fact that *A Better Tomorrow* – with its stylised violence and over-the-top celebration of homosocial bonding – marked a paradigm shift in the local crime film, away from the realist aesthetic that had dominated the genre from the late 1960s onwards. This book proposes the concept of 'criminal realism' to describe this aesthetic, treating it as an enduring mode of the crime film from its earliest years up to the present, not just in Hong Kong but around the world. What, then, is 'criminal realism'? Most simply, the term describes the type of – often sensationalist – realism one finds in crime films, a genre often seen as particularly close to 'real' (urban) life. More specifically, the term also indicates a realism that is 'criminal' in two distinct ways. Taking Hong Kong crime films as an example, it first of all alludes to the extent to which depictions of social reality (including crime) were anxiously policed by colonial censors well into the 1970s – this is a crucial but so far largely ignored factor in the history of the Hong Kong crime film. Second, it also refers to the way crime films tended (and still tend) to confound and transgress critical definitions of realism. Especially during the 1970s and early 1980s, Hong Kong film critics on the one hand promoted the kind of realism familiar from New Wave cinemas around the world, while on the other hand attacking or just ignoring the many local crime films that brought unprecedented levels of realism to film screens thanks to location-shooting, improved sound equipment and the re-creation of actual crimes or criminal environments. It is through the concept of criminal realism that this book understands the nexus of crime films, censorship and society that is its focus.

The next few sections of this Introduction explore the theoretical understanding of film genre this book takes as its starting point, survey the existing literature on the crime film and its relationship to society, and delve more deeply into the definition of criminal realism. The remainder of this Introduction will provide useful background information on the triads, the Hong Kong Police Force, as well as on some of the key values and concepts associated with Hong Kong crime films. These will help to illuminate the arguments made later in the book.

Film Genre

When scholars first started to focus on questions of film genre in the 1960s and 1970s, they did so mainly to seriously and positively engage with popular cinema, and to address some of the shortcomings of auteurism, the then dominant critical approach. For these scholars, genre offered a way to deal with the whole range of popular cinema's output and to chart trends within it (Neale 2000, 10–11).

Thomas Schatz's *Hollywood Genres: Formulas, Filmmaking, and the Studio System* (1981) can be considered the epitome of this earlier period's understanding of film genre: the book devoted individual chapters to what Schatz considered to be the major genres of 'Classical Hollywood' (the western, the gangster film, the hard-boiled-detective film, the screwball comedy, the musical and the family melodrama). Throughout *Hollywood Genres*, Schatz treats genres as unproblematic, clearly definable and bounded categories, and completely bypasses questions of genre hybridity that would stimulate much of the later scholarship on film genre. Building on the writings on literary genre by Northrop Frye (1957) and Tzvetan Todorov (1975) and influenced by the rise of Cultural Studies, film genre theory underwent an important reconfiguration in the 1990s, with a more fluid concept of genre taking hold. One of the figures leading this shift was Rick Altman (1998, 1999), who proposed viewing genre as a 'process' rather than a fixed category. For Altman, genres are discursively constructed and perennially in flux, with each new film, poster, review or even conversation having the potential to change the way genres are commonly understood. Genre theory, in other words, was moving beyond the genre text and started to pay more attention to genres' (discursive) context.

Genre theory's expansion beyond textual concerns allowed critics to explore the broader cultural contexts shaping – and being shaped by – film texts. An excellent example of this approach is Jason Mittell's (2004) work on television genres, which proposes to treat genres as 'cultural categories' which operate 'across the cultural realms of media industries, audiences, policy, critics, and historical contexts' (xii). While Mittell radically shifts attention away from genre texts, other scholars have maintained that genre is still useful in helping us understand how texts function. One such scholar is Celestino Deleyto. In a 2012 article, Deleyto first summarises several ideas that define contemporary genre theory: that genres are 'social and historical chains' rather than groups of films, that they do not have any essential features, and that the relations between different genre films are instead more like family resemblances.[1] Drawing on Derrida (1980), Deleyto further argues that all texts are generic, but do not 'belong' to any specific genre and instead 'participate' in one or many genres (2012, 223). Deleyto then contributes to the current state of the field by drawing on chaos theory to further illuminate genres' textual dimension.

---

[1] For instance, large noses might be common in my family, but that doesn't mean they are essential to being considered a member of my family. The 'family resemblances' idea derives from Ludwig Wittgenstein's critique of categorical thinking. Wittgenstein's influence is felt in George Lakoff's cognitive theory of 'chaining', which implies that categories as chains 'develop historically or sequentially': specific elements in the chain 'are related to those close to them but not to those in further regions of the chain' (Deleyto 2012, 221). Lakoff's ideas were first introduced into genre theory by James Naremore (1998).

In chaos theory, everything and everyone is part of chaotic systems, which are both unpredictable and uncontrollable, at least in the long run. In these complex systems, there is always an unstable balance between order and chaos, which impels their dynamic change over time. Deleyto (2012) continues:

> The internal structure of complex structures is fractal – that is, made up of elements that recall or resemble in themselves the structure of larger systems but are, at the same time, endlessly evolving, mutating, and establishing complex relationships with other elements. At any given point, a series of bifurcations may lead any of these elements to become 'strange attractors' and make the structure of the system converge around them, change its trajectory, create new systems, and occasionally, threaten to destroy the whole structure, which then may or may not reorganize itself in a different way. (221–2)

This is a productive way to understand the way genres function textually: not just how they relate to each other, but also how individual films (or even shots in these films) relate to one another and to genre categories. In this book, I will use the term 'generic landscape' to stress the broader genre context in which crime films exist; it is the total environment of major and minor genres in a given period that informs the genre (or film) under discussion, in varying degrees of intensity. Consistent with the more recent understanding of genre as developed by Altman, Mittell, Deleyto and others, this landscape is constantly changing.

Some scholars have tried to cope with what is now generally recognised as the unstable, ever-evolving nature of film genres by focusing instead on the more limited phenomenon of cycles and clusters. Leger Grindon (2012, 44), for instance, defines a cycle as 'a series of genre films produced during a limited period of time and linked by a dominant trend in their use of the genre's conventions'. A cluster, on the other hand, occurs 'when a group of films appears in the same period but fails to generate a coherent model or common motifs' (Grindon 2012, 45). Scholars like Grindon and Amanda Klein (2011) believe – in my view rightfully – that by studying specific cycles and clusters a more nuanced genre history can be pieced together. This approach, however, also risks resurrecting the oft-criticized practice of explaining genres in an overly sociological manner. Even at the more restricted scale of clusters and cycles, the risk of oversimplification in this practice remains substantial: studying a gangster film cycle might, for instance, lead one to a conclusion about the sociopolitical environment in which it was produced that is very different from the conclusion reached when looking at, say, a cycle of police thrillers appearing around the same time. As this book argues, it is, perhaps paradoxically, by looking at such cycles and clusters within the larger framework of the crime film and over a longer time that we can arrive at a more nuanced understanding of the enduring questions of law, justice and authority that have animated crime cinema since its inception. Different crime (sub)genres, cycles and clusters should thus not be considered in isolation from one another. The fact that questions of law, justice and authority are so prominent during so many decades of Hong Kong filmmaking is itself significant, and by looking at different genres/cycles/clusters together, we can more clearly observe broader tendencies in the crime film, such as the criminal realism focused on in this book. As the earlier discussion of criminal realism already indicated, my approach also considers factors outside the film text (such as censorship, international film trends and so on) as well as the local generic landscape. Taking into account the recent, more fluid reconceptualisation of film genre, the following section will look at some of the existing definitions of the crime film, as well as related genre terms that compete with it.

Crime Film

We can first consider a genre term that overlaps with the crime film significantly, namely the thriller. The thriller in fact preceded the crime film in becoming the subject of genre studies, with several books on it appearing in the 1960s and 1970s (for example, Harper 1969; Davis 1973; Palmer 1979). Since then, interest in the genre has faded, with only two important studies appearing: Charles Derry's *The Suspense Thriller: Films in the Shadow of Alfred Hitchcock* (1988) and Martin Rubin's *Thrillers* (1999). Derry's book promotes a narrower definition of the thriller: he self-consciously excludes certain types of films to which the term 'thriller' often has been attached, such as spy films, police films, heist films, horror films and detective films. He defines the suspense thriller instead as

> a crime work which presents a violent and generally murderous antagonism in which the protagonist becomes either an innocent victim or a nonprofessional criminal within a narrative structure that is significantly unmediated by a traditional figure of detection in a central position. (Derry 1988, 62)

Derry then goes on to describe the suspense thriller as a genre that can be recognised by the appearance of various elements, such as 'murderous passions, conspiracies, assassinations; an innocent protagonist on the run' and so on (Derry 1988, 62–3). While Derry places the suspense thriller under the umbrella of the crime film, Rubin (1999) defines the thriller in a way that more closely aligns it to the less rigorous use of the term in daily life. Considering the various genres to which the term 'thriller' can be applied, he deduces 'the overarching, "thrilleresque" common denominators that link them' (Rubin 1999, 4). These common denominators include the excessive feelings (such as suspense, fright, mystery, exhilaration) that the thriller generates, a central dialectic of control and vulnerability, and thrillers' frequently labyrinthine nature (Rubin 1999, 3–36). In contrast to Derry, who bases his definition on a film's protagonists, Rubin's definition is predominantly based on the affect generated by a film. Furthermore, Rubin historicises the thriller and posits it as an umbrella genre at the same level as – and overlapping with – the crime film, while also encompassing science fiction, monster movies, spy films, action films and disaster movies.

Derry's protagonist-based definition of the suspense thriller proved a major influence on later definitions of the crime film. Derry (1988, 57) himself attributes this approach to the work of (unnamed) earlier scholars of crime literature, who stressed the centrality of and the relationships between three major characters in all crime fiction: the criminal, the detective and the victim. While Derry assigned no less than seven major crime genres to those three main characters, Steve Neale (2000, 65) later simplified the model to just three: the detective film (focusing on an agent of investigation and emphasising detection), the gangster film (focusing on the perpetrators of crime and emphasising criminal activity) and the suspense thriller (focusing on the victims of crime and emphasising their response). In his influential 2002 monograph on the subject, Thomas Leitch similarly uses the figures of the criminal, the victim and the detective/avenger as the foundation upon which to build a more elaborate definition of the crime film. Largely accepted by later scholars (such as Thompson 2007; Benyahia 2012; Sorrento 2012; Elliott 2014), Leitch (2002a, 16) defines the crime film as a genre that 'includes all films that focus on any of the three parties to a crime – criminal, victim, avenger – while exploring that party's links to the other two'. He further specifies that the genre mediates

> between two powerful but blankly contradictory articles of faith: that the social order that every crime challenges is ultimately well-defined, stable, and justified in consigning different people to the mutually exclusive roles of lawbreakers, law enforcers, and the victims who are the audience's natural identification figures; and that every audience member is not only a potential victim but a potential avenger and a potential criminal under the skin. (Leitch 2002a, 15)

The audience's ambivalent attitude towards these two contradictory beliefs and the shifting identifications that result from this is what determines the place of each type of crime film within the larger genre (Leitch 2002a, 15). This also explains why in crime films the roles of the criminal, detective/avenger and victim constantly are undermined or blur into one another, and why crime is always in some sense a metaphor: 'Every crime in every crime film represents a larger critique of the social or institutional order – either the film's critique or some character's' (14). Leitch thus clearly asserts the existence of a link between the crime film and society, a subject we will return to in the next section.

With the crime film serving as an umbrella genre, Leitch devotes separate chapters to the victim film, the gangster film, the film noir, the erotic thriller, the unofficial detective film, the private eye film, the police film, the lawyer film and the crime comedy. The action film is notably not included as a subgenre: Leitch argues that, rather than collapsing one into the other, it is best considered as a separate umbrella genre, albeit one that frequently overlaps with the crime film. After all, 'action films all involve the attempt to right some perceived wrong through physical action' (302). Challenging Leitch's approach, Pribram (2011) uses the term 'justice genres' to cover the same subgenres covered by Leitch, while also including action films and their superhero subgenres. Using the term 'justice genres' rather than 'crime genres', she argues, serves 'to stress a discursive relationship with all judicial institutions and juridical ideologies, not solely the narrower grouping of films based specifically on lawbreakers or the conduct of criminal activities' (Pribram 2011, 57). Pribram thus puts the detective/avenger figure at the centre, while Leitch regards the criminal as the most important. As he writes, 'even when the crime film focuses on a victim or detective or avenger . . . those heroes become interesting, admirable, and heroic precisely to the extent that they begin to act like criminals' (Leitch 2002a, 306). The difference between the two is however mainly one of emphasis, and although I will return to Pribram's theorisation of the justice genres below, in this book I follow Leitch in using the term 'crime film'. The subgenres I include in this term differ significantly from Leitch's, however, as I focus on those that were prominent in Hong Kong cinema during the period covered: gangster films, detective films, suspense thrillers and police films, as well as crime subgenres that had particular local significance, such as unofficial justice fighter films (also known as Jane Bond films or *bangpian* [*bongpin*]), problem youth films, and films sometimes described by the Chinese term *shehui qiqingpian* 會奇情 (*sewui keicingpin*, literally 'society marvellous/strange situations film'). One major subgenre that I do not cover here due to lack of space is the crime comedy, a subgenre so productive in Hong Kong cinema, especially from the 1970s onwards, that it deserves a dedicated study.

While I will return to the names of various subgenres and cycles throughout the book, it may be useful at the outset to also consider the terms used in Chinese for the crime film. As in English, the relevant genre terms are often used quite loosely. For instance, a very popular – but problematic – term for the crime film is *jingfeipian* 匪 (*gingfeipin*, 'cops-and-robbers film'), which is sometimes used to describe crime films in general, but at other times refers specifically to films that focus on police protagonists, which are perhaps more accurately referred to as *jingchapian* 察 (*gingcaatpin*, 'police films'). Po Fung (2018), one of the most knowledgeable researchers of Hong Kong crime films, uses the term *jingfeipian* in this narrower sense. To further confuse matters, some commentators use various Chinese terms for the gangster film – such as *heibangpian* 幫 (*hakbongpin*, 'black gang film') – to refer to crime films in general: Teo (2014), for instance, treats *jingfeipian* and *heibangpian* as largely synonymous, translating them both as gangster film, but in practice using both terms to refer to the crime film in general. Finally, a popular and less ambiguous alternative for *jingfeipian* is *fanzuipian* (*faanzeoipin*), which is a direct translation of 'crime film' and is generally used to indicate a broad range of crime films (prison films, police films, gangster films, and so on). Aside from treating the crime film (*fanzuipian*) as an umbrella genre, I will in this book use the term police film or cop film (*jingchapian*) to describe films that focus predominantly on a police protagonist, and the term cops-and-robbers film (*jingfeipian*) for films that focus on the contest between these two parties and pay roughly equal attention to both. I will also differentiate between the gangster film or *heibangpian* and the triad film or *heishehuipian* 會 (*haksewuipin*, 'black society film'), with the latter indicating films that pay more attention to the cultural traditions and real-life practices of triad gangsters.

Crime Film and Society

The relationship between film and society has been the subject of debate from the medium's very beginning. Studies of film genre have been particularly obsessed with this question, with early film genre theorists drawing on structural anthropology and linguistics to treat genres as the modern equivalent of oral folktales and myths. The idea that genre films fictively solve social contradictions that remain intractable in real life stems from this approach and remains an important article of faith for many genre scholars today, even if the field has largely moved away from an earlier conceptualisation of genres as transhistorical. As Barry Keith Grant (2007, 30) has put it: 'In their mythic capacity, genre films provide a means for cultural dialogue, engaging their audiences in a shared discourse that reaffirms, challenges and tests cultural values and identity.'

If the interest in the genre-society nexus is central to genre studies in general, this is even more the case for the crime film in particular. As García-Mainar (2016, 2) recently noted, the crime film's 'social content' has been a staple of definitions of the genre that can be traced back all the way to early twentieth-century writings on detective fiction, and it remains central to the more recent definitions of the crime film discussed above. Illustrative is the fact that the crime film is the only film genre taken seriously by criminologists and sociologists, who study it as part of a new (sub-)discipline, 'cultural criminology', with at least one dedicated journal: *Crime, Media, Culture* (launched in 2005). A seminal book in this field was Nicole Rafter's *Shots in the Mirror: Crime Films and Society* (2000). Prefiguring Leitch (2002a), Rafter (2000, 3) argues that crime movies make two arguments at once:

> On the one hand, they criticise some aspect of society . . . often by encouraging viewers to identify with a 'good' bad guy who challenges the system. On the other hand, they enable us to identify with a character who restores order at the end, even if that means the punishment or death of the bad-guy hero.

As a criminologist, however, Rafter's interests are somewhat different from those of film scholars. Stressing the importance of crime films to criminology due to the influence they have on popular understandings of crime, criminal justice and the world in general, she argues that crime films present and popularise versions of criminological theory, for instance on the causes of crime.[2]

Given the significant overlap in the works of Leitch and Rafter, despite their different disciplinary backgrounds, it is not surprising that Pribram (2011, 65) proposes to combine what she calls the 'discursive' (criminal justice studies) and 'narrative' (media studies) approaches. Describing the justice genres as 'a generic network that constructs a dominant, collective "reality" based on discourses of justice and injustice' (50), she takes 'a larger cultural view that helps to account for these genres' social meanings and purposes' (51). Similarly, my account of criminal realism and the Hong Kong crime film aims to approach films as texts, while also considering the various contexts and discourses that they partake in. Chapters 3 and 5, for instance, discuss problem youth films, placing these films in the social and political environment of Hong Kong in the 1960s, 1970s and early 1980s that shaped them and that they helped shape. Hong Kong's rapidly changing social and political environment at this time had significant similarities with that of other capitalist economies around the world (for instance, the cultural impact of the baby boomer generation), which facilitated the circulation of films between them and reinforced global dynamics that Hong Kong films energetically participated in.

---

[2] Oddly, Rafter chose a famous shot from John Woo's *The Killer* (喋 *Diphyut soen-ghung*, 1989) for the cover of the second edition of her book (2006), even though Hong Kong cinema is barely touched upon in the text itself. This implies that Rafter's findings based predominantly on Hollywood crime films are supposedly valid for the crime film in other places as well. Naturally, there is some truth to that, but as this book will show, it is productive to consider the Hong Kong crime film against various other contexts as well.

The interaction of Hong Kong cinema with other cinemas is further highlighted in Chapter 2, which deals with the influence of Alfred Hitchcock's suspense thrillers in 1950s and 1960s Hong Kong. Hollywood undeniably was an important reference point for Hong Kong filmmakers, but examples throughout the book illustrate that it was certainly not the only one. My focus on criminal realism as an important tendency of the Hong Kong crime film will illustrate how larger global trends had very particular local dimensions as well.

In the period covered by this study, one crucial aspect of these local dimensions was Hong Kong's status as a British colony. Not only did colonial rule result in a capitalist society significantly different from the communist one that developed in post-war mainland China; it also crafted a unique film censorship regime that was sensitive to the depiction of contemporary crime until well into the 1970s. This sensitivity should come as no surprise, as the depiction of a highly visible colonial institution – the 'Royal' Hong Kong Police – introduced into crime films a political layer that is (largely) missing in crime films from most other places. The triads carry political baggage as well: Han Chinese patriotic resistance against foreign oppression features prominently in their foundation myths. These political connotations of law enforcement and the triads remain relevant in today's Hong Kong and are something that can be activated in multiple ways by both the makers and viewers of crime films. Particularly relevant in this regard is Law Wing-sang's characterisation of Hong Kong's colonialism as 'collaborative colonialism', and his application of this concept to the undercover cop film. Arguing that 'a certain tacit collaborative contract between the British colonisers and the Chinese elites in Hong Kong ... underpinned the city's colonial rule' (2008, 527), Law focuses on the Hong Kong undercover cop genre as a useful site to illuminate the particular 'structure of feeling' created by this collaboration – one characterised by treachery, conspiracy, betrayal and mistrust (522, 528). While the undercover cop figure is the most explicit example of the political tensions and identity-related ambiguities present in Hong Kong cinema (especially since the 1980s), I expand Law's claim to assert that these tensions have been present in the Hong Kong crime film more broadly, from very early on. In Chapter 1, for instance, I write about a brief cycle of films on 'guerrilla gangsters' that appeared in the late 1940s: these action-oriented films focused on gangster heroes who are diegetically redeemed by their patriotic devotion to the anti-Japanese struggle during the then only recently concluded war. These films exhibit a strong sense of Chinese patriotism (and identity) in an atmosphere of 'treachery, conspiracy, betrayal and mistrust' borrowed from spy films, providing an interesting contrast to the exploration of a very ambiguous Hong Kong-specific identity in the more recent films Law writes about.

Criminal Realism

The complex interconnections between crime films, film censorship and society are what the term criminal realism aims to capture. Indeed, the perceived closeness of crime films to the 'real world' frequently leads to evaluative claims about individual crime films' 'realism'. Realism, of course, is a very slippery term. When a film is described as realist, it roughly means that it is an accurate, 'truthful' representation of life. However, as nearly any scholarly discussion of realism points out, what is considered 'realist' can vary significantly. Marris (2001, 50), for instance, writes that films described as realist are perceived to give, 'in contrast to previously established artistic conventions, . . . a more convincing and contemporarily relevant account of the social, offering new insights that speak to their times'. Or as Pomerance (2013, 1) eloquently puts it,

> ['reality' on-screen] is yet one more of the 'effects' of cinema, a cultured stylization that must change with the knowledge, desire, and expectations of those who appreciate it. And the terms in which 'reality' is manifested will shift with what is technically, materially possible in the means of reproduction.

Hallam and Marshment (2000, xii–xiii) add to this that the formal concept of realism is allied to the notion of truth telling: realism is seen as appropriate for, even as obliged to, 'represent social reality in the interests of knowledge and social justice'. Its relevance to the crime film is obvious here.

Berry and Farquhar (2006, 76–7) have argued that realism was the 'hegemonic mode' of twentieth-century Chinese-language cinemas, even if in practice it was a mixed mode that was often highly melodramatic. The prestige and commercial appeal of realism are certainly beyond doubt when one looks through advertisements for Hong Kong crime films from the 1930s to the 1970s: in them the term for 'realist' – *xieshi* 寫實 (*sesat*) – is frequently used as one of a crime film's main selling points. Building on Berry and Farquhar's claims, Chapters 1 and 2 will explore how Hong Kong crime films from the late 1940s to the late 1960s were informed by the melodramas that dominated the generic landscape at the time, but also by action-adventure films with roots in pulp fiction and Shanghai cinema. While melodramas were more prestigious and often pursued a 'realist' aesthetic, the pulp fiction-derived films make less of a claim on reality and instead prefigure certain strands of Hong Kong's famed action cinema. Returning to this theme in Chapter 3, I argue that in the changed generic landscape of the 1970s realism became highly prized at the box office but was now paired primarily with sensationalism in a cycle of films that drew on gruesome real-life crimes, as well as on the 'real' worlds of rebellious youth, local triad gangsters and police officers.

As noted earlier, while the term 'criminal realism' on one level simply describes the type of realism we can find in crime films, it also indicates the illegitimacy of this realism in the eyes of many film critics, especially during its heyday in the 1970s and early 1980s. Interestingly, while major film companies like Shaw Brothers at this time touted the realist credentials of their crime films, many critics were calling for a local New Wave and a realist aesthetic that was defined against these very same studios and their films. As discussed in Chapter 4, these parallel investments in realism indicate the growing awareness of and interest in a distinctive Hong Kong identity at the time. Clearly, different notions of realism were at play here, roughly corresponding to the contrast between realism in the commercial/Hollywood mode and the realism associated with 'art cinema'. Bordwell (1985, 206–9) has described the latter as 'subjective realism', as it emphasises subjectivity, psychological states and realistic characters. Realism in the commercial mode meanwhile refers more simply to films' use of real locations, actual events and real-life figures (often taken from newspaper headlines). The events 1970s commercial crime films focus on – murders, drug deals gone wrong and so on – tend to be beyond most people's daily experience, but they certainly do take place in the real world. Likely due to the critics' disdain for local commercial cinema at the time, these mainstream films' realist credentials were rarely discussed. The realist 'revolution' in commercial Hong Kong cinema of the 1970s is obvious in retrospect, however, and has been noted both by Teo (1997, 97–108) and by Bordwell (2010, 131), who characterises the films of the 1970s as a kind of 'vernacular realism'.

Hong Kong filmmakers' interest in realism ties into transnational cinematic trends, with New Hollywood works such as *Dirty Harry* (1971), *The French Connection* (1971) and *The Godfather* (1972) an undeniable inspiration for the new type of Hong Kong crime film of the 1970s. In a description that could be equally applied to the young Hong Kong filmmakers of the time, Armstrong (2005, 83) writes about the New Hollywood directors: 'their attempt to tackle the times, coupled with an emotionally dislocated, rebellious and populist attitude, brought a realism into American cinema which survives into the contemporary scene'. Despite these broader trends, we should not lose sight of the particularly local implications of realism. Hence, the third and final dimension of criminal realism focused on in this book relates to local censorship practices and politics. As indicated earlier on, colonial censors well into the 1970s were very cautious with films that showed Hong Kong in a less than flattering light or could be interpreted as critical of the authorities: if a film depicted crime too realistically, showed sympathy to gangster figures, or depicted police corruption, it was at risk of being banned or cut. For many years, for instance, the censors distinguished between crime and violence set in contemporary Hong Kong – which was more strictly censored – and similar depictions in films set in another time or place. Engaging with Hong Kong reality in film was therefore almost literally a potentially criminal act, with political implications. Although the history of political censorship in Hong Kong has received substantial attention in recent years, most scholars have focused on the Cold War context and the international relations aspects of this censorship, largely bypassing its more domestic concerns. This book breaks new ground by looking at this more local facet of censorship, which arguably was vastly more important in shaping Hong Kong film production. Censorship is the main subject of the Intermezzo, and frequently returns in discussions of specific crime films, especially in Chapters 3, 4 and 5. These chapters show that the transition between the two main forms of criminal realism discussed in this book was significantly influenced by the government's film censorship standards and filmmakers' reaction to them.

In the following, I will provide brief historical accounts of both the triads and the Hong Kong Police Force, to serve as background knowledge for the various discussions in this book. I will also introduce some of the cultural myths and values associated with these two groups, highlighting the mythical origins that the triads share with Chinese martial arts, as well as the model of traditional Chinese masculinity that Hong Kong crime films frequently reference. Concluding the Introduction is a short overview of this book's structure and chapters.

Triads: Mythology and History

It is useful at the outset of this book to briefly recount the histories and myths surrounding triads and police in Hong Kong. The patriotic guerrilla gangster cycle of the late 1940s mentioned earlier, for instance, makes more sense if one considers the triads' own foundation myth.[3] This origins story usually starts in the early Qing dynasty, with the Kangxi Emperor (1654–1722) calling for the population's help against a barbarian invasion. Monks from the Shaolin monastery, long famed for their martial abilities, came to the rescue and achieved a resounding victory against the barbarians. Their success however led to jealousy at the imperial court and a plot to destroy the monastery. Only a small number of monks escaped the burning of the Shaolin monastery by Qing forces, with five of them subsequently coming upon an incense burner that miraculously appeared from a river. On it, they found a command to 'destroy the Qing and restore the Ming dynasty'. The five men established

---

[3] The following summary is based on Ter Haar (1998, 18–19) and the detailed reproduction of the foundation account in Morgan (1960, 28–49).

the first triad group, taking a solemn blood oath and becoming brothers of the Hong family.[4] After a failed uprising that aimed to install a descendant of the Ming dynasty on the throne, the five founders dispersed and founded triad societies all over China. While the traditional foundation account ends here, Morgan (1960, 49–50) also recorded later triad history as recounted by his triad informants, which connects the triads to various rebellions, starting from the Lin Shuangwen uprising of 1786–7 to the successful 1911 revolution led by Sun Yat-sen that finally overthrew the Qing and established the Republic of China.

Early scholarly work on the triads tended to take the triad foundation account at face value, highlighting the triads' patriotic and religious origins while arguing that since the fall of the Qing, the triads, having lost their original purpose, devolved into criminal gangs. Nationalist historians of the Republican era (1912–49), for instance, often highlighted the patriotic aspects of triad lore to support their own nationalist and anti-Manchu ideals (Ter Haar 1998, 25). Among non-Chinese sources, W. P. Morgan's 1960 book is exemplary of early Western scholarship on the triads. As Morgan was a Sub-Inspector of the Hong Kong Police Force, his book not only recounts the triad foundation myth in detail but is also clearly informed by fear of the triads as a potential threat to British colonial rule in Hong Kong. In the Preface to the book, the then Commissioner of Police Henry W. E. Heath wrote that the goal for the police was to keep triad societies divided, because there was always the risk that 'outside interests may . . . be tempted to assist or encourage such reorganisation for their own purposes' (Morgan 1960, x), which would threaten the stability of the colony. Claims like this illustrate how the police likely exaggerated the threat posed by the triads to justify increased funding and operational flexibility for the force. Heath, for instance, also implausibly notes in his Preface that approximately one in six Hongkongers is a triad member (Morgan 1960, ix). This number justifies his surprisingly modest goal of merely keeping the triad societies divided rather than aiming to destroy them, which is considered simply impossible – a police attitude one can find echoes of even in more recent triad films, such as *Election* (　黑社會 *Haksewui*, 2005) by Johnnie To 杜　峯.

Newly available documents from the Qing archives and elsewhere have since the 1970s resulted in a revised and more historically grounded account of the early triads. The new scholarly consensus is that the triads were mainly a form of non-elite mutual aid organisation that arose in response to the increased commercialisation, migration and instability of seventeenth- and eighteenth-century China. David Ownby's influential work (1996), for example, set out to contextualise triad groups – and Chinese brotherhood associations in general – within mainstream Chinese social

---

[4] Hence, a common name for the triads in Chinese is the *Hongmen*　　.

history, noting their similarity to guilds and urban associations. He argues that brotherhood activities ranged along a continuum: 'from small-scale mutual aid societies, little more than formalised versions of friendships, to large organizations of varying degrees of integration' (Ownby 1993, 16). Importantly, these associations achieved their fullest capacity in contexts where the state was weak or absent. The Southeast Asian variety, the so-called *kongsi*, even evolved into organisations that accumulated property and played an important role in public life in Singapore and Malaya (Murray 2002, 14–16). The activities of brotherhood associations easily led to criminal behaviour. As Ownby (1993, 16) puts it: 'Small-scale mutual aid in a frontier context frequently meant self-defense. Frequent exercises in self-defense could produce mercenaries, strongmen, and gangsters.' These dynamics also explain why triads were likely to get involved in rebellions.

While Ownby and Murray place brotherhood associations into the context of Chinese social history, Barend J. ter Haar (1998) locates 'triad lore' (encompassing the triad initiation ritual, foundation account, jargon and recognition symbols) in the broader history of Chinese culture and religion. Arguing that this lore is what really defined the triads vis-à-vis other similar groups like mutual aid brotherhoods, bandits and smugglers, he contends its main function was to forge unrelated males into a cohesive group. Triad groups were therefore constructed as kinship units: sworn brotherhoods with all members sharing the same surname, structured hierarchically like traditional Chinese families, and even practising collective ancestor worship rituals. Triad lore also gave the group a sociopolitical identity with historical depth, as the putative mission to restore the Ming offered power and legitimacy to otherwise marginalised members of society. Finally, triad groups' elaborate jargon, sign language and recognition dialogues helped to further strengthen internal ties, with secrecy being only a secondary concern (Ter Haar 1998, 461–2). Even though research on contemporary triads is for obvious reasons hard to carry out, most scholars and commentators agree that much of this traditional triad lore, including the elaborate initiation rituals, has now gone out of use. Without this lore, the triads might not be very different from organised crime groups elsewhere. Indeed, Chu Yiu Kong (2000), who studies the triads 'as business', concludes that, in terms of economic activity and organisational structure, the triads are similar to the Sicilian mafia.

Ter Haar's emphasis on triad lore is nevertheless relevant for a study of the Hong Kong crime film, as this lore informs the genre's mythmaking as well as its sociopolitical subtexts to this day. Also important are the cultural affinities between triads and Chinese martial arts groups. This connection is perhaps not so surprising: groups for which violence is crucial for protecting and furthering interests will welcome members with strong fighting skills. Nevertheless, the linkages between the two go much deeper, extending to their respective myths of origin, with Chinese martial arts schools similarly tracing back their origins to the Shaolin monastery (Ng 1980, 56). One version of this myth credits the founding of the five main schools of Southern Chinese martial arts to the same five refugee monks from the Shaolin monastery that in the triad foundation account established the first triad societies (Ng 1980, 59–60). As Meir Shahar (2008, 185) has pointed out, it is likely that triad societies traced their origins to the Shaolin monastery – then already famed for its martial arts and support for the Ming – to enhance their military standing and assume an aura of Ming loyalism. In terms of their social organisation, martial arts schools tap into the same broader cultural patterns and traditions that the triads draw on: both are almost exclusively male groups that turn unrelated individuals into members of a 'family' through initiation rites, with the internal hierarchy of the group based on that of the traditional Chinese family. As Jeff Takacs (2003, 885–6) has shown, members of some martial arts groups even behave as if they are biological descendants of their school's founder, participating in ancestor worship – again, much like the members of some triad societies did for their founders. As we will see below, the worlds of triads, martial arts and police are further connected to each other through the concepts of *jianghu* (*gongwu*) and *wu* 武 (*mou*) masculinity.

Hong Kong Police Force: Paramilitary Force, Corruption and Legitimacy

Although less shrouded in mystery and myth, the history of the Hong Kong Police Force is also a dramatic one.[5] Established in 1844 – only a few years after Hong Kong became a British colony – the force for much of its history recruited senior officers in Britain, with the bulk of its staff consisting of Indians and Chinese. Plagued by rapid staff turnover and poor-quality recruits, the early years of the Hong Kong Police Force do not seem to have been very glorious. In 1867, a new Police Commissioner, Walter Meredith Deane, dismissed much of the force and replaced them with a contingent of Sikhs recruited from the Indian province of Sind. As the Sind police had earlier been reorganised on the model of the Royal Irish Constabulary, Deane's reforms turned the Hong Kong Police Force into an efficient paramilitary organisation, with the prime aim of maintaining public order (Gaylord and Traver 1995, 25–7). With much of the force recruited overseas until 1945, it is easy to imagine how the police 'appeared to the indigenous Chinese as an occupying

---

[5] In recognition of its performance during the 1967 riots, the Hong Kong Police Force became the *Royal* Hong Kong Police Force in 1969. With the 1997 Handover, it lost this Royal title.

army and therefore enjoyed very little legitimacy' (Deflem et al. 2008, 351). The colonial administration relaxed the limits on local recruitment after 1945, in large part due to the loss of other colonies which had served for many years as important sources of police recruits (Jiao 2007, 3–4). Still, the localisation of the higher levels of police hierarchy moved more slowly than that of other government departments, so that even in the mid-1990s, most senior-level police officers were still expatriates (Deflem et al. 2008, 351).

Aware of its image problem, the Hong Kong Police Force in the 1960s started to invest in public relations, in the hope that this would increase public cooperation and help to counter criticism. In this effort, they were – ironically – helped by the Leftist Riots of 1967, which in their later phase devolved into terrorist bombings that resulted in civilian casualties. Given their success in bringing an end to this violence, the force's popularity received a boost (Lethbridge 1985, 69; Gaylord and Traver 1995, 30). Although the riots inspired even more police investment in public relations, the force's reputation declined again in the following years. An important reason for this was the growing public outrage with police corruption, and, possibly, the perception of an uncontrollable (youth) crime wave in the colony. These two phenomena may have been related: Lethbridge (1985, 72–3) speculates that triad collaboration with the police during the 1967 riots played a part in the crime wave that followed, as it made the police go soft on organised crime and worsened the problem of police corruption.[6] This period of the late 1960s and early 1970s saw the rise of powerful drug lords with high-ranking members of the police force on their payroll, followed by both groups' downfall after the establishment of the Independent Commission Against Corruption (ICAC) in 1974 and the launch of several Fight Crime Campaigns from 1973 onwards. These dramatic events were crucial to the appearance in the 1970s of what in this book I will call the 'modern Hong Kong crime film' and they continue to inspire filmmakers to this day.[7] These developments will be discussed in more detail in Chapters 3, 4 and 5.

The successful dismantling of corruption syndicates within the police force by the ICAC and the police's success in taking down some of the most well-known drug lords improved the legitimacy of the police and the colonial government. Along with massive spending on infrastructure, public housing, healthcare and education, the

---

[6] This outcome, it should be noted, was the reverse of the aftermath of the 1956 riots, which the police blamed on the triads, and which was followed by a crackdown on triad activity (Jones and Vagg 2007, 362–3).

[7] Most recently, Philip Yung 子光 revisited this period's events in *Where the Wind Blows* (再 時 *Fung zoi hei si*, 2022). A few years ago, the Hong Kong-mainland co-production *Chasing the Dragon* (*Zeoilung*, 2017), directed by Wong Jing 晶 and Jason Kwan 智 , also drew on this history and became a major box office success in mainland China.

1970s also saw an intensification of the localisation drive within the government. All this ended up fostering local pride and the much-noted growth of a distinct Hong Kong identity. For the police, these changes happened so rapidly that by 1983, journalist Kevin Sinclair could – without too much irony – describe them as 'Asia's Finest'. The force's high level of public support was lost only recently, when its sometimes violent suppression of protest movements in 2014 and in 2019 turned a large segment of the population against it. If anything, these recent events highlighted the long-obscured paramilitary nature of the police force and illustrated – in a kind of replay of 1967 – the police's loyalty to the central authorities. This time, of course, these authorities were not based in London, but in Beijing.

Key Values and Concepts in Hong Kong Crime Films

Even occasional viewers of Hong Kong martial arts and gangster films will have encountered the concept of *jianghu* (literally 'rivers and lakes'), a term with multiple connotations. As used in daily life, it indicates a precarious existence by one's wits alone (for instance, as one enters the world of commerce or becomes a migrant worker, one can refer to oneself as 'entering the *jianghu*'). Very often nowadays, it is also taken to refer specifically to the criminal underworld. In popular culture, the *jianghu* represents a dangerous and morally ambiguous imaginary realm, one, according to Boretz (2011, 32), that 'parallels the everyday', but is 'never mundane, more an intensification than an exaggeration of the ordinary' – a description that indicates *jianghu*'s affinity with the concept of criminal realism discussed above. In martial arts fiction, the term *jianghu* evokes the fantastic world of Robin Hood-like bandits, adventurers, thieves and gamblers, in which swordsmen and other martial adepts roam about looking for fame through acts of heroism. In films, comic books and novels with a contemporary setting, the *jianghu* is the lawless world of gamblers, gangsters and prostitutes in which *yiqi*　　(*jihei*, 'honour, righteousness and loyalty') is paramount and in a sense replaces the laws of family, society and state (Shahar 2001, 380; Boretz 2011, 35–6). *Jianghu* is often seen as closely connected to working-class life: Boretz (2011, 35) for instance argues that *jianghu* 'is intrinsic to, and in some ways constitutive of, working-class society, not a separate sphere of deviance'. As a world that can only exist 'beyond the stability and security of village and family and conventional occupations' (33), it is moreover a sphere bound to increase in relevance in the process of modernisation and urbanisation.

Just as *jianghu* connects the (imaginary) worlds of martial arts, modern-day crime and working-class life, so does *wu* masculinity. The *wen-wu* 文武 (*man-mou*, 'civil-military') dyad structured many areas of (traditional) Chinese culture, including the imperial bureaucracy, religious rituals and theatre. This dyad has been used by Kam Louie to theorise Chinese masculinity. Louie argues that *wen* and *wu* offer two models for Chinese masculinity, with *wen* associated primarily with the figure of the Confucian scholar and *wu* with the martial hero. Both *wen* and *wu* are acceptable models of masculinity, although the ideal man should possess both, and *wen* has historically often been valued more highly than *wu* (Louie 2002, 1–21). Louie further distinguishes between two types of *wu* masculinity, each exemplified by a famous character from China's literary classics. One type is the *yingxiong* (*jinghung*, 'hero'), associated more with upper-class men and exemplified by the famous general Guan Yu from the literary classic *Sanguo yanyi* 三國 (*Saamgwok jinji*, *Romance of the Three Kingdoms*); the other is the *haohan* 好 (*houhon*, 'good fellow'), associated with working-class men and exemplified by the outlaw Wu Song from another classic novel, *Shuihuzhuan* 傳 (*Seoiwuzyun*, *Water Margin*). While triads worship Guan Yu, they arguably have more in common with Wu Song. Wu Song is known for his enormous appetite for alcohol and meat, his barehanded slaying of a tiger when drunk, and his rather casual attitude towards murder (Louie 2002, 78–83). The translation of *haohan* as 'good fellow' indicates the importance a *haohan* places on brotherhood – another possible translation for the above-mentioned *yiqi*. As Jenner (1996, 2) writes, a *haohan* is someone willing to 'take a knife in the ribs for a mate'. Indeed, 'the recklessness of the big destructive gesture is . . . central to the *haohan* ethic' (5). With their shared myth of origins, familial organisational structures, *jianghu* universe, and *wu* masculinity, the world of triads and martial artists are connected to one another at multiple levels. Tellingly, when Louie (2002, 140–59) discusses the contemporary internationalisation of *wu* masculinity he focuses on the international success of Hong Kong stars Bruce Lee 李小 , Jackie Chan 成 and Chow Yun-fat 周 – the first two famed martial arts performers, the latter a heroic gangster icon. The significant overlap between the crime film and the action film in Hong Kong is therefore not surprising, and the two often feed into one another.

The affinities between policemen and triads in Hong Kong films similarly have deep cultural roots. Like the triads, Hong Kong policemen traditionally worship Guan Yu. This worship of a deity embodying brotherhood indicates how both groups share in some of the same values. Indeed, separated from ordinary citizens and often faced with public hostility, police anywhere tend to have strong group loyalty. In a further similarity to the triads, most policemen tend to be working class and aspire to a *haohan* masculinity (Jenner 1996, 7). Although Hong Kong cops are supposed to enforce the law – which, as a symbol of rationality, order and state authority, is antithetical to the *jianghu* – their job frequently requires them to operate in the *jianghu*, with some unambiguously becoming a part of it (such as corrupt cops and undercover agents). In this regard, Lethbridge (1985, 34–5) makes the following relevant observation:

> Corruption is a latent occupational disease for all law enforcers, if only because they maintain a symbiotic relationship with the underworld; they participate in, to a lesser or greater degree, a criminal subculture, they frequent the same milieux . . . This is not a black-and-white world, of good and bad, but a grey *terrain vague*, where hunter and hunted may come to share the same ambiguous values and grow estranged from the conventional world.

While Lethbridge never uses the term *jianghu*, this is actually a pretty good description for it. Hence, although the blurred boundary between cops and gangsters is common in crime films around the world, Hong Kong cinema's particularly frequent elaboration of this theme can in part be attributed to this broader cultural context, in which the affinity between the two groups is explicitly acknowledged.

Chapter Overview

To trace the history of the Hong Kong crime film and its two main forms of criminal realism from the late 1940s to the mid-1980s, this book is divided into two parts. The Intermezzo connects these two parts and is different from the other chapters in that it focuses squarely on the Hong Kong censorship apparatus in the late 1960s and 1970s and the changes in the censorship of cinematic crime and violence at this time – changes that this book argues were crucial in the appearance of the modern Hong Kong crime film and the form of criminal realism that dominated it from the late 1960s to the mid-1980s. All the other chapters focus mainly on film texts: they outline significant subgenres and cycles in the crime film, situate them in the broader generic landscape, and sketch out the various local, regional and international contexts they interacted with. The advantage of this structure is that it brings into sharper focus the continuities but also the contrasts between the two distinct eras of Hong Kong crime cinema covered here: the first one from the late 1940s to the mid-1960s (Part I), and the second from the late 1960s to the mid-1980s (Part II). This mix of difference and continuity is reflected in my use of the term 'criminal realism' for films of both periods, alongside the distinction I make between the two periods by talking of the appearance in the 1970s of the modern Hong Kong crime film.

Chapter 1 sketches out the contours of the post-war Hong Kong crime film and the criminal realism of this period. Against the larger generic landscape from the late 1940s to the late 1960s, it deals with crime films that focus on a criminal protagonist, primarily gangster films and what I call 'unofficial justice fighter films'. A dominant (sub)genre in later decades, the gangster film was a minor category at the time. Still, a few distinct albeit brief cycles can be discerned, such as the patriotic gangster-turned-guerrilla fighter film of the late 1940s and early 1950s, and the reformed gangster films of the late 1960s. The unofficial justice fighter film is a rather unique (sub)genre with pre-1949 Shanghai roots that flourished in Hong Kong from the late 1950s to the late 1960s. Translating tropes from traditional martial arts novels to a modern urban setting and absorbing elements from detective, cat burglar and American superhero/vigilante tales, these films usually featured female action heroes and are sometimes referred to as 'Jane Bond' films, even though their appearance actually predates the global popularity of James Bond. Alongside an overview of these two subgenres, this chapter also pinpoints two 'strange attractors' in the generic landscape of Hong Kong cinema during this period and their influence on the crime film: melodrama and pulp fiction-derived action-adventure. It is mainly in melodramas that the criminal realism of this period can be located. Pulp fiction-derived action-adventure is no less important, however, as it prefigured later Hong Kong action cinema. The modern Hong Kong crime film and the criminal realism of the 1970s can in fact be considered as a combination of these two forms.

Chapter 2 completes the overview of the post-war crime film by focusing on films organised around the two other central protagonists of crime films besides criminals: detectives (the detective film) and victims (the suspense thriller). Unlike the gangster film, these were very productive genres during the 1950s and 1960s, and my account of both is limited to a few key film cycles and figures. In my discussion of the detective film, I highlight the late 1940s influence of Hollywood and Shanghai cinema in the form of local versions of the famous Chinese American film detective, Charlie Chan. I also single out for attention the action star Tso Tat-wah 曹　, an icon of *haohan* masculinity and someone so known for his detective roles that decades later people still referred to him affectionately as 'Detective Tso'. Next, my overview of the suspense thriller deals with the role of the Kong Ngee film studio and the influential '999' series of crime films it produced, which at the time marked a shift away from the teary realist melodramas of the early post-war years towards a more light-hearted, urban and middle-class type of cinema. Aside from sketching out these two genres, this chapter also engages questions surrounding the role of the individual director vis-à-vis a genre, and the relationship between Hong Kong and transnational cinema. It initially does this by taking a closer look at *Murderer in Town* (　城兇影 *Hoengsing hungjing*, 1958), by celebrated director Lee Tit, whose gangster films are covered in Chapter 1. Then, a close analysis of *Backyard Adventures* (後　 *Haucoeng*, 1955), a remake of Alfred Hitchcock's *Rear Window* (1954) provides a case study on how Hong Kong (crime) cinema relates to other (crime) cinemas. A comparative analysis of the two films highlights how the local generic landscape and other contextual factors shape local remakes of foreign films.

As a bridge between the two main parts of this book, the Intermezzo temporarily leaves behind the textual analysis that dominates the other chapters and instead sets out to show how the colonial government's changing practice of film censorship shaped genre filmmaking in the late 1960s and early 1970s, playing a role in the successive fads for swordplay, kung fu and crime films. Unlike in earlier decades, Hong Kong censors in the 1970s became more responsive to the public, with archival documents shedding light on the ways they mediated between different social, economic and political forces and interests. Departing from most of the existing literature on the history of film censorship in Hong Kong, which has looked mainly at political censorship in the Cold War context, I focus on the rapidly changing censorship standards for crime, violence and sex in films. I argue that the censors' approach during this time can be described as one of 'liberal (de)colonisation', a somewhat counter-intuitive double process whereby senior British officials were able to impose their comparatively liberal views on the censorship of sex, violence and crime in spite of persistent media criticism, while at the same time also overseeing an effort towards localising the censorship bureaucracy and giving Hong Kong citizens a greater say in how the city should be run. In this way, the film censors played an important role in the appearance of the modern Hong Kong crime film and a new form of criminal realism.

Covering roughly the same period as the Intermezzo (late 1960s to mid 1970s), Chapter 3 shifts the focus back to the film texts themselves to track the emergence of the modern Hong Kong crime film. The censors' reluctance to tolerate depictions of crime and other social problems in contemporary Hong Kong arguably increased the commercial appeal of realism, with filmmakers constantly pushing boundaries to show more of Hong Kong's sordid side to viewers. This trend was further reinforced by moral panics surrounding crime and juvenile delinquency in this same period, and by the fact that crime was constantly in the news: as described above, the 1960s and 1970s saw the rise and fall of major drug lords and corrupt policemen, and the government's launching of annual Fight Crime campaigns. After a cycle of problem youth films in the late 1960s and of kung fu crime films in the early 1970s, these circumstances mid-decade gave rise to a fad for so-called *shehui qiqingpian*, which often purported to offer an honest look at sensational true crimes. The new form of criminal realism was thus very different from that found in the 1950s and 1960s. In a sense it combined the two major tendencies of this earlier period (realist melodrama and pulp fiction-derived action-adventure) and amplified them, with the realism at times overshadowed by sensationalism. This chapter additionally shows that, contrary to its popular perception as being stuck in the past, the Shaw Brothers studio played a pioneering role in the local crime film during these years, its dominant position in the local industry seemingly enabling it to push the boundaries of what could be shown on the silver screen.

Towards the end of the 1970s, the true crime trend gradually shifted towards exposés of the worlds of triads and policemen – the figures that would come to dominate Hong Kong cinema for much of the next thirty years. Marked by the move away from the studio to Hong Kong's mean streets and by the increasing return of Cantonese (after a brief disappearance of the language in the early 1970s), these films were prime participants in the localisation of Hong Kong cinema. Chapter 4 focuses on how, by providing a discursive space in which different perspectives on Hong Kong society, politics and culture could be voiced indirectly and ambiguously, the crime film forged a close connection with Hong Kong identity that has lasted to the present. This chapter also asks why the modern Hong Kong crime film came to focus especially on the figures of the cop and the gangster, suggesting that, besides local news headlines and Hollywood influences, the nature of the triads and the police as groups with distinctive cultures and power dynamics made them fertile ground for storytelling. In addition, as social groups involved in transgressing/enforcing the Law and in asserting their authority over territory, triads and police easily lend themselves to allegorical commentary on broader cultural and sociopolitical tensions, especially in a context where it remained risky to broach such subjects directly. The chapter concludes with a closer look at the figure of the immigrant gangster, usually from mainland China: from the late 1970s onwards, this figure was regularly deployed by filmmakers to reflect on the Hong Kong-mainland China relationship and, later, on the city's predicament in view of the approaching Handover. The complex Self/Other dynamic at work in these films is one of the most obvious ways in which the genre has been used to engage the broader discourse on Hong Kong identity.

The final chapter of this book looks mainly at the Hong Kong New Wave in the late 1970s and the early 1980s. Although sometimes presented as a radical break in Hong Kong film history, I argue that the New Wave in many respects was the culmination of the various changes that had taken place in Hong Kong cinema since the late 1960s. As directors' New Wave status was largely a discursive product of what Hector Rodriguez (2001) has called the 'film cultural field', I employ the term 'New Hong Kong Cinema' (popularised in English by Ackbar Abbas and Wimal Dissanayake) to indicate the broader generational change that took place in Hong Kong cinema at this time, which went beyond the narrow group of New Wave directors and was accompanied by increased sophistication in film style as well as changes in the industry as a whole. I highlight the continuity with the preceding decade by first discussing a fresh cycle of problem youth films, which arose partly in response to renewed societal and political alarm surrounding juvenile delinquency. While some films followed the familiar patterns of the earlier cycle, *Dangerous Encounter of the First Kind* (一 型危 *Dai jat leoijing ngaihim*, 1980) broke out of the cycle's ideological constraints, resulting in a famous clash with the film censors. Like the new problem youth films and the immigrant gangster films, police films further enriched the discourse surrounding Hong Kong identity. They did this by exploring the distinctive local police culture and engaging contemporary perceptions of the police, which were then in rapid flux. This chapter concludes by detailing the transition to the new paradigm fully inaugurated with the release and success of *A Better Tomorrow* in 1986. Of the various 'precursor' films to Woo's heroic bloodshed classic, perhaps the most interesting is the nearly forgotten *Outlaw Genes* (性 *Caaksing*, 1982). This film, based on the same 1967 film that inspired *A Better Tomorrow*, is a prime example of the dominant crime film aesthetic of the late 1970s and early 1980s, and is thus a fitting film with which to conclude this account of criminal realism.

The Afterword brings the discussion up to the present moment, which undoubtedly is another turning point for Hong Kong and its cinema. Following the massive protests of 2019, the introduction of the National Security Law in 2020 and the drastic 2021 changes in film censorship legislation, Hong Kong filmmakers are coping with an increasingly politicised and restricted environment. Since the new censorship rules prohibit the representation of certain aspects of the Hong Kong experience – such as the memory of the 2019 protests – several important Hong Kong films have been released overseas but cannot be screened in Hong Kong itself. The Afterword compares one of these films, *May You Stay Forever Young* (少年 *Siunin*, 2021), to some of the problem youth films discussed in Chapters 3 and 5 of this book, arguing that criminal realism has become relevant once again, albeit in a radically altered format.

PART I
THE GENERIC LANDSCAPE OF THE POST-WAR HONG KONG CRIME FILM, 1947–1969

1 Gangsters and Unofficial Justice Fighters: Realist *Lunlipian* versus Action-Adventure Films

WHERE TO START a history of the Hong Kong crime film? One could conceivably start at the very beginning of film production in Hong Kong in the 1910s, as some of the territory's earliest known films – *Stealing a Roasted Duck* (偷　　 *Tau siungaap*, 1914) and *Righting a Wrong with Earthenware Dish* (　　冤 *Ngaapun sanjyun*, 1914) – suggest in their titles a thematic concern with issues of crime and justice. Hong Kong only became a significant place for film production in the early 1930s, however, when the introduction of sound helped to turn the city into a centre for Cantonese-language cinema. This decade saw the occasional crime film appear, such as *House Number Sixty-Six* (六十六　屋 *Luksapluk hou nguk*, 1936), directed by Lee Tit 李　 and based on an actual murder that took place in Canton (Guangzhou) in 1923. The 1930s would certainly be a plausible starting point for a history of the Hong Kong crime film.

But then how about the crime films produced in Shanghai since the early 1920s? The then-dominant centre for Chinese-language filmmaking was after all closely connected to Hong Kong, with film talent and capital moving between the two cities before and during the Second Sino-Japanese war (1937–45), during the ensuing civil war between the Kuomintang (KMT) and the Chinese Communist Party (CCP), and immediately after the victory of the Communists in 1949.[1] This connection is exemplified by director Yam Pang-nin 任彭年, who made *Yan Ruisheng* (　　 *Jim Seoisaang*, 1921) – both the first feature-length Chinese film and the first Chinese crime film, based on a 1920 murder in Shanghai. Suggestive of the connections between action and crime cinema that run throughout the history of

---

[1] For accounts of this period focusing on various regional cinematic connections, see Fu (2003) and Yeh (2018).

Chinese-language film, Yam later in the decade became a prominent martial arts director, making films with his wife Wu Lai-chu, China's first female martial arts star. Both moved to Hong Kong in the 1940s, where they continued making first spy and then mainly action-crime films until the 1960s. Even before their move, *Yan Ruisheng* itself was in 1938 remade in Hong Kong by Kwan Man-ching 文, an important figure in early Hong Kong film history.²

This book on the history of the Hong Kong crime film nevertheless only starts its account in the late 1940s. One important reason for this is practical: very few pre-war Hong Kong film prints have survived, meaning we must mostly rely on second-hand information to get an idea of this era's films. The Second Sino-Japanese war also constitutes an important turning point, as it resulted in a much-reshaped world order that would come to profoundly influence the colony and its films. One outcome of this new world order was the closing of borders, separating Hong Kong and Taiwan from mainland China, with these three societies over time accumulating very different historical experiences and, as a result, developing distinct identities. One contention of this book is that the crime film and criminal realism were closely tied to the growth of a distinct Hong Kong identity, so this is an additional reason to start my account in the late 1940s.³

This period saw the beginning of the Cold War. British-ruled Hong Kong became the prime ideological battleground between the American-backed KMT on Taiwan and the CCP in mainland China. This was reflected in the period's colonial censorship policies (discussed in the Intermezzo), but also in the creation of leftist and rightist unions that divided the film industry into two competing camps. While these developments cut across the Cantonese and Mandarin divide that then existed in Hong Kong cinema, Cantonese filmmakers arguably adapted faster, with the early 1950s now recognised as a first golden era for Cantonese cinema. Mandarin film companies had more difficult transitions to make as the mainland market was first unstable and then largely closed – even for leftist companies – while access to the

---

² The English title of the remake is *The Tragedy of Shanghai*, but the Chinese title is the same.

³ The examples of *House Number Sixty-Six* and *Yan Ruisheng* suggest that the concept of criminal realism is relevant to these earlier films as well. Promotional materials for *House Number Sixty-Six* repeatedly stress the film's 'realism' – even its 'documentary' nature – and tout the assistance the filmmakers received from the Guangzhou police. This type of film based on sensational real-life crimes was quite popular in the 1920s, even though it was criticised by intellectuals and occasionally subjected to censorship (Qin 2013). Like the films discussed in this book, these films participated in a public sphere that was coping with the challenges of modernisation and urbanisation, but they are crucially not about the experience in Hong Kong specifically.

sizeable Taiwanese market depended on displaying political allegiance to the KMT. The strategy for both Cantonese and Mandarin studios was to cater to the Southeast Asian market (especially the then British colonies of Malaya, Singapore and Borneo, which had sizeable ethnically Chinese populations). The companies that would eventually lead Mandarin cinema to a period of prosperity from the late 1950s onwards not coincidentally had strong roots in Southeast Asia: Motion Picture & General Investment Company (MP&GI) and Shaw Brothers both invested heavily in Mandarin film production in Hong Kong to feed their Southeast Asian theatre chains (Law K. 2000, 118).[4] The films made by these two companies largely avoided politics and aimed for pure entertainment, a trend also observable in Cantonese cinema from the mid-1950s onwards.

Throughout this book, I stress the importance of what I call the 'generic landscape', the total environment of major and minor genres in a given period that informs the particular crime genre (or particular crime film) under discussion, in various degrees of intensity. For the period covered in this chapter and the next, this requires some discussion of the concept of melodrama, a term as notoriously slippery as it is popular, as well as two related terms in Chinese, *lunlipian* 倫 (*leonleipin*, 'ethics film') and *xieshipian* 寫實 (*sesatpin*, 'realist film'). Besides the critically celebrated tradition of Cantonese melodrama, this chapter and the next also draw attention to the equally important but often neglected connections of local cinema to popular pulp literature and radio plays (the so-called 'airwave novels'). (Realist) *lunlipian* generally provided the more welcoming environment for sociopolitical commentary, while pulp literature was a prime source for Hong Kong's famed action film traditions. With the overall generic landscape established, the main sections of this chapter will discuss the in the 1950s and 1960s still minor genre of the gangster film, focusing on the figure of the reformed gangster. The final section will look at the highly productive mid-1960s action-crime cycle featuring mostly female 'unofficial justice fighters'. My account of 1950s and 1960s crime film genres is continued in Chapter 2, where I cover detective films and suspense thrillers.

---

[4] For an excellent account of the left-right struggle in the Mandarin film industry, see Fu (2018). Fu points out that initially the left-wing, PRC-supported studios were more successful, but that the efforts by right-wing, US- and KMT-supported studios to contain the Communist influence started to bear fruit by the end of the 1950s. Shaw Brothers and MP&GI are generally considered to belong to the right-wing camp.

The Generic Landscape

The generic landscape of Hong Kong cinema shifted dramatically in the 1950s and 1960s, marking the transition from a comparatively traditional and conservative sensibility to a more modern, liberal and urban one. During this period, genres in Cantonese and Mandarin cinema witnessed different as well as overlapping developments. When a certain Cantonese film proved successful, the Mandarin studios would sometimes try to capitalise on this success, and vice versa. Still, the difference between the two industries was substantial and had to do with the different market segments they were addressing. As Chu Yingchi (2003, 17) points out:

> It was commonly acknowledged that the Mandarin audience was generally the white-collar class, the modernised urban population, who preferred Hollywood and Shanghai films. By contrast, the Cantonese film audience was comprised mainly of the working classes from a rural background, who were likely to be superstitious followers of Buddhism and Taoism, and with little or no formal education.

Over the years, as the post-war baby boomer generation came of age, the tastes of the Cantonese audience became increasingly like those of the Mandarin audience. Given the generally higher production values of the Mandarin film studios, this probably contributed to the temporary demise of Cantonese filmmaking in the late 1960s and early 1970s.

The immediate post-war generic landscape resembled the pre-war one. Important Cantonese genres in the 1950s included the Cantonese opera film, the costume drama, the kung fu film, ghost films and comedies. In addition, horror, spy and detective films made regular appearances. Starting in the late 1950s, Cantonese opera films declined in prominence, whereas detective films, suspense thrillers, fantasy martial arts films and horror films became more popular, existing alongside several cycles of youth movies. The mid-1960s also witnessed a major cycle of James Bond-inspired action films. Capping the drastic changes over these years was the proliferation, towards the late 1960s, of soft-core erotic films. Although Mandarin filmmakers worked in many of the same genres as their Cantonese colleagues, they tended to create films in a less slapdash manner, with higher budgets and better production values. In the late 1950s, MP&GI and Shaw Brothers developed distinctive strengths in musicals and *huangmeidiao* 梅 (*wongmuidiu*) opera films respectively, followed by Shaw Brothers' phenomenal success with 'new-style' martial arts films from the mid-1960s onwards.

While the generic landscape of the 1950s and 1960s was clearly very varied, one of the major centres of gravity – or, borrowing Celestino Deleyto's (2012) term, 'strange attractors' – in this landscape was what we can for the sake of convenience call 'melodrama'. A more detailed discussion of melodrama is appropriate here, as it is complexly intertwined with local crime cinema in this period and beyond. As various scholars of Hollywood cinema have pointed out, the meaning of the term melodrama has shifted over the years: in the first half of the twentieth century, it was broadly associated with films of action and suspense and was used as a synonym for 'thriller', whereas in more recent decades the term has been associated more with the 'woman's film' (Neale 2000, 3–4, 179–204). Typically, when people discuss 'Cantonese melodramas of the 1950s', they are using the term in its more restricted, recent sense, as referring to films narrating highly emotional stories full of sudden twists, usually set in the private sphere, focusing on suffering, and featuring stereotyped characters. In this vein, several scholars (Law K. 1986; Zhang Z. 2012) – citing Tsai Kuo Jung's pioneering 1985 study on the subject – have argued that the two dominant strains of melodrama in Chinese-language cinemas are the romantic and the family melodrama, both of which first appeared in the 1920s. Some consideration of a few of the Chinese terms used to describe these films can help us further pinpoint their salient features.[5]

Two such terms are *lunlipian* (ethics film) and *xieshipian* (realist film). Both are commonly used to describe the critically acclaimed Cantonese melodramas of the 1950s, which I will argue below were an important intertext for some of the crime films that appeared in the post-war decades. While they are often used to describe the same films, *lunli* – implying a Confucian- and May Fourth-inspired didactic function for film – and *xieshi* – indicating a claim on the truthful representation of reality – might at first seem to contradict one another: wouldn't a film's educational purpose compromise its attempt to be true to the 'real world'?[6] Of course, as discussed in the Introduction, realism is

---

[5] A term sometimes proposed as the Chinese translation or equivalent of melodrama is *wenyi* 文 (*manngai*, 'letters and arts'). The problem with this term is that it is even more fluid in meaning than the term melodrama itself. As Emilie Yueh-yu Yeh (2013) has pointed out, the meaning of *wenyi* has shifted over time: she traces its modern usage back to the late nineteenth and early twentieth centuries, when it referred to translations from foreign/Western literature and Western-style literary works. In the 1920s, it also started to be used to refer to films adapted from such literature. Since then, however, the meaning of the term has further expanded to broadly refer to films dealing with emotions and sentiments (Tsai 1985, 2) or even contemporary dramas in general (J. Chang 2019, 109). Yeh, it should be noted, rejects treating *wenyi* as the Chinese equivalent of melodrama. To avoid unnecessary complications, I here will not further engage with the debates surrounding *wenyi*.

[6] For a detailed discussion of *lunli*'s Confucian and May Fourth roots, see J. Chang (2019, 75–124).

a slippery concept. Not unlike post-war Italian neorealism, in post-war Hong Kong it usually implied films depicting the life of struggling working-class people. This often happened in the form of so-called tenement films, in which a large ensemble cast represented a cross-section of society living in the cramped conditions common at the time. Some of the most well-known *xieshipian* are Lee Tit's *In the Face of Demolition* (危樓春曉 *Ngailau ceonhiu*, 1953) and Ng Wui 吳回's *Father and Son* (　子 *Fu jyu zi*, 1954). Incidentally, these two celebrated *xieshipian* are often also seen to respectively exemplify two sub-varieties of *lunlipian*: the *shehui lunlipian* 　會倫 (*sewui leonleipin*, 'social ethics film') and the *jiating lunlipian* 家庭倫 (*gaating leonleipin*, 'family ethics film'). This overlapping terminology is not contradictory per se: perhaps *lunli* should be considered as a 'style of address' and *xieshi* as a 'mode', with each term latching on to different aspects of (occasionally) the same films.[7] Since both realism and ethics are common topics in discussions of (Western) melodrama, the terms *lunlipian*, *xieshipian* and melodrama overlap to a significant extent. As Berry and Farquhar (2006, 243) write in a related discussion, 'all of these so-called subgenres are arguably a single genre and mode: melodrama with its tears, coincidences, virtuous victims, and family reunions'. Throughout this book, I will nevertheless continue to use the different terms outlined here as they enable a more precise characterisation of specific films.

The Confucian and May Fourth-inspired moral didacticism of post-war Cantonese cinema would, in tandem with stringent censorship rules, powerfully shape the Hong Kong crime films of this era, as would the pursuit by some filmmakers of a critical engagement with social problems. These are, to again use Deleyto's term, powerful 'strange attractors' in the generic landscape of 1950s and 1960s Hong Kong cinema. The dominant position of melodrama meant that when crimes such as murder, theft and robbery were depicted, they appeared often as just one more reason for the protagonists' melodramatic suffering (or, occasionally, as a reaction to this suffering), rather than as, say, an object of suspenseful investigation or exotic fascination.[8] As we shall see in the next section, a sensational, action-oriented tradition rooted in pulp fiction as well as older Chinese literary archetypes flourished in

---

[7] I borrow the term 'style of address' from J. Chang (2019), who has used it to describe *lunli*'s persistence beyond the realist Cantonese films of the early 1950s. My use of the term 'mode' to describe realism derives from Gledhill (2000, 235), who defines realism as 'that modality which makes a claim on the real', but I am also drawing on Williams (1998, 42) who argues that 'supposedly realist cinematic *effects* . . . most often operate in the service of melodramatic *affects*' (emphasis in original).

[8] The focus on suffering victims also provides a suggestive reason for the popularity of suspense thrillers from the mid-1950s to the early 1960s: their focus on the victim's perspective easily blended with that found in family and romantic melodramas (see Chapter 2).

parallel to the critically more respected *lunlipian* and *xieshipian*, representing another powerful 'strange attractor' in the post-war generic landscape.

The Action-Adventure Strain: Patriotic Gangster Heroes and Chinese Tradition

As discussed in the Introduction, most analysts of the crime film agree that focusing on the three major parties to a crime can help us chart the genre. These three parties are the criminal, the victim, and the agent of law and order (Neale 2000, 72). The gangster and caper film focus on criminals; the *policier*, detective film and lawyer film concentrate on the agent of law and order; and the victim's perspective is central to suspense thrillers (Leitch 2002a, 16). While these positions and their respective genres frequently overlap and cross-fertilise, they usually remain recognisable as general tendencies and provide a workable grid to map Hong Kong's crime cinema. Given the centrality of gangsters in post-1960s Hong Kong crime films, we will start with some of the ancestors of this archetypal figure.

In the immediate post-war years, several films featured gangsters who turn into patriotic anti-Japanese resistance fighters. Two significant Cantonese-language films in this cycle – which unfortunately have been lost – were *Hot-Tempered Leung's Adventure in Hong Kong* (　　大　　 *Ngauzing Loeng daainaau Hoenggong*, 1947) and *The Guangzhou Adventure of the Fearless* (　　廣州 *Zau Sandaam naau Gwongzau*, 1947), both scripted by Yam Wu-fa 任　 , a newspaper boss who was also an active editor, author, film critic and film director. A pioneer of American-influenced pulp literature (Law K. 2005, 162), Yam was the original author (under the alias Chow Pak-ping 周　) of the popular *Hot-Tempered Leung* serialised novels, the first of which had come out in 1947. Although Yam claimed that the Hot-Tempered Leung character was based on an actual bandit who joined the anti-Japanese resistance (Law K. 2006a, 76), Wong Chung-ming (2014, 46–51) has described the *Hot-Tempered Leung* stories – as well as Yam's earlier *Man Killer of China* (中國殺人　 *Zunggwok saatjanwong*) series – as '*haohan* fiction', i.e. as modelled on the outlaw heroes of the classic Chinese novel, the *Shuihuzhuan*.[9]

---

[9] The *Man Killer of China* series centred on a Chinese professional killer who gets into various adventures in the United States and in major cities around the world. The Man Killer often doubled as an adviser to Chinatown bosses in their struggles against abusive white people or competing mafia gangs. A film adaptation, *The Man Killer against the Tricky Man* (殺人　大戰扭　 *Saatjanwong daaizin Naugai Sam*), appeared in 1961. The film is a clear precursor to the James Bond-influenced cycle discussed later in this chapter, complete with sensational action, disguises, gadgets and a supremely self-confident hero. For more on Yam and his cultural endeavours, see Law K. 2005, 152–69.

Figure 1.1 Newspaper ad for *Hot-Tempered Leung's Adventure in Hong Kong* (1947). Image reproduced from *Wah Kiu Yat Po*, 14 November 1947.

Further cementing their place in the history of Hong Kong gangster films, Ng Ho (2008, 173) describes the *Hot-Tempered Leung* and *Man Killer of China* stories as forerunners of the 1980s heroic bloodshed films. The films in this minor cycle – which also included the surviving Mandarin-language film *Lion-Hearted Warriors* (兒 *Tithyut naamji*, 1948) – were indeed very action-heavy, as highlighted in their promotional materials. *The Guangzhou Adventure of the Fearless* even starred Kwan Tak-hing 德, the martial arts performer who would over the next two decades play Wong Feihung in dozens of kung fu films. Government censorship possibly hindered the further development of this type of *haohan* film in the late 1940s, however. While *Hot-Tempered Leung's Adventure in Hong Kong* was eventually cleared for release, it was only after initially encountering a ban by the Hong Kong censors – a fact highlighted by the filmmakers in their newspaper ad for the film ('Hot-Tempered Leung's Adventure in Hong Kong', *Wah Kiu Yat Po*, 13 November 1947).

Films focusing on gangsters were exceedingly rare in the early 1950s, but they picked up in popularity slightly from the mid-1950s onwards. These films occasionally focused on the conflict between rival gangs, sometimes from the (safer) perspective of outsiders caught in the middle, as in Li Pingqian 李 倩's

Mandarin-language *The Green Swan Nightclub* (天 夜 會 *Luk tinngo jezungwui*, 1958), but sometimes also without such intermediaries, as in But Fu 's Cantonese-language *The Five Tiger Heroes* (五 將 *Ng fu zoeng*, 1955). The latter film is particularly interesting, not only because promotional materials positioned it in the same *haohan* tradition as the gangster-turned-guerrilla films discussed above – describing *Five Tiger Heroes* (rather hyperbolically) as a 'modern-day *Shuihuzhuan*' ('Five Tiger Heroes', *Wah Kiu Yat Po*, 4 September 1955) – but also because of the prominent role of women in the film, with one of them even participating in the film's final brawl. As we shall see below, the presence of fighting women was not uncommon in films at this time, and they could already be found in the *Shuihuzhuan* and in other classics of Chinese literature. Notwithstanding its alluring promotional slogans, *Five Tiger Heroes* pays little attention to the gangster background and values of the characters, playing instead more like a battle of wits and brawn between generic 'good' and 'bad' guys. Despite its surprising paucity of fight scenes, the Hong Kong Film Archive therefore not unreasonably classifies the film as an 'adventure/action' film.

Other films focused less on action and more on the internal machinations of a crime family, depicting its internal struggles and decline. These films never coalesced into a cycle and instead were produced when a work in another medium proved to have commercial appeal. It was a very common practice in Hong Kong cinema from the 1930s to the 1960 to adapt popular books, newspaper serials, radio plays, Chinese operas and even comic strips. Such was the case with three gangster films that prefigure in many ways the gangster cinema of the 1970s and beyond: *Tradition* (傳 *Cyuntung*, 1954), *Bloodshed on Wedding Day* (新婚大 案 *Sanfan daaihyut ngon*, 1965) and *Adventure in Fishing Harbor* (恩仇 *Jyugong jansau*, 1967).[10] Chan Lit-bun 品's *Adventure in Fishing Harbor* is arguably the shoddiest production of the three, but perhaps best exemplifies the media crossover strategies of the period. The film is based on a novel written by Yee Tat 伊 (also known as John Yip), a pulp fiction writer working for Universal Publisher. Universal's owner Law Bun 斌 had started his career in Shanghai and early on realised the commercial rewards of media crossover, routinely turning the newspaper and magazine serials his companies produced first into books and then into films (Wong 2002; Yung and Rea 2014). This was also the case for *Adventure*, which was produced by Law's Hong Kong Film Company, otherwise most noted for its Cantonese-language swordplay films. Rare for Cantonese cinema at the time, the film was shot in colour and on location in Taiwan, indicating a rather substantial investment in an industry known for

---

[10] Some sources give 1955 as the year in which *Tradition* came out: the film was first shown in Taiwan in 1954, with its Hong Kong release following in 1955.

its shoestring budgets. With Connie Chan 寶 as an undercover police officer, the film was in part trying to cash in on the contemporary action films that followed in the wake of the James Bond phenomenon (see below). Still, the film's focus on the conflict between two gangster brothers who represent the clash between 'traditional' and 'modern/capitalist' values already prefigures the gangster films to follow in the 1970s and 1980s.[11]

The 'modernity' versus 'tradition' conflict in fact can be traced back to Tang Huang 唐 's *Tradition* (1954), which Po Fung (2014b, 10) has described as the only 'real' Hong Kong gangster movie of the 1950s and 1960s.[12] The film is based on a story by Xu Xu 徐 , a writer who had risen to fame in wartime Shanghai and Chongqing and had relocated to Hong Kong in 1950. The first production of the short-lived American-sponsored Asia Pictures company, *Tradition* reflects some of the common concerns of the intellectual exiles from the north, who rejected what they considered the destructive effects of capitalism and colonialism on traditional moral values in Hong Kong – an attitude that in fact cut across the left and right divide in the Mandarin film industry at the time (Law and Bren 2004, 157). The film is set in Hangzhou before and during the war and focuses on a local crime family. Its leader Hong Jiu – played by Wang Yuan-long 元 , an actor associated with several of the gangster films discussed in this section – runs the gang with righteousness, upholding the tradition of not getting involved in gambling and other 'unjust' businesses. Like Hot-Tempered Leung, Hong is a patriot, lending logistical assistance to the fight against the Japanese when the war breaks out. Before succumbing to illness, he hands over the leadership of the gang to his competent protégé Xiang Cheng (Wong Ho), passing over his own son in the process. Xiang continues to run the gang righteously, but trouble starts when a modern city woman, Cao San (Lau Kei 劉), convinces Hong Jiu's widow and daughter to go with her to Shanghai. Upon their return to Hangzhou two years later, the mother and daughter appear completely transformed by the modern city. Cao San convinces Hong Jiu's widow and son to open a casino, and when Xiang Cheng opposes this infraction of family rules, she tips off the local pro-Japanese police chief about Xiang's involvement in transporting Chinese war supplies. Xiang manages to escape the police and kill Cao San, but subsequently is shot dead by the old boss's widow. Hence, rather than adopting the

---

[11] Also noteworthy in *Adventure in Fishing Harbor* is the (probably) first ever depiction of the execution of the *jiafa* 家 (*gaafaat*, 'family law'), the system of rules that govern Triad societies and that would be glorified in several 1970s films.

[12] As my earlier discussion of the *Hot-Tempered Leung* stories indicates, this claim can be contested. Still, *Tradition* is likely the first local film to explore the conflict between traditional and modern values in the gangster world, which would become a major theme in Hong Kong gangster films for several decades.

individual's 'rise-and-fall' narrative of 1930s Hollywood gangster films, *Tradition* instead focuses on the confrontation between modern capitalist gangsters who pursue wealth no matter what the cost, and traditional, community-oriented and moral gangsters. Remarkably, the role of modern capitalist gangsters is here taken up mainly by women, tapping into anxieties surrounding the 'modern' woman familiar from 1930s Shanghai cinema (see, for example, Zhang Y. 1994; Pang 2002; Zhang Z. 2005).

The corrupting influence of the modern woman is even more on display in *Bloodshed on Wedding Day* (1965). The source of inspiration for this film was one of the period's most popular gangster stories, Niu Ge 哥's *Feuds in a Gambling City* (國仇城 *Dougwok causing*).¹³ As the title suggests, the story is set in Macau. First published as a book in 1953, Niu Ge's *Feuds* inspired no less than four movie adaptations, several plays and a 1970s television series. The first of these films came out in Hong Kong in 1958 under the name *Love and Hate in Jianghu* (恩仇 *Gongwu jansau*) and was co-directed by *Tradition*'s Tang Huang. Two other versions were produced in Taiwan (released in 1964 and 1979), where the story seems to have had a more lasting impact. Chronologically the third adaptation, *Bloodshed on Wedding Day* was a Hong Kong production directed by Wang Yin 引, a well-known actor-director from 1930s Shanghai, who had continued his career successfully in Hong Kong after the Second Sino-Japanese War.¹⁴ Wang also acts in the film, taking up the role of Pan Dasheng, a gang boss jailed for seven years due to the betrayal of his lover, Zhang Lifang (Lily Mo 愁). A true femme fatale, Zhang manipulates her gangster allies as well as her current boyfriend, police inspector Zhu Guodong (Liu Wei-bin 劉 斌), to thwart Pan's attempts to get his fortune back. The film ends in tragedy: Pan, who has discovered that Zhu is the son he abandoned years ago, resorts to killing Zhang when she is about to marry Zhu. He is promptly shot by Zhu himself, who only afterwards finds out Pan was his father.

---

¹³ Niu Ge was the pen name of Li Jingguang 李敬光, also known as Fei Meng , a celebrated comic-book artist. In a preface to a later edition of *Feuds in a Gambling City*, Niu Ge (2007, 2) wrote he was personally familiar with the triads due to his time in Hong Kong in the turbulent 1940s, where he claimed connections with the triads were essential if one wanted to make a living.

¹⁴ I have opted to focus on Wang Yin's adaptation, as *Love and Hate in Jianghu* appears to be lost. Wang Yin's presence in this film hints at a connection to two earlier texts, as he played a very similar role in *Blood Will Tell* (棠 *Hoitong hung*, 1955), itself a remake of *Blood-Stained Begonia* (染 棠 *Hyutjim hoitong hung*, 1949), now considered a classic Hong Kong film noir. These two films also featured some of the fiercest femmes fatales in Hong Kong film history, played respectively by Li Li-hua 李 and Bai Guang 光. For more on post-war Hong Kong noirs, see the excellent overview by Law K. (2017, 30–50).

Bloodshed on Wedding Day is different from *Tradition* and *Adventure in Fishing Harbor* in that the tradition versus modernity conflict plays no central role: everyone is already corrupted by modernity, giving the film the definite air of a film noir. With Pan Dasheng showing regret for his past criminal behaviour and trying to make amends, the film does come close to another subgenre of note in this period, the reformed gangster film. It is to this subgenre that we now turn.

The Realist *Lunlipian* Tradition: Reformed Gangsters

While the amount of action in the gangster films discussed so far varies, they are united in their lack of realist intentions and/or social critique. Meanwhile, gangster films in the realist *lunlipian* tradition focused frequently on the specific figure of the reformed gangster, so this section will mainly deal with this subgenre, and especially the films leading up to and including *Story of a Discharged Prisoner* (本 *Jinghun bunsik*, 1967). I argue that this film is significant not only because it was the inspiration for the most influential gangster film in Hong Kong history, *A Better Tomorrow* (1986), but also because the film itself marked an important turning point in this history.

A film that illustrates clearly how melodrama intertwined with crime cinema in this period is Lee Tit's *We Want to Live* (我 下去 *Ngo jiu wuthaaheoi*, 1960), possibly the only Hong Kong heist film in the twenty years before the late 1960s.[15] Considered one of the greatest directors of Cantonese cinema in the 1950s and 1960s, Lee Tit is also a crucial figure in the history of the Hong Kong crime film. As mentioned earlier, he was responsible for one of the first local crime films, *House Number Sixty-Six*, and in the post-war period he occasionally returned to the genre. Adapted from the Italian neorealist crime film *Four Ways Out* (*La città si difende*, 1951), *We Want to Live* starts with four men committing a robbery of the Jockey Club racecourse and going their separate ways afterwards. The robbery itself, depicted in a for that time strikingly rapid montage and nearly without dialogue, only takes up the first ten minutes of the film, with the bulk of *We Want to Live* devoted to establishing the robbers' backstories and eventual demise. While suspense is generated from their 'man-on-the-run' status, melodramatic suffering dominates this section of the film. Rather than the detailed depiction of the heist, the celebration of the robbers' cooperation, or the eventual betrayal and demise common to heist films, Lee's film

---

[15] Based on their plot synopses, Evan Yang 易文's Mandarin film *48 Hours in Escape* (亡 48 小時 *Toumong 48 siusi*, 1959) and Yuan Qiufeng 楓's Cantonese film *Duel in Black Dragon Street* (*Hyutsaa haklunggaai*, 1961) might qualify as heist films too, but these films appear to be lost, so this cannot be verified.

asks us to look at these men primarily as victims driven to crime by circumstances: we have the jobless father with a sick daughter at home, the failed artist, the faded soccer star jilted in love, and the young boy who grew up in abject poverty and has to provide for an ailing parent. None of them escape their fate: capture by the police, or death. The sympathetic depiction of the down-and-out robbers as victims of a ruthless capitalist society clearly connects the film to the realist melodramas of the early and mid-1950s to which Lee Tit was an important contributor. At the same time, the sensationalist focus on a robbery hints at the changes taking place in Hong Kong cinema at the turn of a new decade. Indeed, the film was praised by the leftist newspaper *Ta Kung Pao* for its 'laying bare of social reality', but simultaneously also criticised for its 'unprincipled sympathy with the robbers' (*Ta Kung Pao*, 15 November 1960, cited in Tsang Siu Wang 2013, 43, note 22).

Lee Tit is not only sympathetic towards the robbers in his film, his depiction of the police is also subtly negative. When one of the robbers is being interrogated, for instance, Lee Tit shows the cops' threatening, semi-villainous character in a striking series of short shots: a high-angle shot of the robber surrounded by several policemen is followed by a series of low-angle, chiaroscuro close-ups of the cops' faces, with one of them questioning the robber aggressively. Visually, these men resemble gangsters more than police officers. The same officers also repeatedly show little concern for the robbers' lives, unnecessarily killing one of them when he runs away and having no patience when the captured young robber bids a tearful farewell to his parents. *We Want to Live* therefore hints at a dynamic we will see returning in Hong Kong crime films over the decades: an intense dislike of the colonial Hong Kong Police Force inversely correlates to sympathy with lawbreakers. This ambiguous attitude towards law enforcers and lawbreakers is not unique to Hong Kong crime films: Thomas Leitch (2002a, 13–15) has identified a similar dynamic in his study of (mostly) Hollywood crime films and argues this ambiguity is central to the genre. The colonial condition of Hong Kong and the Chinese cultural traditions its filmmakers could draw on (such as the popular anti-government outlaws in the *Shuihuzhuan*) nevertheless strengthened Hong Kong crime cinema's proclivity towards favouring gangsters over cops, and towards blurring the boundary between them.

Like Lee Tit's heist film, the reformed gangster cycle of the 1960s offers a good snapshot of the various forces at work in Hong Kong cinema at the time, while giving a taste of what was to come. The narrative of a reforming gangster is in fact an old one: in a revisionist study of early Hollywood gangster cinema of the 1920s and 1930s, Amanda Ann Klein (2011, 35) has argued that what she calls the 'melodramatic-redemption' cycle was central to the gangster genre in this period and continues to exert an influence on recent gangster films and television programmes.

Figure 1.2 Shots from the interrogation scene in *We Want to Live* (1960).

One of the dominant narratives in this early cycle, according to Klein (2011, 41), was the 'reforming-mentor' narrative, in which a reforming figure convinces the gangster to return to the straight and narrow. Usually, the change in the gangster's behaviour comes too late and he, or someone close to him, loses his/her life as a symbolic punishment for his past crimes. The appeal of this kind of narrative to 1960s Hong Kong directors should not surprise us: it fit within the local *lunlipian* tradition – which, like the *Ta Kung Pao* reviewer cited above, frowned upon 'unprincipled sympathy' with criminals – while also responding to the audience's increasing appetite for sensational crime and violence – the dynamic already touched on in the analysis of *We Want to Live*. Unlike *Bloodshed on Wedding Day* and the films Klein focuses on, the Cantonese reformed gangster films of the 1960s focus on the difficulties faced by the ex-convict in staying on the right side of the law after his release. Invariably, circumstances force him to break the law again, which, paradoxically, leads both to the recognition of his essential goodness, and, in most cases, to his reimprisonment.

We Want to Live's director, Lee Tit, would in fact repeatedly tap into the reformed gangster narrative in the 1960s. In his analysis of Lee's *Father Is Back* (幽

Fofat jaulaan, 1961), Timmy Chen Chih-ting (2019) posits the film as an important transitional work between the early 1950s family ethics and tenement films and 1967's *Story of a Discharged Prisoner*. The link to the early 1950s realist melodramas is here reinforced by the presence of Ng Cho-fan 吳楚帆, the actor central to the establishment in 1952 of Union Film Enterprises, the film collective most associated with the progressive movement in Cantonese cinema. Reportedly inspired by a walk through the poverty-stricken Yau Ma Tei area ten years earlier, Ng provided the story for *Father Is Back*, and the film's realist credentials were further bolstered through 'consultations with experts on social problems' (Hong Kong Film Archive PR2187X, Programme for *The Ghost That Was Not*, 1961). Ng also starred in the film, playing Chan For, a criminal released after ten years in jail. On his instructions, Chan's wife never revealed to their children what really happened to him – a secret she takes to the grave after leaving the children in the care of a friendly neighbour, To Chung-man (Cheung Ying 張   ). Pretending to be a friend of their father, Chan moves into the children's tenement flat to look after them. When his son has a bout of acute appendicitis and his daughter Ah Lan (Kong Suet   ) is about to sell her body to solve their financial problems, Chan agrees to carry out a burglary for his former partner-in-crime. He is later arrested and returns to jail, but not before he pays off his family's debts. Chung-man, Ah Lan and his son come to visit him in jail, and the just-married couple pay their respects to him in a makeshift wedding tea ceremony. This ending of a self-sacrificing parent who can only be a distant witness to his child's (marital) happiness, evokes that of many 'maternal melodramas' in Hollywood and beyond, such as the numerous versions of *Stella Dallas*.[16] In *Father Is Back*, of course, the melodrama is paternal.

Another, more immediate inspiration for *Story of a Discharged Prisoner* was *Once a Thief* (1965), a US-France co-production starring Alain Delon (Law 2010, 95). Although the film was not a great box office success in Hong Kong and played only briefly, it inspired several local remakes in the mid-1960s, and appears to have had a lasting impact on John Woo.[17] A review published in the *Wah Kiu Yat Po* soon after the film's Hong Kong release hints at what might have appealed to local filmmakers

---

[16] For an influential article on *Stella Dallas*, which became a key film in 1980s debates on feminist film theory, see Williams (1984). For an analysis of Hong Kong and Shanghai remakes of this film, see Wang (2013, 18–47).

[17] As mentioned earlier, Woo's *A Better Tomorrow* was a remake of *Story of a Discharged Prisoner*, which in turn was inspired by *Once a Thief*. Woo was clearly also aware of the 1965 film: he used the title *Once a Thief* for a 1991 film he directed (橫四   *Zungwaang seihoi*), while using the translated Chinese title of the Delon film, 喋   *Diphyut gaaitau*, for his *Bullet in the Head* (1990). Mark (Chow Yun-fat) in *A Better Tomorrow* was moreover styled after Alain Delon's character in Jean-Pierre Melville's *Le Samouraï* (1967).

and audiences: the reviewer praises Delon's ability to be both *wen* (civil) and *wu* (martial) (*Wah Kiu Yat Po*, 31 May 1965). This not only indicates Delon's approximation of ideal 'Chinese' masculinity (see Introduction), but also hints at an ideal combination of melodrama (*wen*) and action (*wu*) elements – clearly what directors like Lee Tit, Patrick Lung 剛 and others were striving for at the time. Like *Father Is Back*, *Once a Thief*'s plot focuses on an ex-convict who is forced to return to a life of crime, but it differs from the 1961 film in that it also includes a policeman who harasses the ex-con, as he does not believe in the ability of criminals to reform. This character would return in the local reformed gangster films that followed in *Once a Thief*'s wake: not just in *Story of a Discharged Prisoner*, but also in Wong Yiu 堯's *Treasure Hunt* (剛 奪寶 *Titgamgong hoihung dyutbou*, 1965), a more action-oriented film made in the wake of the James Bond craze, and in another Lee Tit film, *Between Justice and Love* (情 *Faatmong cingsi*, 1966).

The first of these films, *Treasure Hunt*, came out only months after the local release of *Once a Thief* in May 1965. While Wong Yiu retains the figure of the harassing cop, he becomes mainly a source of slapstick humour. Another important difference is the absence of the ex-con's brother, who in *Once a Thief* and the two later Hong Kong remakes is the main reason for the ex-con's return to crime. Giving the story a more light-hearted twist, the ex-con in *Treasure Hunt* instead manages to prove his innocence and aids in the arrest of his former gang. In contrast, Lee Tit's 1966 remake of *Once a Thief*, *Between Justice and Love*, is a more serious drama and, like his *We Want to Live* and *Father Is Back*, presents crime as the product of a corrupt society.[18] An interesting variation on this theme in *Between Justice and Love* is the film's spotlighting of the nefarious influence of consumer culture: the ex-con is made more vulnerable to the pressure from his former gangster pals as he has recently bought several consumer items and a new apartment on credit. The cop character here is not only sceptical about criminals' ability to reform, but also bears a personal grudge: the ex-con had shot him during a robbery a few years earlier. The cop eventually comes to realise his mistake and helps the ex-con in a final showdown with the gang boss. This makes the film in fact the closest local remake of *Once a Thief*.

Story of a Discharged Prisoner (hereafter *Story*) falls somewhere between *Treasure Hunt* and *Between Justice and Love* in terms of the action-melodrama balance. It shows some influence from the James Bond craze through the inclusion of several accomplished action sequences, the opening credits featuring a girl in a catsuit and mask dancing in front of a rotating globe, and the macho characterisation of

---

[18] The film in some ways feels like a conscious attempt to improve on Wong Yiu's 1965 film, with several of the same lead actors, such as Cheung Ying-choi 張 才 and Nam Hung 南 , taking up the same roles.

the protagonist played by Patrick Tse. Director Patrick Lung on the other hand also inherited the social awareness and didacticism of the older generation of Cantonese filmmakers. While these older filmmakers tended to promote communal solidarity as the answer to rampant inequality and hardship, Lung in his celebrated late 1960s works stressed the importance of institutions: the Discharged Prisoners Aid Society (DPAS) in *Story*, a home for the blind run by nuns in *The Window* (Coeng, 1968), and a reform school for girls in *Teddy Girls* (女正傳 *Feineoi zingcyun*, 1969). A negative view of the police and the positive representation of government-organised social work and civil society initiatives are recurrent features of his films at this time.[19]

Aside from the action scenes, it is Lung's variation on the characters of the cop and the ex-con's brother that seems to have most influenced John Woo and subsequent Hong Kong crime cinema. Woo followed Lung's example in playing the part of the cop himself, but the figure has a more critical function in the 1967 film: unlike all the preceding films from *Once a Thief* onwards, the cop in *Story* remains convinced until the very end that the ex-con is guilty and that criminals cannot reform. The conversation between this cop and the head of DPAS concludes the film, and, significantly, the two are shown walking out of the Supreme Court Building in Central as they talk. The cop says he feels vindicated by the imprisonment of the ex-con, seeing it as proof that he was right all along and that the head of DPAS was naïve to trust in a crook's ability to change. As both the DPAS head and the film spectator know that the ex-con was in fact innocent and is just trying to keep his brother out of jail, Lung's implied criticism of the police and the judicial system is obvious. The film concludes with several short shots of the busy Central district and finally a slow pan from a higher location looking down on the city, indicating the whole society's responsibility for the injustice that has taken place. This subtle expression of dissatisfaction with the police and the courts in Hong Kong is more concrete than that found in Lee Tit's *We Want to Live* and prefigures the similar but much more direct criticism in 1970s crime films. Also important to later Hong Kong crime cinema is Lung's portrayal of the bond between brothers, with the ex-con choosing to take the rap for his younger brother's crime – a melodramatic aspect of the film amplified in Woo's 1986 remake. Aside from over-the-top

---

[19] Cunliffe (2021) and Lee (2020, 115–23) have recently also highlighted this aspect of Lung's films, with Lee characterising Lung's position as rather conservative and Cunliffe in response stressing Lung's critical attitude towards the colonial status quo. To frame Lung's position in terms of progressiveness and conservatism is perhaps too black and white. It may be more useful to see Lung as having a reformist – rather than a revolutionary – mindset: he wants to change the system from within, not simply destroy it.

action, this celebration of the bonds between men would define the late 1980s cycle of crime films that *A Better Tomorrow* initiated.[20]

The importance of the brief reformed gangster cycle in the late 1960s can hardly be overstated, as it encapsulated much of the crime cinema that had come before while hinting at much of what was to come. The cycle highlights the importance of realist melodrama in Hong Kong crime cinema, by focusing on family ties and on the bonds between brothers. It also indicates how some directors found the gangster film a commercially viable way to engage in social and even political criticism, whether it was by highlighting the economic inequality that caused crime or by subtly expressing dissatisfaction with the city's law and order regime. In general, crime films' commercial appeal lay in their sensational character – the thrill of action, the suspense of mystery, the emotional rollercoaster of melodrama. While violence was relatively scarce in the genre prior to the 1970s, several of the reformed gangster films already gestured towards the genre's suitability for staging spectacular action sequences. For most of the 1950s and 1960s, however, contemporary action was featured more often in films focusing on 'unofficial justice fighters', ambiguous figures that most fully exemplify the pulp fiction-inspired action-adventure strand in the period's crime films.

Unofficial Justice Fighters

Although Thomas Leitch (2002a) placed the blurring of boundaries between victims, criminals and 'avengers' at the heart of his definition of the crime film, his book surprisingly pays little attention to vigilante films, even though they illustrate his theory most clearly. Certainly, in Hong Kong crime cinema, some of the most prominent and enduring figures have been these 'unofficial justice fighters'. I prefer to use this somewhat clumsy term as it includes a broader range of protagonists than that covered by the term 'vigilante': while many of the films discussed in this section focus on crime-fighting vigilantes and Robin Hood-like social justice warriors, I will also include films that focus on secret agents and undercover cops – characters whose actions are usually legally legitimate, but who hide this fact to other characters in the film and occasionally even to the viewer. What connects these four different types is their shared effort to hide their identity, especially where it comes

---

[20] Lung was certainly not the first to include this element: it is for instance present in the earlier-discussed *Tradition* and *Adventure in Fishing Harbor*, while in 1966 Patrick Tse had already portrayed a heroic gangster with a 'brother' on the other side of the law in Chan Man 文's *The Dreadnaught* (Titdaam). Chan's film can be taken as another important intertext for *Story of a Discharged Prisoner*.

to their position vis-à-vis the law and the state. In other words, they all operate in a liminal space. This grouping together is motivated by the films that are the focus of this section: the so-called 'Jane Bond' cycle of unofficial justice fighter films that dominated Hong Kong cinema between 1965 and 1967, marking the first time that a crime film genre exerted this kind of influence. These films are precursors to the undercover cop in more recent Hong Kong cinema, a figure often interpreted as a stand-in for Hong Kong's complex identity and (post)colonial condition.[21] Unlike these more recent films, however, they don't take the undercover's identity confusion as their subject, instead adopting a more light-hearted good-versus-evil structure.

Coined by Sam Ho in a 1996 article, the term 'Jane Bond' highlights two important aspects of the 1965–7 cycle: the influence of global James Bond mania, and the prominent role of women fighters in these local action films. The trend was broader and had deeper roots than this term suggests, however, featuring not only female but also male Bond figures, and drawing on heroes and tropes from both local and foreign literature and cinema going back decades, if not centuries.[22] The woman warrior, as noted earlier, has a long and illustrious history in Chinese culture: the most famous woman warrior myth of all, the Hua Mulan 木 story, has its roots in the sixth century CE. Similarly, the English legend of Robin Hood goes back several centuries, while stories of masked avengers date back at least to the nineteenth century CE, when figures such as Spring Heeled Jack and Rocambole began to appear in European literature. Of particular importance in the Chinese/Hong Kong context are the French Arsène Lupin stories, about a gentleman thief and master of disguise: they inspired Sun Liaohong 孫了 's popular stories about the chivalrous thief Lu Ping 平, which appeared from the 1920s to the 1940s. These types quickly made their way onto the silver screen in pre-war China and Hong Kong. Hong Kong filmmakers in the 1960s were clearly aware of these various lineages. For instance, one of the Jane Bonds was called Muk Lan-fa 木 (Mu Lanhua) in an obvious reference to Hua Mulan, while 1967 saw the release of *Bat Girl* (女殺星 *Jukmin neoi saatsing*, also known as *The Lady Killer*), which made direct reference to the Batman story. The most important predecessor to the Jane Bond cycle, however, is a somewhat lesser-known figure: Yellow Oriole, sometimes also referred to as Wong Ang .

---

[21] See, for instance, Law Wing-sang (2006, 2008) and Fu (2014). The undercover trope will be revisited in Chapter 5.
[22] Gates (2011) has written an informative history of the figure of the female detective in Hollywood cinema, including its roots in nineteenth-century English-language detective fiction.

Figure 1.3 Publicity picture for *How Wong Ang the Heroine Solved the Case of the Three Bodies* (1959). Image provided by the Hong Kong Film Archive, Leisure and Cultural Services Department, with the permission of Kong Chiao Film Company.

Yellow Oriole is a good example of the fluidity between the different character types described above: not only is this woman warrior frequently described as a chivalrous 'flying thief' – a *feizei* (*feicaak*), or cat burglar – but in the stories she also often appears as a detective and sometimes even as a patriotic secret agent fighting against Japanese spies and Chinese traitors. Written by an author known under the pen name Xiao Ping 小平, Yellow Oriole's adventures were first serialised in Shanghai in 1948 by pulp king Law Bun's *Blue Cover Detective Magazine* (書 *Lanpishu*) and resumed publication in Hong Kong when Law relocated his company there (Yung and Rea 2014, 158–9).[23] New Yellow Oriole adventures were published until the late 1950s and, given their popularity, were quickly adapted into films.

---

[23] Yung (2007, 334) has speculated that the author of the Yellow Oriole series might have been Zheng Dike 克, a known contributor to *Blue Cover Detective Magazine*. In contrast, Ng Ho (2008, 238–9) suggests Xiao Ping continued to send in the stories from Shanghai, until he was arrested by the PRC's public security agents. After the arrest, several writers in Hong Kong supposedly continued to publish stories under the name of Xiao Ping.

While the first adaptation was a Mandarin film titled *White-Dappled Snake* (*Baakfaase*, 1954), the other ten, starting from *The Fascinating Messenger* (勾 使 *Ngauwan saize*, 1956), were all Cantonese productions. The popularity of the Oriole films peaked between 1959 and 1962, after female martial arts stars Wu Lai-chu and Yu So-chau 于　　 teamed up to star in two Yellow Oriole films directed by Yam Pang-nin: *How Wong Ang the Heroine Solved the Case of the Three Dead Bodies* (女俠　　夜　三屍案 *Neoihap Wong Ang je po saam si ngon*, 1959) and *How Wong Ang the Heroine Caught the Murderer* (女俠　　擒兇　*Neoihap Wong Ang kamhung gei*, 1959). Other filmmakers quickly tried to capitalise on the success of these films, with seven more Yellow Oriole films appearing over the next three years. As the above film titles indicate, the plots usually revolve around a crime investigation and the struggle against a criminal gang, with the female vigilantes often working in an (uneasy) partnership with a male police detective. This type of partnership reappears frequently in many of the later Jane Bond films, indicating that one's official status vis-à-vis the law and the state is of limited importance in these films, with plots instead revolving around the unambiguous struggle between 'good' and 'evil'. Although action and adventure therefore clearly take precedence over characterisation and sociopolitical commentary in the Yellow Oriole films and most of the later Jane Bond films, there are a few important exceptions that will be discussed below.

The Yellow Oriole novels and films were an important step towards modernising the woman warrior figure already familiar from period martial arts stories and films, providing a crucial transition towards the Jane Bond cycle of the mid-1960s. Embodying this connection is Connie Chan, the star most associated with the Jane Bond cycle, who portrayed one of Yellow Oriole's two female companions in the last film adaptation, *Yellow Giant* (　　毛怪人 *Wongmou gwaaijan*, 1962). Chan would soon star in the chivalrous thief film often credited with kicking off the Jane Bond cycle: Chor Yuen 楚原's *Black Rose* (　　　 *Hak muigwai*, 1965). In this film, Chan portrays one of two sisters who pose as rich society ladies while leading a double life as chivalrous thieves: their name 'Black Rose' stems from their habit of leaving behind this flower whenever they steal from the rich and give to the poor. The film's sequel *Spy with My Face* (　　　　　　　　 *Hak muigwai jyu hak muigwai*, 1966) more obviously marked the arrival of Bond-mania in Hong Kong, following the local release – in September 1965 – of *Goldfinger* (1964). Indeed, although Chor Yuen claimed *Black Rose* was inspired by the Bond films (Ng and Kwok 2006, 29) and explicitly 'cited' them (by including a fragment of the trademark Bond tune and referring casually to James Bond in a dialogue), the film generally remained more rooted in local traditions, including a socially didactic message and a focus on the localised figure of the female unofficial justice fighter. By contrast, the sequel abandons most of this in favour of a much less restrained borrowing from *Goldfinger*'s soundtrack and the inclusion of typical Bond elements, such as technological gadgets, a masked supervillain in his lair, and more action sequences.

The elements we associate with Bond films were not completely new to Hong Kong cinema. Indeed, the Bond films themselves can be placed in the traditions of British and American pulp literature and B movies going back at least to the 1910s. The American serial-queen melodramas of the 1910s, for instance, have many similarities with the Jane Bond phenomenon, including the focus on an active heroine, the importance of action and stunts, and their serial nature.[24] These pulp traditions were introduced in Hong Kong early on – the earlier-mentioned Yam Wu-fa, active from the 1930s to the 1950s and author of the *Hot-Tempered Leung* and the *Man Killer of China* stories, was a pioneer in this regard.[25] It is therefore not unusual to find hidden doors, gadgets, disguises and the like in earlier Hong Kong cinema. The influence of the Bond films in Hong Kong is instead best understood in the context of their broader influence on transnational action cinema. As Kristin Thompson and David Bordwell (1994, 394) have pointed out, the 1950s saw an 'upscaling' of genres, with previously low-budget fare (such as horror, science fiction and the thriller) receiving big-budget treatment. They cite the big-budget espionage film as the most prominent example of this trend. With previously denigrated genres gaining new respectability and achieving great commercial success, the Bond films were a milestone in the transition to the contemporary era of action blockbusters (Chapman 2000, 21). The changes in Hong Kong cinema paralleled these global trends, with the Jane Bond films an important transitional moment paving the way for the swordplay and kung fu films of the late 1960s and 1970s.

In 1966 and 1967, about seventy films focusing on unofficial justice fighters were produced in Hong Kong, accounting for more than one third of total film output in these years.[26] Production sharply dropped off in 1968, at least in part due to the phenomenal success of Chang Cheh 張徹's *One-Armed Swordsman* (刀 *Dukbei dou*, 1967), which inaugurated a fad for 'new-style' period martial arts films led by

---

[24] Several series were constructed around Jane Bond figures like Black Rose, Black Cat, Golden Butterfly, Muk Lan-fa and Lady Bond.

[25] Also worth mentioning is Mong Wan 望 (pen name of Cheung Man-ping 張文), another icon of Southern Chinese pulp fiction, whose Dark Hero (俠 *Heixia*) stories appeared in the late 1930s and were adapted into film in 1941 and 1948. Yung and Rea (2014, 162) consider the Dark Hero an influence on Muk Lan-fa.

[26] This is only a rough count based on information available in the sixth volume of the *Hong Kong Filmography* (1965–9) published by the Hong Kong Film Archive (2007). Not all films from this period have surviving prints, so for some we must go by their title and plot description. While unofficial justice fighters are also a staple of period martial arts films, I am here only considering films with a contemporary setting.

the Shaw Brothers studio (Ng H. 2005, 2). While the Jane Bond films shared many similarities, focusing on the four different types of unofficial justice fighters outlined earlier reveals some distinctive patterns. Judging by the number of sequels that were produced, the two most popular Jane Bond characters were Lady Bond (女殺手 *Neoi saatsau*, four films) and Muk Lan-fa (three films), portrayed by Connie Chan and Suet Nei 妮 respectively. Both start out in an ambiguous relation to the law: Lady Bond is the adopted daughter of a gangster boss, while Muk is a chivalrous thief (even though this aspect of her character receives scant attention in the films). Both are predominantly crime-fighting vigilantes, and in later entries of their respective series, they gradually cooperate more closely with the police, with Lady Bond even joining the force in her third film. Usually acting as independent agents, their goals are generally aligned with those of the police force, even though the latter is sometimes shown to contain undercover villains. Lady Bond and Muk Lan-fa therefore form less of an ideological challenge to the colonial-capitalist society of Hong Kong compared to some of the films that will be discussed below. Instead, films in these two series are distinguished by their outstanding action choreography – a result of the joint efforts by Lau Kar-leung 劉家 and Tong Kai 唐佳, who would soon bring their talents to the Shaw Brothers studio.[27]

Although the secret agent and undercover cop operate with more legal and institutional sanction, in films it is often hard to tell them apart from the crime-fighting vigilantes, as they typically act with scant attention for the law. Since international Cold War politics was a particularly sensitive point for the Hong Kong censors (see the Intermezzo), films frequently blurred the boundaries between secret agent and undercover cop, with the secret agent often simply appearing not as a spy but as an international crime fighter working for Interpol, an explicitly apolitical organisation. Indeed, an Interpol-affiliated secret agent and a Hong Kong cop often team up to bring down local or international crime syndicates. Unlike in the British Bond films, references to the Soviet bloc and the contemporary world order are absent, and while the villains adopt some of the trappings of Bond villains (such as high-tech hidden bases and a megalomaniac style), their aspirations are usually much more modest. Given their (hidden) official and legal authority, the secret agent and undercover cop are even more ideologically conservative than crime-fighting vigilantes such as Lady Bond and Muk Lan-fa. Unsurprisingly perhaps, men are

---

[27] Another person linking the Jane Bond phenomenon and the Shaw Brothers martial arts films that followed is Ni Kuang 倪匡, who penned the original Muk Lan-fa stories for Law Bun's Universal Publisher, and who provided the script for Chang Cheh's *One-Armed Swordsman*, kicking off an extremely productive career as a scriptwriter, mostly for Shaw Brothers.

relatively more prominent in these two roles, with Cantonese stars like Patrick Tse, Cheung Ying-choi and Kenneth Tsang 曾 occasionally appearing as James Bond-like figures in mid-1960s films. Even so, these male Bonds often still operate in a (competitive) partnership with a fighting woman.

One somewhat unusual film in this strand of undercover cop films was the Connie Chan vehicle *Girl Detective 001* (第一女探員 *Dai jat hou neoi taamjyun*, 1966). Chan plays an undercover cop in the film, but her identity as a cop is revealed early on, and, in a few scenes, she even dons a police uniform – something exceedingly rare for this period's heroes. An image of Chan in police attire was also used for the film's promotional materials, which can perhaps be explained by the relative novelty of female police officers in Hong Kong.[28] Made with the cooperation of the police and including shots of real uniformed officers marching at a police training school, the film can be considered a precursor to the 1970s police thriller, even though it lacks the interest in actual police culture and practices that marked the genre in later years. Although she dons the uniform, Chan in fact rarely comes across as a 'real' Hong Kong cop. Indeed, the film treats the police uniform and the location shots at the school mostly as gimmicks, with the noteworthy exception of two short scenes that are seemingly meant to indicate the competence of the Hong Kong Police Force and are perhaps the filmmakers' way of thanking the police for their assistance. One of these scenes is particularly interesting, as it shows Chan in police uniform stopping two men – likely triad gangsters – from harassing an illegal hawker for protection fees. Given that police harassment of illegal hawkers – among the poorest people in the colony – was highly unpopular (more on this in Chapter 5), the scene comes across as either a clumsy effort to show the police in a positive light, or, alternatively, to distance Chan's star image from negative perceptions of the police at the time.

Interestingly, most of the ten-odd Shaw Brothers entries in the unofficial justice fighter cycle of the mid-1960s focus on international secret agents and/or undercover cops.[29] These Mandarin films are distinct from the Cantonese ones that otherwise dominated the cycle.[30] First, Shaw Brothers clearly saw these contemporary

---

[28] It was only in the 1950s that women officers were recruited in significant numbers and became visible on city streets. A few years earlier, *The Lady Detective* (女偵探 *Noei zingtaam*, 1963) also included a few brief shots of a uniformed female officer that similarly seem motivated by a fascination with this new phenomenon.

[29] Examples are *Angel with the Iron Fists* (鐵觀音 *Tit gunjam*, 1967), *Operation Lipstick* (嬌娃 *Dipmong giuwaa*, 1967), *Asia-Pol* (亞洲秘密警察 *Ngaazau beimat gingcaat*, 1967) and *Inter-Pol* (零零九 *Dakging ling ling gau*, 1967).

[30] MP&GI, the other major Mandarin studio, also attempted to cash in on the trend, producing a handful of Bond-inspired films in 1967 and 1968. Then already in serious decline, the studio's entries in the cycle did not leave much of a mark.

thrillers as a way to modernise and technically upgrade their output, expanding beyond the period films that had been their flagship productions since the late 1950s (Tan 2015). They assigned much of the Japanese and Korean talent they hired in this period to these films: Furukawa Takumi 古川卓巳, Murayama Mitsuo 村山三 and Inoue Umetsugu 井上梅次 each directed two films in the Shaw Brothers cycle, whereas Matsuo Akinori 松尾昭典, Nakahira Koh 中平康 and Chung Chang-hwa 昌和 each contributed one film.[31] By assigning foreign directors, the studio clearly hoped to break into international markets. The one exception was Lo Wei , who helmed four Bond-inspired films for Shaw Brothers between 1966 and 1969. Second, these films stayed closer to the Western James Bond model by more frequently starring a male Bond figure – usually Paul Chang 張 and Tang Ching 唐 – and by being less sexually conservative than the Cantonese films, featuring more daring (female) nudity and sex scenes. While women still played important parts in these films, they frequently appeared as femme fatale villains – a relatively rare phenomenon in the Cantonese unofficial justice fighter films. Third, perhaps due to the higher production values Shaw Brothers could afford, their Bond films are more cosmopolitan in nature, with frequent location shooting in other Asian localities and a highlighting of international air travel (most often by including scenes at airports) (Tan 2015). Finally, the Shaw Brothers Bond clones also reproduced the upper-middle-class identity of the original Bond, highlighting the pleasures of luxury consumption. In contrast, while the Cantonese Jane Bond films also often showed their heroines wearing the latest fashions, they simultaneously, and almost without exception, stress these characters' working-class origins. Their heroic deeds are frequently also committed on behalf of the common people.

The distinctions between the three different character types discussed so far – crime-fighting vigilantes, undercover cops and secret agents – are arguably negligible. Offering scenes of sensational action and adventure was clearly the main goal of these films, and by staging straightforward battles between 'good' and 'evil', they usually avoided raising any troubling questions about justice, law and their enforcement that could make them more interesting as crime films. The differentiation between character types however bears fruit when we consider the fourth group of protagonists: Robin Hood-like social justice warriors. This is the variant of unofficial justice fighter film that remains most closely aligned with the realist, leftist and *lunlipian* traditions of earlier Cantonese cinema. They are particularly fascinating given the sociopolitical turbulence against which the whole unofficial justice fighter cycle played out: the 1966 Star Ferry Riots and the 1967 Leftist Riots, both seen as crucial

---

[31] For Shaw Brothers' strategy of recruiting Japanese talent, see Yau (2009) and Poon (2020). On Chung Chang-hwa, see Magnan-Park (2011).

Figure 1.4 Medium close-up of a masked heroine in *Black Rose* (1965).

turning points in Hong Kong history. Lasting seven months, resulting in dozens of deaths and thousands of arrests, the 1967 Riots was the most severe social unrest Hong Kong has faced in the last seventy years, except for the recent 2019 protests. Indeed, several commentators have noted the rebelliousness and discontent bubbling underneath the surface of these popular entertainment films (Ng H. 2008, 201–40; Wei 2016, 150–1). With the 2019 protests fresh in one's memory, the sight of young, black-clad and masked hero(in)es fighting against injustice certainly strengthens the suspicion that these late 1960s films, despite their ostensible light-heartedness, spoke in some way to the social discontent of their time.

A few unofficial justice fighter films certainly indicate that some filmmakers were aware of the sociopolitical critique these figures could be mobilised towards. In *Black Rose*, for instance, one brief conversation seems somewhat incongruous with the generally frivolous atmosphere of the film. As Chan Mei-yu (Nam Hung), one of the two Black Rose sisters, gets romantically involved with the insurance investigator on their trail (Patrick Tse), she confesses her identity to him. She explains that, because her parents were driven to death by corrupt businessmen and officials when she was still a teenager, she and her sister decided to take revenge by stealing from the rich and helping the poor. The investigator retorts that the money they give to the poor will eventually run out and that they will still be poor, while the rich will continue to bully them. Pointedly, he then asks: 'How much can one person do to change society?' Chan avoids answering the question, saying only that she hopes that one day he will agree with her. In addition to the film's depiction of the police as powerless and partial to the rich and powerful, this brief scene can be seen as a (modest) call for social activism.

Films that featured chivalrous thieves in this period were more likely to contain this kind of political message, although filmmakers could of course take this figure into different directions. Likely due to Connie Chan's girl-next-door star image, Chiang Wai-kwong 偉光's *Lady Black Cat* (女 *Neoicaak hakjemaau*, 1966) for instance simply evades the criminal nature of Black Cat's activities, focusing the story instead squarely on a battle of wits (and brawn) between Black Cat and a rich smuggler. A more puzzling film is Chan Wan 's *The Girl with Long Hair* (姑娘 *Coengfaat gunoeng*, 1967), in which Connie Chan's heroine plays second fiddle to a male masked avenger named the Filial Thief. His goal is to punish overly 'Westernised' rich people who have abandoned the 'traditionally Chinese' value of filial piety, and therefore neglect and even harm their parents and siblings. The film is a somewhat quirky variation on the tradition versus modernity conflict that was a persistent theme in Hong Kong gangster films, as discussed earlier. Mok Hong-si 康時's *Golden Butterfly, The Lady Thief* (女 *Neoicaak gamwudip*, 1965) offers a more standard conservative alternative, in line with older Cantonese crime films, such as the Lee Tit films discussed earlier. An important part in the film is given to Shek Kin 堅, usually typecast as a villain but here in a good guy role: as a reformed thief just released from jail and as the father of Golden Butterfly (Ting Ying 丁), he helps to convince his daughter to abandon her well-intentioned but illegal activities. After some complications, Golden Butterfly retires and promptly marries a police detective's son.

On the other end of the spectrum, there are the two Bus Money films, based on a character from a newspaper comic: *The Girl in the Bus* (巴士 巧 *Baasi Ngan haaupo houmungai*, 1965) and *Bus Money Wiped out the Evils* (巴士 妙 三害 *Baasi Ngan miugai ceoi saamhoi*, 1966) – both directed by Mok Hong-si and starring Pak Yan as Bus Money. The key person behind these films was Lo Duen 敦, who served as scriptwriter, producer and actor in them. One of the leading leftists in Cantonese cinema and drama since the 1930s, Lo infused the unofficial justice fighter formula with an unabashedly leftist and feminist agenda. In the films, rich and powerful men are repeatedly shown to be exploiting the poor and to be preying on innocent girls. Bus Money not only punishes these villains personally, but even leads the proletariat in fighting back collectively.[32] Further stressing her

---

[32] For a discussion of Lo Duen's life and some of his work in film, see Lo (2019, 75–91).

identity as 'one of the people', Bus Money never dons the black outfit and mask most other Jane Bonds appear in. And while she often disguises herself, the films tend to skip over the details: appearing unexplained and in disguise in unlikely settings, she is ghost-like, as if she were the embodiment of the bourgeoisie's guilty conscience. Her feminist credentials are established by a routine that gives her the nickname Bus Money, shown in both films: pretending to be out of small change on a bus, she scams men who use the borrowing of a few cents as an excuse to flirt with her.

Of the two films, the sequel is the richest in political subtexts. The film starts with Bus Money assisting workers in a labour dispute involving a greedy industrialist – played by Lo Duen – who knowingly puts workers' lives at risk. The same industrialist is later plotting to burn down a squatter area to make way for a property development and is also shown to be behind a scheme involving the drug rape of young female workers. Bus Money organises the inhabitants of the slum into a militia and the film concludes with their victory in a brawl with the gangsters. While in the first film the rich villain is merely punished by having his face pushed into a cake, the stakes in the second film are considerably higher: the industrialist is killed when a burning wall falls on him during the final brawl. In a perhaps unintentionally chilling moment, Bus Money and her friends don't make any effort to help him, and just stand by and watch. These films are certainly not subtle, but the anger driving them is palpable. *Bus Money Wiped out the Evils* arguably channelled some of the widespread discontent of the time: the Star Ferry Riots of 1966 would break out just two months after its release.

The two Bus Money films are a fitting conclusion to this chapter: relatively light on action compared to other unofficial justice fighter films, they infused this action-adventure cycle with *lunli* and *xieshi* elements familiar from the 1950s and offered a fiery leftist critique of economic and gender inequality in 1960s Hong Kong. In later chapters I will argue that the 1970s saw a more thorough mixing of these traditions, resulting in a new form of criminal realism. First, however, I will shift my focus from criminals and unofficial justice fighters to protagonists that are more firmly on the 'right' side of the law, such as police and private detectives, as well as crime victims. Whereas the current chapter has aimed to place Hong Kong crime films in their larger generic landscape and historical contexts, the next one will highlight the role of the auteur in genre filmmaking as well as the international circulation of films. There is no better way to do this than to look at local remakes and adaptations of Alfred Hitchcock's films.

2 Detectives and Suspense Thrillers: Remaking Hitchcock in Hong Kong

THE PREVIOUS CHAPTER has argued that the 1950s and 1960s crime film was pulled towards the 'strange attractors' of (realist) *lunlipian* and pulp fiction-inspired action-adventure. This chapter will broaden the scope to consider other powerful forces shaping the Hong Kong crime film in the post-war decades and beyond: transnational cinematic trends, auteurs, stars and studios. At the same time, it will complete the historical overview of the 1940s, 1950s and 1960s Hong Kong crime film by looking at two crime genres that were prominent during this period but have faded since: detective films and suspense thrillers.[1] Unlike gangster and unofficial justice fighter films, these are works that generally deal with characters on the 'right' side of the law – professional investigators and crime victims – even if individual films tend to blur this boundary. Chapter 1 already hinted that Hong Kong crime films took much inspiration from foreign sources, especially from the US, Europe and Japan, often via pre-1949 Shanghai. Obviously, Hong Kong popular culture cannot be considered in isolation, so this chapter will more directly conceptualise the relationship between the local and the transnational through the phenomenon of the remake. By taking a closer look at local remakes of the oeuvre of the 'Master of Suspense', Alfred Hitchcock, we can strike two birds with the same stone: not only can we scrutinise how foreign films were translated into the local generic landscape, but we can also more broadly consider the role of the auteur in genre cinema. In

---

[1] Given the pervasiveness of genre blending, any appraisal of the popularity of different crime genres from 1947 to 1969 is of necessity an imprecise one. Based mainly on the information available in the Hong Kong Film Archive's *Hong Kong Filmography*, it is however clear that suspense/horror films were the dominant crime film genre at this time, followed respectively by unofficial justice fighter films, detective films and gangster films.

addition to auteurs, this chapter's survey of detective films and suspense thrillers also highlights particular film stars and studios that played a major role in shaping these genres.

Through an analysis of *Murderer in Town* (1958), helmed by one of the era's most prominent crime film directors, Lee Tit, this chapter's first section will consider how a director can shape a genre film to express his/her world view, and will explore how Hong Kong (crime) cinema relates to other (crime) cinemas. For this latter point, I will draw parallels between transnational film remakes and the broader processes of genre, taking inspiration from Wang Yiman's (2013) argument that remakes sometimes enable the formation of local/regional/national identity. Next, I will give brief overviews of the detective film and the suspense thriller in post-war Hong Kong cinema, suggesting their affinity with each other, as well as with unofficial justice warrior films, *jiating lunlipian* ('family ethics film'), and horror movies. While my discussion of the detective film will highlight several fictional detective figures as well as the career of Tso Tat-wah, the star who became locally known as 'Detective Tso' for his many appearances in this role, my overview of the suspense thriller will zoom in on the impact of the Kong Ngee film studio on the genre, taking the studio's so-called '*999*' series of suspense thrillers as a case study. Finally, I will move on to Hitchcock, giving an overview of local remakes of his films and then proceeding to a close reading of *Backyard Adventures* (1955), a remake of Hitchcock's *Rear Window* (1954). This reading will show how the local generic landscape and various other contextual factors shaped *Backyard Adventures*, with the differences between the remake and the original pointing towards the broader particularities of Cantonese-language cinema at this time. Indirectly, this comparative analysis sheds light on the relationship between Hong Kong and other local/regional/national/transnational cinemas, illustrating how the ambiguous boundaries between cinemas mirror the ambiguous boundaries between genres.

(Criminal) realism is relatively less important for the films discussed in this chapter, which mostly derived from local pulp fiction and which rarely strayed close the realist *lunlipian* mode, even if the analyses of *Murderer in Town*, *Backyard Adventures*, and the '*999*' series indicate how local realities sometimes still filtered through. The main objective of this chapter is therefore twofold. First, to expand the scope of reference for this book's conceptualisation of the Hong Kong crime film beyond the generic landscape to consider the role of director, star, studio and transnational cinematic trends. Second, to create a fuller picture of the 1940s, 1950s and 1960s crime film that will serve as a necessary context for understanding the drastic changes that took place in the Hong Kong crime film and criminal realism in the 1970s, as detailed in the following chapters.

Auteur, Remake and Genre: Lee Tit's *Murderer in Town* (1958)

Historically, the study of genres became popular in the late 1960s and early 1970s as a response to the perceived shortcomings of 'auteurism'. Popularised by French critics at *Cahiers du Cinéma* in the 1950s and 1960s, auteurism had asserted that cinema could be a medium of individual artistic expression, with the role of author/artist taken up by the director of the film. Most controversially, these critics asserted that auteurs could be found in the ranks of Hollywood directors – Hitchcock being one of their main examples. The reading of films through the artistic personality of one individual often led to interpretations that disregarded various contextual elements, such as the industrial processes of Hollywood, the role of other contributors to a film (scriptwriter, producer, cinematographer, star and so on), and the broader conventions of popular cinema. Early proponents of genre studies aimed to address these obvious oversights. Somewhat paradoxically, however, many of these studies continued to approach genres through the work of one, or several, celebrated directors: Jim Kitses' landmark study *Horizons West* (1969), for instance, approached the western through the work of Anthony Mann, Budd Boetticher and Sam Peckinpah. Even today it is not uncommon to see the work of recognised auteurs take centre stage in the study of a genre. Frequently, this approach is justified with the assertion that a certain director manages to express his/her own idiosyncratic preoccupations within, or even despite, the constraints of the genre.

The difficulty in separating auteur from genre studies arguably stems from both approaches' shared interest in 'mapping' the vast field of cinematic production. As Michel Foucault (1992, 304) noted in his famous 'What Is an Author?' lecture, the presence of an author's name 'is functional in that it serves as a means of classification. A name can group together a number of texts and thus differentiate them from others.' This taxonomical desire is of course also what drives genre studies. Genre and auteur studies both aim to provide maps of cinema, albeit at different scales and according to different principles – and in this sense they can indeed be complementary. This is an idea also expressed by Robin Wood (1989, 288–302) in his argument for a 'synthetic criticism' that pays attention to the interactions of genre, auteur and ideology. Wood's article juxtaposes Frank Capra's *It's a Wonderful Life* (1946) with Hitchcock's *Shadow of a Doubt* (1943) to show how each director's personality inflects the treatment of the American capitalist ideology that underlies the genres they both work in. Wood's view of the roles of the director, genre and ideology, as well as his project of 'synthetic criticism', mesh well with the approach of this book – even if Wood's conception of ideology is perhaps a bit too monolithic. My reading in the previous chapter of the mid-1960s unofficial justice fighter cycle, as well as Lee Tit's *We Want to Live* (1960), *Father Is Back* (1961) and *Between Justice and*

Love (1966), already indicated the productiveness of considering director, genre and ideology together. As Lee Tit was arguably the most noteworthy director of crime films in 1950s and 1960s Hong Kong cinema, let me reinforce this point by briefly looking at his detective film *Murderer in Town* (1958).

While Lee directed around a dozen crime films in the post-war decades, he largely avoided detective films. Even when adapting well-known detective stories – such as *The Bloody Sucker* (吸 婦 *Kaphyutfu*, 1962), based on the Sherlock Holmes story 'The Adventure of the Sussex Vampire', and *The Bloody Paper Man* (人 *Hyutzijan*, 1964), based on 1940s Shanghai detective novelist Sun Liaohong's story of the same name – Lee removed the detective figure from them (Po 2013a, 92–3). As the previous chapter argued that Lee's *We Want to Live* hinted at his dislike of the police, a closer look at *Murderer in Town* – his only film with a police detective as the central character – enables us to see more clearly the interplay between genre, auteur and ideology. Considered one of Lee's best crime films, *Murderer in Town* follows the police investigation into a bank robbery that ended in murder. Detective Chong Chung-yan (Ng Cho-fan) tracks down three suspects, but each of them is murdered before they can reveal the main culprit. With its occasional chiaroscuro lighting and hard-boiled detective hero, local critics almost unanimously agree that the film is influenced by Hollywood film noir (Ho and Chan 2013). Indeed, Chong's costume seems to come straight out of 1940s Hollywood detective films, as he goes around wearing a long beige overcoat and fedora. In line with the hard-boiled tradition, Chong is a morally ambiguous character: his pursuit of the murderer is at least partly motivated by his desire to avenge his brother's death at the villain's hands, and he does not hesitate to use an innocent woman as bait to lure out the criminals. Ng Cho-fan gives an unusual performance, portraying the detective as a domineering and patriarchal figure, who imperiously bosses his subordinates around, aggressively shouts at suspects and has his face in a near-constant angry frown.

The film implicitly also depicts Chong as rather incompetent and out of control, despite his self-confident façade: several times the criminals manage to murder a suspect in his very presence, and he is undermined by a mole within the police force who informs the criminal mastermind of his every move.[2] These elements can perhaps be attributed to the hard-boiled tradition, but the film delivers a twist at the end that serves to more fully undermine the detective figure: unlike his

---

[2] This depiction of the police as incompetent and even corrupt seems quite daring given the censorship standards at the time. No records are available that indicate that Lee Tit ran into problems with the censors with this film, but he did seem to like pushing the boundaries of the permissible, as the initial ban on his *Hot-Tempered Leung's Adventure in Hong Kong* indicates (see Chapter 1).

Figure 2.1 Publicity picture showing Ng Cho-fan as detective Chong Chung-yan in *Murderer in Town* (1958). Image provided by the Hong Kong Film Archive, Leisure and Cultural Services Department, with the permission of Television Broadcasts Limited.

Hollywood counterparts, Chong is only able to survive and defeat the gang because his colleagues appear at the last moment to save the day. This twist was a conscious choice by Lee Tit, who claimed he wanted to avoid glorifying the individual hero in the manner of Hollywood cinema (Tsang Siu Wang 2013, 37). This, in turn, was in line with the leftist ideology of Union Film Enterprises, the company that Lee co-founded and that produced the film. The result is a further diminished image of the police that is not too different from the one presented in Lee's heist film *We Want to Live*. While the cops are undoubtedly the 'good guys' in *Murderer in Town*, they have been shown to be potentially corrupt and frequently incompetent: they are no heroes, although as a modern collective, they can achieve results. This vaguely negative representation of the police is reinforced by a variation on the interrogation scene that Lee would restage in *We Want to Live* two years later, already discussed in Chapter 1 (see Figure 1.2). The visual similarities between these two scenes are unmistakable, from a high-angle establishing shot that gives a prominent place to a lamp hanging overhead, to the chiaroscuro lighting, and a series of quick close-ups of the threatening silent faces of the police officers doing the interrogation.

This connection between *Murderer in Town* and *We Want to Live* – respectively a detective film and a heist film – illustrates the importance of not considering a genre in isolation, but to also account for the agency of the director and the influence of ideology. While genre conventions result in differing representations of the police in the two films, the presence of the director and the broader ideological environment make them more similar than one would expect.

Lee Tit's crime films raise another issue relevant to our consideration of Hong Kong crime cinema more broadly, as several of them are clearly influenced by foreign examples or even direct remakes of foreign films. As we saw previously, Lee's *We Want to Live* was based on the Italian neorealist film *Four Ways Out* (1951) and his *Between Justice and Love* was a close remake of French-US co-production *Once a Thief* (1965). To this list can be added his *Sisters in Crime* (橫刀奪愛 *Waangdou dyutngoi*, also known as 999 姊妹情殺案 *999 zimui cingsaatngon*, 1958), based on Michael Curtiz's *Mildred Pierce* (1945). Influences from foreign cinema are also present in his work at a more general level, from the already-mentioned detective outfit in *Murderer in Town*, to the copying of certain plot twists or shooting styles which are harder to pin down with certainty. Lee was certainly not the only Hong Kong filmmaker who found inspiration in foreign cinema; Hollywood, European and Japanese movies were on many a local filmmaker's radar. This seeming derivativeness of Hong Kong crime films has likely been a factor in their relative critical neglect. This chapter will later focus on remakes of Hitchcock's films to acknowledge the extent of the practice of remaking, especially in 1950s and 1960s Hong Kong cinema. These remakes were not simply copies of foreign originals but were often self-consciously localised to fit within the local 'generic landscape' – a process we have also seen at work in the Jane Bond films discussed in the previous chapter.

Remakes are a particularly useful vehicle to explore the workings of film genre. Based on the same principle of repetition and variation that underlies genre filmmaking, remakes offer a more concentrated example of this process. In recent years, many scholars have noted the remake's affinity with genre, as well as with other activities of repetition and variation, such as quotation, allusion, adaptation, parody and serial filmmaking (Braudy 1998; Naremore 2000; Leitch 2002b; Loock and Verevis 2012). Most of these scholars would tend to agree with Jennifer Forrest and Leonard R. Koos (2002b), who assert that, while quality varies, most remakes are

> interesting for what they reveal, either about different cultures, about different directorial styles and aesthetic orientations, about class or gender perceptions, about different social-historical periods and changing audience expectations, about the dynamics of the genre film, or simply about the evolution of economic practices in the industry. (4–5)

In her study of remakes in Chinese cinema, Wang Yiman (2013) goes even further, asserting that 'the remake may facilitate the emergence ... of a collective, location-specific subject positioning' (2). Rather than being a potentially embarrassing copycat with little importance or value in local film history, the remake in Wang's view takes a central role in producing a distinctive local/regional/national cinema. Wang's bold assertion in fact rings true for the genre of the Hong Kong crime film in general: while clearly influenced and frequently inspired by foreign literature and cinema, the crime film, especially from the 1970s onwards, became central to the definition of what we now know as 'Hong Kong cinema', and even to 'Hong Kong identity' in general, as will be discussed in Part 2 of this book. The local remakes of Alfred Hitchcock's films allow us to explore this process in 1950s and 1960s Hong Kong. First, however, an overview of the local detective film and suspense thriller is in order, as is a consideration of two further factors shaping films and film genres: stars and studios.

Detective Films: Genre and Star

Charles Derry (1988, 57–8) has pointed out that professional detectives in cinema fall into three main categories: the classical detective who solves crimes primarily through ratiocination, the hard-boiled detective who goes on an investigative adventure in the underworld, and the police detective whose crime solving is framed within the institutions and procedures of the modern police force. In Hong Kong cinema, it is significant that the latter type is nearly absent prior to the 1970s: even if very occasionally the detective protagonist belongs to the police force, he/she in practice mostly behaves like a private detective – Lee Tit's *Murderer in Town* is a case in point. As most detectives in 1950s and 1960s Hong Kong film are closer to the hard-boiled, action-oriented type than to the classical detective, there is moreover significant overlap between the detective film and the unofficial justice fighter film discussed in the previous chapter. We already saw, for example, that the female vigilante in the Yellow Oriole novels and films often worked in tense partnership with a male detective.

Like the chivalrous thief and other unofficial justice fighters, the post-war Hong Kong detective had clear precedents in pre-1949 Shanghai, and in European and American literature and film. A good example is Charlie Chan, the fictional Chinese American police detective created by Earl Derr Biggers in the 1920s who became the subject of dozens of Hollywood films produced mainly in the 1930s and 1940s. While Charlie Chan is now regarded by many as an embarrassing racist stereotype and in films was routinely portrayed by Caucasian actors in yellowface, he was considered a relatively progressive character at the time – a corrective

Figure 2.2 Chui San-yuen as Detective Charlie Chan in *The Net of Divine Retribution* (1947). Image provided by the Hong Kong Film Archive, Leisure and Cultural Services Department, with the permission of Kong Chiao Film Company.

for the 'evil mandarin' stereotype represented by Fu Manchu (Mayer 2012, 74). Perhaps because of this, Charlie Chan films were well received in China, where even a luminary like Lu Xun was reportedly a fan (Xu 2000, 79). The Shanghai film industry was soon churning out its own Charlie Chan films: at least four such films were made between 1937 and 1941, usually with actor Chui San-yuen 徐 園 portraying the Charlie Chan character. After relocating to Hong Kong, Chui resumed the role twice, in *The Net of Divine Retribution* (天 恢恢 *Tinmong fuifui*, 1947) and *Hero of Our Time* (一代梟 *Jatdoi hiuhung*, 1948). Noteworthy about all these films is that Chan is no longer a police detective but a private detective, while his assistant, when present, is no longer his 'Number One' son, but his daughter Meina. In *Hero of Our Time*, Meina in fact seems to have taken a prominent role in assisting her father's investigation, suggesting an affinity with the Yellow Oriole stories that began to come out in that same year.[3] On the one hand, this indicates how the Charlie Chan detective stories were

---

[3] I am basing myself here on the plot synopsis of *Hero of Our Time* provided by the Hong Kong Film Archive – I was unable to locate a copy of the film.

adapted to the local generic landscape in Hong Kong (and, earlier, Shanghai). On the other, it confirms the murky boundary between unofficial justice fighters and private detectives.

This murkiness can be traced back even further, to Maurice Leblanc's Arsène Lupin stories, which began to appear in 1905 and which were crucial intertexts for Shanghai detective films and literature. Leblanc conceived of the gentleman thief Lupin as the French answer to Arthur Conan Doyle's Sherlock Holmes, going so far as to have both characters engage in a battle of wits in several of his stories. Both the Holmes and the Lupin stories were translated into Chinese in the early twentieth century, and were widely imitated, with Cheng Xiaoqing 小 's detective Huo Sang 桑 and Sun Liaohong's gentleman thief Lu Ping the most successful. In a detailed comparative study, Jeffrey C. Kinkley (2000, 171) places the heyday of these stories in the 1920s, with a significant revival in the 1940s. As the previous chapter already indicated, it is mainly the Lu Ping chivalrous thief tradition that flourished in Hong Kong, with the prevalence of 'disguises, spies, doubles, socially invisible bodyguards, and James Bond-like devices, not to mention secret tunnels and stairways' (Kinkley 2000, 211) distinguishing them from the more cerebral whodunnit epitomised by the Holmes stories. Although the unofficial justice fighter and private detective are clearly connected and are often treated together by critics and scholars, they are dealt with separately in this book because their attitudes to the law and the authorities differ. This is mainly a difference in degree: while detective stories frequently ridicule the police and occasionally show the hero acting outside – or even as – the law in the service of 'justice' or 'morality', an anti-establishment attitude is even more pronounced in stories focusing on unofficial justice fighters who conceal their identity, as discussed in Chapter 1. From this perspective, the (near) absence of classical detectives and police detectives compared to the prevalence of hard-boiled detectives and various unofficial justice fighters in post-war Hong Kong is significant. Kinkley (2000, 170; 203–8) hypothesises that similar tendencies in Shanghai detective fiction are connected to China's humiliating experience with unequal treaties and Western policing (for instance, in Shanghai's foreign concessions), a painful experience that was arguably even more intense in Hong Kong. As Ng Ho (2008, 216) has argued, given widespread police corruption in 1950s Hong Kong, it was in fact hard to tell cops and crooks apart in real life. He posits that in response Hong Kong writers focused on the traditional Chinese chivalrous thief and combined this type with Western detective and film noir characteristics to develop a local detective paradigm, in which common people (such as reporters) solve criminal cases.

Examples of local detectives are Sima Fu 司 夫, Dai Sum 戴森, Lui Hak 克, Lui Tat , and Leung Tai-yim 梁 , who all made it to the silver screen after they proved popular on the radio or in newspaper serials.[4] The most significant of these fictional detectives was arguably Sima Fu, a creation of Hui Tak 德. Hui Tak was one of the many pseudonyms used by the writer and newspaper editor Gou Dakhung 德, who is perhaps best known by his pen name Saam Sou 三. Hui wrote most of the Sima Fu stories between 1946 and 1948, with a final story serialised in 1957. In a 2009 MPhil thesis, Cheung Ka Chun links Sima Fu to various other texts that we have previously encountered, such as the Yam Fu-wah's *Man Killer of China* and *Hot-Tempered Leung* series (53), but also notes that the Sima Fu stories have a strong *jiating lunli* flavour, as the crimes in them usually take place in a family setting (125). They are, in other words, a remarkable blend of the era's 'strange attractors' as sketched out in the previous chapter. Three film adaptations appeared when the Sima Fu stories were at their most popular in the late 1940s: *Coming Back to Life in a Dead Body* (借屍 *Zesi waanwan*, 1947), *Return of the Black Hero* (俠歸來 *Hakhap gwailoi*, 1948) and *Sima Fu's Encounter with the Honey Gang* (司 夫大 *Simaa Fu daaipo mattong dong*, 1949). *Return of the Black Hero* is a particularly interesting case: it is based on a Sima Fu story, but borrows the chivalrous thief character Black Hero from Mong Wan, whose self-directed *The Black Hero and Lee Ching-mei* (俠 李 *Hakhap jyu Lei Cingmei*, 1948) came out just weeks before *Return of the Black Hero*. To further confuse matters, Ng Cho-fan took up the role of the detective in all three Sima Fu films and the role of the Black Hero in Mong Wan's film. If any was still needed, these adaptations provide further evidence of the close links between unofficial justice fighter and detective films.[5]

A discussion of 1950s and 1960s Hong Kong detective films demands mention of Tso Tat-wah, the star who became so known for his portrayal of film detectives that decades later people still refer to him as 'Detective Tso' or 'Detective Wah'. During a career that started in the late 1930s and lasted until the late 1990s, Tso appeared in over 400 films, with the 1950s and 1960s being his most prolific

---

[4] Inspector Dai Sum appeared in an early 1940s newspaper serial, and was adapted for the silver screen in 1950 as *How Inspector Dai Sum Shattered the Strange Cloaks Gang* (戴森奇案: 大 怪 *Daai Sam kei ngon: Daaipo gwaaijidong*). Detectives Leung Tai-yim, Lui Hak and Lui Tat were all originally the subject of popular radio shows. A Leung Tai-yim story was adapted as *The Mystery of the Human Head* (人 奇案 *Jantau kei ngon*) in 1955. Lui Hak was the subject of two films, *The Valiant Brothers* (克探案之 手凶刀 *Leoi Hak taam ngon zi hyutsau hungdou*, 1961) and *The Shadow* (克探案之 影 *Leoi Hak taam ngon zi hyutjing gingwan*, 1961), while Lui Tat appeared in *Hound Murderer Case* (兇 *Mohyun zeoihung*, 1961) and *The Motor Car Murder* (兇殺案 *Heice hungsaat ngon*, 1962).

[5] One more Sima Fu adaptation, directed by Chor Yuen and starring Patrick Tse, came out in 1966. It likely aimed to capitalise on the James Bond craze.

period. Nicknamed *yingtan tiehan* 影壇 (*jingtaan tithon*, 'the film world's strong fellow'), he was mainly known for his action roles: as Wong Feihung's most prominent student Leung Foon in dozens of kung fu films, as swordsman Lung Gimfei in the *Buddha's Palm* series (如來 掌 *Jyuloi sanzoeng*, 1963–4), and as a detective or special agent in many contemporary thrillers, including some of the ones already mentioned (Lin and Ng 2017, 38–9). While Paul Fonoroff (1997, 100) claims Tso appeared in about fifty detective films between 1955 and 1970, his 'Detective Tso' persona was firmly established only in the early 1960s. A key turning point was his appearance as a detective in the Yellow Oriole film, *House No. 13* (十三 兇殺案 *Sapsaam hou hungsaat ngon*, 1960). His being cast for this role was not so surprising, as in the preceding years he had already been routinely paired up in numerous period martial arts films with Yu So-chau, the actress playing Yellow Oriole. Strikingly, Tso received top billing in the two Yellow Oriole films he appeared in, despite Yu playing the series' titular heroine.⁶ When subsequently female unofficial justice fighters took a backseat following the conclusion of the Yellow Oriole series, Tso's career as a film detective really took off, with well over twenty appearances as a detective between 1960 and 1966. In this way, Tso became the key figure linking the Yellow Oriole series and the James Bond-influenced films that became popular from 1965 onwards. In 1965, he in fact portrayed a detective with James Bond's Chinese name (剛 Titgamgong) in *A Chase of the Murderer at the Canidrome* (剛 場 兇 *Titgamgong gaucoeng zeoihung*), one of the earliest local Bond copycats. While he would take up the special agent role a few more times, the era clearly favoured more youthful stars and the veteran actor who in 1965 still appeared in over twenty films suddenly found himself out of work. Only in the 1980s would he start reappearing regularly in films, mostly in supporting roles.

Tso is not only significant as a precursor of the Hong Kong action-crime heroes of the 1970s and beyond; his career also more broadly illustrates the importance of film stars in 1950s and 1960s Hong Kong cinema. As an emblem of *wu* or martial masculinity, Tso's name signalled to the audience what to expect of a film at least as much as the genre terms used to promote it – his presence promised a narrative full of action and adventure, as well as a focus on a tough, macho hero. Romance, on the other hand, was likely to take a back seat. The main difference with later male action stars was his age: at the peak of his career, Tso was already well into his forties.⁷

---

⁶ The second Yellow Oriole film starring Tso was *Yellow Giant* (1962).
⁷ Similarly, his main competitor for *wu* masculinity role model, Kwan Tak-hing, was already over forty when he first took up the role of Wong Feihung that would define his acting career. In the Wong Feihung films, Kwan's Wong represented a more Confucian, restrained

Figure 2.3 'Detective Tso' (centre) investigates in *The Mystery of the Human Head* (1955). Image provided by the Hong Kong Film Archive, Leisure and Cultural Services Department, with the permission of Television Broadcasts Limited.

In general, the star images of the era were exceedingly clear and straightforward, established and repeated in dozens, if not hundreds, of films. As a result, the combination of star and genre created, in John Ellis (1982) and Steve Neale's (2000) words, a very clear 'narrative image' for films. Tso is a perfect example of this dynamic: Fonoroff (1997, 100) appropriately compares his presence in detective films to John Wayne's presence in American westerns.

While other stars' images were perhaps not quite as clear-cut, a similar marriage of star and genre can be found in suspense thrillers starring Patrick Tse in the late 1950s and early 1960s. Unlike Tso, Tse's youth and good looks lent themselves more easily to romance. Tse was never cast as a professional detective in this period, instead portraying amateur investigators or innocent men-on-the-run in numerous suspense thrillers. In his case, however, equal, if not more, attention needs to be paid

> masculinity, while Tso's Leung Foon was more of a *haohan* type in the *Shuihuzhuan* tradition – aggressive and rebellious while also displaying more interest in the opposite sex. Although the Wong Feihung films clearly promoted the self-moderating masculinity of Wong, Tso's Leung Foon was so popular that he was brought back in later entries in the series despite being killed off in the fourth film.

to Kong Ngee, the film studio that produced many of the films that starred him and which in the late 1950s brought a boost to the local suspense thriller genre.

Suspense Thrillers: Genre and Studio

In his influential study of the genre, Charles Derry (1988, 62) defines the suspense thriller as

> a crime work which presents a violent and generally murderous antagonism in which the protagonist becomes either an innocent victim or a nonprofessional criminal within a narrative structure that is significantly unmediated by a traditional figure of detection in a central position.

There are two points to note about this definition. First, it allows for a (non-professional) criminal to be the protagonist, indicating proximity to the gangster film, and second, it posits the lack of centrality of a 'traditional figure of detection' as a major distinguishing characteristic of the suspense thriller. Since an investigation by a (potential) victim is often central to the suspense thriller, however, the genre retains significant overlap with the detective film. Once again, then, the boundaries between the three main types of crime film are less than clear-cut.

Aside from the above examples of overlap, there are important affinities between the suspense thriller and two other genres. The first is between the suspense thriller and melodrama – or more specifically in the Hong Kong context, the *jiating lunlipian*. Both genres usually focus on a victim: in melodrama (and *jiating lunlipian*) the victim is typically a passive, suffering protagonist whose innocence is misrecognised (Gledhill 1987, 30), while in suspense thrillers the focus is usually on how an innocent victim survives an ordeal and actively discovers/defeats the real culprit. Consequently, both are centrally concerned with issues of morality: where Peter Brooks (1995) argued that the central function of melodrama is to uncover the 'moral occult', Noël Carroll's influential theory of suspense holds that 'suspense occurs when a moral outcome is improbable and, conversely, ... *does not* occur when an immoral outcome is improbable' (1996, 111, italics in original). The connection between the two genres is obvious in 1950s and 1960s Hong Kong cinema: the typical suspense thriller is set against a background of family and/or romantic intrigue, often after an old patriarch is found murdered, with both the inheritance and the life of the protagonist in the balance. The main difference between suspense thrillers and the many *jiating lunlipian* of the period was merely a shift of focus from suffering and pathos to a suspenseful search for the murderer. One can even argue that to some extent the suspense thriller replaced the *jiating lunlipian*, with the former rising in popularity in the late 1950s as the latter declined.

A final genre proximate to the suspense thriller is the horror film. Hitchcock, the 'Master of Suspense', is not coincidentally also considered one of the formative figures in the history of the horror film, especially thanks to his *Psycho* (1960). Moreover, as Noël Carroll (1990, 128) notes, 'a key narrative element in most horror stories is suspense'. In 1950s and 1960s Hong Kong films, the suspense thriller and the (Gothic) horror film are often very hard to tell apart, with dozens of films taking place in old, haunted mansions. Almost without exception, the ghosts in these mansions are eventually revealed to be fake, with people pretending to be ghosts either to commit crimes, as in *The Ghostly Murderer* (兇手 *Gwai hungsau*, 1964), or to expose criminals, as in *The Ghost That Was Not in the Moon-Light* (殘月 *Caanjyut leiwan*, 1962). If we accept Carroll's (1990) argument that the presence of a monster is central to the horror film, then these films are suspense thrillers that only temporarily pretend to be horror films. This convention of the fake ghost has precedents in Western Gothic literature and 1930s 'shudder pulps' (N. Carroll 1990, 15), but can also be attributed to the edifying mission of many of the era's filmmakers, who, inspired by the May Fourth enlightenment movement, aimed to fight superstition and challenge feudal customs.

The narrative predictability resulting from the 'fake ghost' convention, seemingly at odds with the goal of creating suspense, in fact extends to other aspects of these films, whether it is other narrative tropes (such as the prevalence of long-lost twins and villains who fall to their death at the end of the film), or the typecasting of actors. Shot by one of the era's most productive suspense thriller directors, Ng Wui's *Ghost Chasers* (夜半影 *Jebun dik gwaijing*, 1966) is a typical example, albeit with a distinct mid-1960s youthful vibe. With a story about two servants in a remote, Gothic-style mansion staging ghostly appearances to scare away intruders and keep their drug smuggling activities from view, the film contains all the elements described above, except for a long-lost twin. Still, for good measure, one character is eventually revealed to be the half-sister of another in a brief melodramatic sequence that connects the horror, haunted-mansion part of the film to the final half hour that focuses on the chase of (and by) the main villain in typical suspense thriller fashion. Rehashing a (by the mid-1960s) very familiar plot, *Ghost Chasers* in this way offers a typical example of the interweaving of horror, melodrama and suspense in dozens of similar films made from the late 1940s to the mid-1960s, both in Cantonese and in Mandarin.

Although the post-war years saw a steady trickle of suspense thrillers produced in Hong Kong, the genre really blossomed in the late 1950s and early 1960s, largely thanks to the efforts of one Cantonese-language film studio, Kong Ngee. Film historians regard Kong Ngee as the prime successor of the celebrated Union Film Enterprises (hereafter Union), which had been behind many of the acclaimed realist *lunlipian* of the early to mid-1950s. The brainchild of Chun Kim 劍, who had previously been involved in Union, Kong Ngee was financed by the Ho 何 brothers, owners of a theatre chain in Singapore and Malaya. Instead of the serious *lunlipian* that made Union's reputation, Kong Ngee quickly established itself as the Cantonese equivalent of the Mandarin-language Motion Picture and General Investment (MP&GI) company, which produced sophisticated and 'modern' entertainment films catering to a younger, more affluent segment of the population (Wong A. 2006b, 16). The company produced over eighty films between 1955 and 1968, with its various affiliates churning out dozens more. The earlier-mentioned shift from *jiating lunlipian* to suspense thrillers can largely be attributed to this influential studio. Law Kar (2006b, 114), for instance, argues that Kong Ngee's successful first film (and the film that launched Patrick Tse's stardom), Chun Kim's *The Rouge Tigress* (*Jinzifu*, 1955) was a combination of romantic melodrama and mystery/thriller elements that he aptly dubs a 'romance-thriller'. Several other films in the same mould followed. In addition, thanks to the success of his *Dragnet* (aka *Dial 999 for Murder*, 九九九命案 *Gau gau gau ming ngon*, 1956), Chun soon launched a related trend for what Law (2006b, 114) describes as more straightforward 'detective/crime thrillers'.

Based on a newspaper serial that had previously already been successfully adapted for radio, *Dragnet* kicked off the '999' series of crime films, which took their name from the local emergency number introduced in 1951. Nine films can be considered part of this series, with the first five produced by Kong Ngee and directed by people who, like Chun Kim, had been involved with Union, such as Chan Man, Lee Tit, Ng Wui and Tso Kea 左几. After 1962, other companies borrowed the 999 title for their own productions, including for two detective films starring Tso Tat-wah.[8] Despite taking its title from the police emergency number and despite coinciding with the government's proud advertising of the number's success in the mid-1950s (Jones and Vagg 2007, 212), *Dragnet* and its Kong Ngee-produced sequels are in fact typical suspense thrillers, not police procedurals. Although the police detective played by character actor Lee Pang-fei 李 is featured in all five Kong Ngee 999 films, the focus is squarely on the activities of the victims and perpetrators of crimes. Although marketed as part of the same series and featuring a nearly identical cast, each of the five Kong Ngee films is markedly different from the

---

[8] They were *Twin Corpses Mystery* (九九九 屍案 *Gau gau gau sanbei soengsi ngon*, 1965) and *Dial 999 for the Three Murderers* (九九九 奇三兇手 *Gau gau gau leikei saam hungsau*, 1965).

Figure 2.4 The signature shot of the '999' series: a hand dialling the new emergency number in *Dragnet* (1956).

others, challenging the common belief that sequels are 'recycled scripts' (Simonet 1987). The differences between the films suggest both the personal preferences of the different directors in charge, but also the broad range of generic options that filmmakers could draw on within the common frame of the suspense thriller. A closer look the Kong Ngee-produced *999* films gives a good idea of the diversity of the genre at this time.

Possibly reflecting what Grace Mak (2006, 88) describes as Chun Kim's inclination towards 'romantic sentimentalism', *Dragnet* spends a great amount of screen time on depicting the budding romance between journalist Ling Wan (Patrick Tse) and the initial murder suspect, the victim's step-daughter Tse Siu-king (Patsy Kar 嘉). This romance faintly evokes Hollywood film noir tropes, as Tse Siu-king at least at first appears to be a 'dangerous' woman, potentially a murderer. Furthermore, confirming the film's ties to the *jiating lunlipian*, Ling Wan's investigation eventually reveals an elaborate conspiracy by Tse's fiancé and stepfather to cheat her and her mother out of their fortune. In contrast, the second entry in the series, Chan Man's *Murder on the Beach* (九九九 命案 *Gau gau gau hoitaan ming ngon*, 1957) downplays both the investigative aspect (the identity of the killer is known virtually from the outset), as well as the romance: the focus is instead on the victim gathering evidence of the killer's misdeeds while trying to survive until the latter is captured. The series' third film, Lee Tit's *Sisters in Crime* goes into yet another direction. Structured around several flashback confessions, it downplays the whodunnit element to focus instead on a sensitive melodrama about two sisters who fell victim to the same sexual predator. The fourth film in the series, Tso Kea's *Dial 999 for 24-Hour Murder Case* (九九九廿四小時奇案 *Gau gau gau jaasei xiusi kei ngon*, 1961), comes the closest to a traditional detective film. Lee Pang-fei here portrays the police detective in Sherlock Holmes fashion, with his own Watson who offers possible, but incorrect, solutions to the mystery. The focus also here, however, are the investigative activities of Lee Man-chung (Patrick Tse), the man framed for the murder. Of all Kong Ngee sequels, Tso Kea's film comes closest to *Dragnet*, but unlike the earlier film it only hints at the possibility of romance at the very end. Finally, Ng Wui's *999 Grotesque Corpse* (九九九怪屍案 *Gau gau gau gwaai si ngon*, 1962) focuses – in a rather daring way for the Cantonese cinema of the time – on the activities of a psychopathic murderer (Patrick Lung), edging the film towards the horror genre.

As mentioned earlier, Kong Ngee's films constituted a transition in Hong Kong cinema, signalling a shift from the *jiating* and *shehui lunlipian* appreciated mainly by the older generation to the more modern, youthful and urban cinema of the 1960s. The *999* films are a manifestation of this transition, as these films' depiction of crime, the police and the law generally exhibit a more stereotypically middle-class attitude. On the one hand, the surprising downplaying of the police in these films which take the police emergency number as their starting point is consistent with the veiled leftist, anti-colonial attitudes in some of the films we earlier encountered – in this regard, it is perhaps no coincidence that Lee Tit's entry in the series is the one that diminishes the role of the police the most. On the other hand, the *999* films were at least partly conceived as a kind of civics lesson for life in a modern, westernised metropolis: not only did they help to further popularise the use of the new police emergency number, several of the films also explicitly stressed the importance of cooperating with the police and of reporting crimes, and generally demanded respect for the law. In *Dragnet*, for instance, it is mentioned multiple times that people should report any information they have about a crime to the police. When the two protagonists fail to do so and are found out, the police detective reminds them that they are committing a crime. In *Murder on the Beach*, the police detective lectures one of the protagonists for attempting to avenge her husband's death by killing the murderer: 'After all', he says, 'we have the Law [to deal with this]!' Perhaps most strikingly, *999 Grotesque Corpse* ends with this stilted expression of gratitude by the police detective: 'Thank you for helping the police to crack this case and for bringing this scoundrel who destroys the social order to face judgement under the Law.' So, even as the promotion of the law and its execution by the police are the superficial themes of this series, the decentring of the police in favour of the actions by common citizens belies this theme and betrays a certain ambivalence.

Ng Wui's *999 Grotesque Corpse* deserves some special mention here, not just for being one of Hong Kong's earliest psychopath killer films, but also for its Hitchcockian overtones. The killer as portrayed by Patrick Lung is a charismatic and intelligent figure, bringing to mind similar characters in Hitchcock films such as *Shadow of a Doubt*, *Rope* (1948) and *Psycho*. Ng Wui's direction not only turns the killer into the film's central character, but also seduces us to identify with him and become complicit in his crimes – an approach often associated with Hitchcock (Wood 1989, 98). No wonder that Ng Wui was known as the local *jinzhang dashi* 張大師 (*ganzoeng daaisi*, 'Master of Suspense'), in a direct comparison to Hitchcock.[9] The remainder of this essay will look at Hitchcock's influence on Hong Kong cinema and the phenomenon of local remakes of his films, focusing on Ng Wui's *Backyard Adventures*.

Hitchcock in Hong Kong

While the below will focus on Hitchcock's influence on Hong Kong cinema on the narrative and genre level, his shadow certainly extended beyond these aspects of local filmmaking. Ng Wui for instance claimed that although critics often placed him in the 'Hitchcock school', he went to see Western films 'primarily for their techniques and camera movements rather than for their plots' (Nip and Lam 1985, 31). Indeed, in an oeuvre spanning dozens of crime films, *Backyard Adventures* is Ng's only direct remake of a Hitchcock film. Pinpointing specific stylistic borrowings is however a tricky business. Some camera movements and editing techniques are frequently associated with Hitchcock (forward tracking shots, manipulation of identification through point-of-view, use of montage), but he was hardly the only one to use these techniques, and they are naturally not limited to the crime and spy film genres he did most of his work in. Also in terms of themes one can think of certain recurrent motifs in Hitchcock's films ('innocent-man-on-the-run', 'guilty woman', 'voyeurism', the use of McGuffins, the psychology of murder and so on), which are not unique to the crime films he explored them in, nor to Hitchcock himself, making the attribution of such motifs in Hong Kong films to him rather unconvincing. Hence, this section will

---

[9] For an example of the use of this description, see *Wah Kiu Yat Po*, '"Ganzoeng daaisi" Ng Wui ' 張大師' 吳回 ('Master of Suspense' Ng Wui), 11 July 1966.

Table 2.1. Hitchcock Remakes in Hong Kong (1947–1970)

Title (Year of Release)	Hitchcock Film	Director	Cast	Language
Backyard Adventures (1955)	Rear Window (1954)	Ng Wui	Cheung Ying, Chow Kwun-ling 周坤	Cantonese
Black Cat, The Cat Burglar (Feicaak hakmaau, 1956)	To Catch a Thief (1955)	Wong Hang	Ng Cho-fan, Tsang Nam-sze 曾 施	Cantonese
Ghost That Was Not (夜半幽 Jebun jauling, 1961)	Vertigo (1958)	Chor Yuen	Patrick Tse, Patsy Kar, Woo Fung 楓	Cantonese
The Night the Spirit Returns (回 夜 Wuiwanje, 1962)	Vertigo (1958)	Cheung Ying, Choi Cheung 昌	Cheung Ying, Pak Yin	Cantonese
Bedside Horror (枕 Zambin gingwan, 1963)	Suspicion (1941)	Chow Sze-luk 周	Cheung Ying, Ha Ping 夏	Cantonese
The Ghost Returns at Midnight (午夜招 Ngje ziuwan, 1964)	Rebecca (1940)	Cheung Ying	Cheung Ying, Lee Man 李敏	Cantonese
The Singing Thief (大 歌 Daaidou gowong, 1969)	To Catch a Thief (1955)	Chang Cheh	Lam Chung 林 , Lily Ho 何	Mandarin
A Cause to Kill (殺機 Saatgei, 1970)	Dial M for Murder (1954)	Murayama Mitsuo	Ivy Ling 凌 , Guan Shan 山	Mandarin

limit itself to remakes: Hong Kong films that clearly and substantially are based on films by Hitchcock. An overview of these films can be found in Table 2.1.[10]

Not included here are films that seem strongly influenced by specific Hitchcock movies, without directly copying from them. For instance, the earlier-mentioned *Dial 999 for 24-Hour Murder Case* seems to take inspiration from *Dial M for Murder* (for example, the framing of the murder on an innocent man, clever tampering with evidence and the presence of a smart detective who sees through the deception), without directly borrowing from that film, so it is not listed. The films included also display varying degrees of fidelity to the original. *The Night the Spirit Returns*, for example, is a much closer remake of *Vertigo* than *Ghost That Was Not*, although direct and extensive borrowing from this Hitchcock film is unmistakable in both.

Without going further into detailed comparisons between these various remakes and their originals, a few generalisations can be made. First, aside from the films based on *To Catch a Thief*, all Hong Kong remakes centre on a story about the (attempted) murder of one's spouse. This type of narrative is prominent in Hitchcock's oeuvre, but his range was certainly wider: Hong Kong filmmakers in

---

[10] Only films I was able to watch are included in this table.

the 1950s and 1960s rarely, if ever, drew on his spy thrillers or his films about psychopaths. The remakes thus tended to fit within the local generic landscape as earlier outlined, with the influence of the *jiating lunlipian* particularly obvious. There were various reasons for this: films about murders in the domestic sphere didn't require a large budget and were also less at risk of encountering censorship for moral reasons (as psycho-killer films would be) or for political ones (as spy thrillers would be). Second, as can be seen from Table 2.1, Cheung Ying, a major star in this period, starred in four of the Hitchcock remakes and directed two of them.[11] While Cheung starred in hundreds of films over his career, it seems that Hitchcock remakes were one of his niches in the 1950s and early 1960s. He was recognised for this, as when the leftist *Ta Kung Pao* newspaper on 18 January 1960 pictured him together with Ng Wui, under the caption 'Ng Wui and Cheung Ying compete with each other in suspense'. A final point to note is that the three remakes based on *Rebecca* and *Vertigo* turned the possibility of ghostly possession or the presence of ghosts hinted at in the originals into actual encounters with ghosts. Although these ghosts eventually turn out to be fake, the remakes evidently edge closer to the horror film than Hitchcock's films do.

Let me now focus on the first Hong Kong remake of a Hitchcock film, *Backyard Adventures*, based on *Rear Window*. Although *Rear Window* premiered in New York in August 1954, the film was first screened in Hong Kong only months later, in March 1955. The plans for a local remake were announced soon after, on 15 May 1955. As the *Kung Sheung Daily News* reported, this happened in the wake of the death of celebrated comedian and Cantonese opera actor, Yee Chau-shui 伊 . Yee, who was known – in another example of Hollywood's local influence – as the 'Eastern Charlie Chaplin', had suffered from throat cancer for two years, and the medical bills incurred over this period had left his family penniless. Testifying to the collective spirit that characterised the Cantonese film industry at the time, Yee's friends and colleagues promptly decided to produce a film of which the proceeds would go to his widow and children. The filmmakers also filmed Yee's funeral and eventually had it screened alongside *Backyard Adventures* to further commemorate his life. Ng Wui volunteered to serve as *Backyard Adventure*'s 'executive director', to be assisted by directors Chan Pei and Chu Kea , while the cast became a veritable who's who of the contemporary Cantonese movie and opera scenes, with major stars like Ng Cho-fan, Cheung Ying, Leung Sing-po 梁 , Hung Sin-nui 女, Yam Kim-fai 任劍 and many others making appearances. As Ng Wui later explained, one important reason for remaking *Rear Window* was that the story

---

[11] He also starred in *Over My Dead Body* (殺妻案 *Saatcai ngon*, 1958), which I was unable to see, but which has a plot that resembles Hitchcock's *Strangers on a Train* (1951).

offered an opportunity for many performers to participate (Nip and Lam 1985, 31). Together, the filmmakers involved set up the Liangyou Film Company to manage the production.

Typical for the Cantonese film industry at the time was a relatively fast production process. According to the news report on the day after Yee's passing, the shoot was even to start five days later! This was however postponed multiple times, until 11 July 1955 – the official reason being the persistent rainy weather. One can assume that the building of an elaborate set was an additional reason for the repeated delays. As Scott Curtis (2000, 21) has pointed out in his detailed account of *Rear Window*'s production, 'designing, constructing, dressing, and lighting the set accounted for 25 percent of the total cost of the picture, compared to 12 percent for the cast'. It was considered one of the biggest productions on a Paramount studio lot up to that time. While the Hong Kong set, constructed near the Wader studio in Kwai Chung under the direction of acclaimed set designer Chan King-sam 景森, was more modest than Hitchcock's, it still required the building of several three-story Western-style buildings. This made it one of the more ambitious films made by the typically underfunded Cantonese film industry at the time. Giving a rough idea of the film's budget, an article in the *Ta Kung Pao* on 12 July 1955 mentions that the local screening rights for the film were sold for HK$50,000 to two distributors, which was enough to cover the production cost. *Backyard Adventures* was eventually released on 7 December 1955 at twenty cinemas in Hong Kong and Kowloon, with one actor and one actress going to each of these cinemas to personally promote the film. Further confirming the film's near-blockbuster status, newspaper advertisements claimed this was the largest-scale release of a film in the history of Hong Kong. The release also coincided – perhaps not accidentally – with a widely reported visit of Hitchcock and his wife to the city on 8 December.[12]

Comparing the two films, one major change in the Hong Kong version involves the crucial element of suspense. Both films share the premise of a photographer stranded at home with a broken leg, who takes up the habit of observing his neighbours' apartments and who begins to suspect one neighbour may have murdered his (ex-)wife. While the original plot is followed quite closely and both films are of roughly similar length (around 115 minutes), *Backyard Adventures* begins to develop the suspected murder story and the accompanying suspense much later than *Rear Window* – about 70 minutes into the film, compared to roughly 30 minutes

---

[12] *Kung Sheung Daily News* on 9 December 1955 reported that a special screening of Hitchcock's *The Trouble with Harry* (1955) was organised for the occasion, while his newest film, *To Catch a Thief*, was due to be released locally later that month. In terms of Hitchcock 'fever' in Hong Kong, 1955 was certainly a peak year.

in the original. This most likely is an outcome of the remake's need to showcase the many stars participating in the film. Hence, we get to see several lengthy sketches taking place in the apartment building opposite from the photographer with the broken leg – named Jefferies in the original, and Yu Mong-yuen, whose name literally translates as 'I see far', in the remake. These sketches are mostly humorous, and provide something of a cross-section of 1950s Hong Kong society, depicting a rebellious and fashionable young girl and her conservative father; a taxi dancer, her boyfriend and her middle-aged, already-married suitor; a fortune teller who dupes his clients; a divorced man pursuing a rich widow; a couple of newly-weds; and two young lovers too poor to marry. In addition to the comic sketches, there are several of the musical intermezzos common in the Cantonese and Mandarin films of the period: a love duet sung by two actors, a *nanyin* 南 (*naamyam*) song performed by two blind street beggars, and even a ten-minute long Cantonese opera segment. Eventually, the murder story is introduced to give the film a dramatic ending and bring some coherence to the whole.

Given the financial and technical constraints of the Cantonese film industry, *Backyard Adventure*'s mise-en-scène and cinematography are naturally more modest compared to *Rear Window*'s. Aside from the simpler set, some specific changes in the remake highlight – through contrast – the accomplishments of Hitchcock's film, often considered one of his best. A remarkable aspect of *Rear Window* was for instance Hitchcock's decision to shoot the whole film in or from Jefferies' apartment, which strengthens the suggestive parallels between the voyeuristic Jefferies and the practice of cinemagoing in general (see below). In *Backyard Adventures*, in contrast, this strategy is not consistently followed: the film starts with shots of the front side of the apartment, showing Yu Mong-yuen's taxi arriving. This side of the building, invisible from the apartment itself, reappears several times later in the film, as when Yu's girlfriend Man-wah goes to investigate the suspected murderer. This arguably breaks our identification with Yu and his voyeuristic activities and weakens the original's commentary on the nature of cinema more broadly. A more purely technical weakness of the remake involves another of the point-of-view strategies employed by Hitchcock. Throughout *Rear Window*, the sound is restricted realistically to correspond to what one can expect to hear from Jefferies' apartment – as a result, many of the activities taking place in the apartments on the other side appear as silent film. *Backyard Adventures*, however, switches jarringly from perfect and unrealistic audibility during the various sketches in the first two thirds of the film to complete inaudibility once the murder story begins, contributing to the film's already fragmented nature. One can add to these inconsistencies the variation in shot distance, which, unlike in Hitchcock's film, does not always convincingly correspond to the binoculars and long-focus lens used by Yu Mong-yuen to assist his spying.

These changes arguably merely illustrate the filmmakers' different priorities. The comparison of the two films certainly becomes more interesting when we start to investigate more thoroughly what happens to *Rear Window*'s themes in the Hong Kong remake. Hitchcock's film has frequently been interpreted as a film about film viewing, as the director's ultimate statement about 'cinema'. John Belton (2000b, 11), for instance, compares Jefferies' activity to that of a typical movie viewer: 'He constructs a narrative out of the disparate actions that occur within his view. This is what all film spectators do.' Psychoanalytic film critics added to this reading the insight that what Jefferies looks at is what he wants to see: we are shown a 'projection of Jeff's fears and desires' (Lemire 2000, 58). Most influential in the psychoanalytic vein of film criticism was Laura Mulvey's use of *Rear Window* in her seminal 1975 article on the role of gender in structuring cinematic spectatorship, 'Visual Pleasure and Narrative Cinema'. Mulvey argued that classical Hollywood films adopt the 'male gaze', with women appearing as objects-to-be-looked-at. For Mulvey, Hitchcock's oeuvre – especially his *Rear Window*, *Vertigo* and *Marnie* (1964) – exemplifies what she calls classical Hollywood cinema's tendency of 'sadistic voyeurism', with Hitchcock's films noteworthy for their critical self-reflexivity in this respect.

Both the American and the Hong Kong film treat voyeurism ambivalently. While Jefferies spies on his neighbours to avoid his relationship with his girlfriend Lisa and to regain a sense of power in his emasculated state, he is frequently chastised for this deviant behaviour by the other characters in the film and is at the end punished with a second broken leg. Paradoxically, these other characters are ultimately unable to resist participating in Jefferies' voyeurism, which finally leads to the arrest of a murderer – undeniably a positive outcome. The whole experience moreover helps Jefferies come to terms with his romantic relationship. In *Backyard Adventures*, on the other hand, voyeurism is more trivialised. Given the extremely cramped living conditions in Hong Kong and with privacy an unattainable luxury for many, this is perhaps not so surprising. At the beginning of the film, it is in fact Man-wah who encourages Yu Mong-yuen to look at their neighbours when he is bored, and throughout the film they do most of their viewing together – the 'gaze' is certainly not exclusively male in *Backyard Adventures*. Spying on the neighbours' lives is also presented as a mostly harmless form of entertainment, and we frequently see reaction shots of the couple laughing at the comic situations that unfold in the other building. Only one character, Yu's policeman friend, chastises him for this behaviour. Perhaps because of the film's depiction of voyeuristic activity as mostly harmless, Yu's peeping does not have the therapeutic effects it has for Jefferies. While he also ends up with another broken leg, his suspicions of murder turn out to be unfounded and he comes off as rather silly indeed. While this might seem to imply a condemnation of voyeurism, the final scene of the film has Man-wah comforting

Figure 2.5 The male and female gazes in *Backyard Adventures* (1955).

the disgruntled and incapacitated Yu by providing him with the latest news on all the neighbours. With his curiosity satisfied, he peacefully falls asleep and the movie comes to an end. In *Backyard Adventures* then, voyeurism is ultimately presented as a natural and harmless activity, a form of entertainment that should not be taken too seriously.

While the issue of voyeurism can hardly be avoided, Robin Wood, one of the most influential Hitchcock scholars, has suggested a rather different reading of *Rear Window*. A persistent thread running through Wood's analyses of Hitchcock's films is his focus on their sexual politics. As he writes, these films 'provide a thoroughgoing and radical analysis of the difficulties placed on successful heterosexual union by the social structures and sexual organisation of patriarchal capitalism' (Wood 1989, 248). For Wood, *Rear Window* crucially deals with two interrelated themes: castration and marriage. Like Mulvey, Wood (377) sees the film as a 'dramatization of fundamental male sexual anxieties', which are 'rooted in the fear of castration'. Castration in the film is represented not only by Jefferies' broken leg, but also by his smashed camera, which stands for his 'masculine' recklessness and initiative.

Throughout the film, Jefferies tries to 'assert his "possession of the phallus" through the power of the look' – which takes up increasingly 'larger' proportions as the film progresses, from eyes, to binoculars, to telephoto lens (378). Nevertheless, this attempt to assert his power only confirms his essential impotence: he is unable to help Lisa when she is in danger, and he cannot effectively defend himself when the murderer Thorwald comes to find him in his apartment. The second, related theme that Wood recognises in *Rear Window* is marriage. He argues that the film reflects on the contradictory values that operate in American culture, in particular the 'wandering vs. settling' antinomy. This paradox is often at the core of the American western, where 'settling' (usually accompanied by marriage) is the goal, but also implies a loss of power and freedom. In Wood's view, Hitchcock calls into question the American concept of 'potency' (masculinity), as well as the impossible demands it places on both sexes (378–9). The people Jefferies observes all relate to this theme: 'they variously embody the twin hells of marriage and singleness, in a civilisation that demands the former while rendering its success impossible' (378). Thorwald and his wife in particular can be seen as the macabre doubles of Jefferies and Lisa, with Thorwald's murder of his wife reflecting Jefferies' unconscious desire to get rid of Lisa. It is only by overcoming Thorwald that Jefferies can cast out this desire. Despite the ostensibly happy ending, the film only shows us an uneasy equilibrium between Lisa and Jefferies: 'none of the problems between them have been solved; but the fact of their engagement, and Jefferies' symbolic back-to-window position indicate that they have been at least in a sense accepted' (106).

The complex sexual politics and tensions surrounding marriage described by Wood are strikingly absent in *Backyard Adventures*. Man-wah, like Lisa, is an elegantly dressed working woman, but her professional life is played down compared to Lisa's, with her occupation never even revealed. In addition, her suitability for marriage is – from a traditional, patriarchal point of view – enhanced, as she also adopts the role of Yu's nurse, a separate character in *Rear Window* that is written out of the Hong Kong remake. Man-wah is clearly well off, and it is in her well-furnished and spacious apartment that Yu Mong-yuen recovers. This creates a very different dynamic from that of Hitchcock's couple, as Lisa repeatedly visits – intrudes into? – Jefferies' apartment. Indeed, Yu is not in the least conflicted about his relationship with Man-wah. At the beginning of the film, the couple is already engaged, and marriage is something Yu is eagerly looking forward to. Unlike Jefferies, Yu is happy to give up his job as a photographer – and thus also his freedom – to get married. *Backyard Adventures* finally also plays down the tensions surrounding marriage in the original by making the suspected murderer an alcoholic and a divorcee. In the world of the film, this clearly signals socially deviant behaviour and implicitly gives credence to the suspicions that this man might in fact be a murderer. Removing *Rear*

Window's anxieties surrounding marriage and sexual politics, *Backyard Adventures* can be considered conservative in comparison, but in the Hong Kong context it actually contained a progressive message, in typical *lunlipian* fashion. Several of the sketches make fun of the 'wrong' kind of relationship – a married man pursuing a taxi dancer and an older man blocking his son's marriage to take the girl as his own concubine serve as the butt of the jokes in two separate sketches.[13] The equal, monogamous relationship of Yu Mong-yuen and Man-wah in contrast is based on love and in this context functions as a progressive model for emulation rather than as a site of tension.

This comparative reading of *Backyard Adventures* and *Rear Window* confirms Wang Yiman's thesis that border-crossing remakes are a particularly rich terrain for studying the '(re)formation of a location-specific collective consciousness' (2013, 2). While Hitchcock's film resonated with the anxieties surrounding marriage and sexuality that animated significant segments of American culture and society in the 1950s (Lemire 2000), Ng's remake presents this theme in a way that spoke to large portions of Hong Kong's population. This same process is observable in the other Hong Kong Hitchcock remakes as well: *The Night the Spirit Returns*, for instance, translates *Vertigo*'s Christian references into a rich display of Buddhist and Taoist practices, beliefs and sites of worship. Evidently, neither Hong Kong nor American culture and society were monolithic, then nor now, and we should not overgeneralise. Class – and, more ambiguously, gender – are additional axes along which the remaking process in *Backyard Adventures* took place. It is for instance likely that *Rear Window* appealed more to a Hong Kong (upper) middle-class audience than *Backyard Adventures* did, as the latter, like most Cantonese cinema of the period, seems addressed primarily to working-class spectators. At the same time, the film's setting and lighter tone can also be seen to prefigure the films aimed at younger, middle-class urbanites that Kong Ngee would soon become famous for. Kong Ngee in fact released its first film, *The Rouge Tigress*, in the same year *Backyard Adventures* came out.

What I would like to stress here, however, is how Hitchcock's film is translated to the distinct generic landscape of Hong Kong cinema. What sets *Backyard Adventures* apart from the other local remakes of Hitchcock's work is the way it downplays the suspense thriller nature of its source and instead uses its sketches to create connections to the Cantonese opera film, still very popular at the time, as well as to the perennially popular genre of Cantonese comedy. The need to find a place for a large and varied group of stars arguably encouraged the transformation of the film into a cross-section of Hong Kong film genres popular at the time. The broader ideological

---

[13] The practice of taking a concubine was outlawed in Hong Kong only in 1971.

background is important as well, with many of the leading filmmakers involved carrying the torch of May Fourth intellectuals – Ng Wui, for one, had directed two of his most acclaimed Union *lunlipian* in the two years preceding the making of *Backyard Adventures*: the Ba Jin 巴 adaptation *Family* (家 *Gaa*, 1953) and *Father and Son* (1954). The gentle fun poked at superstition in the fortune-teller's segment and the promotion of equal and monogamous marriage certainly fit within this ideological project. The film can even be considered an upscale variation of the socially conscious tenement dramas that contributed so much to the Union's reputation: Lee Tit's *In the Face of Demolition* (1953) was another film in recent memory when *Backyard Adventures* was made.

This chapter and the preceding one have sketched out the generic landscape of the Hong Kong crime film in the 1950s and 1960s. While the films discussed have been largely neglected in histories of Hong Kong cinema, it should be clear that they encompass a fascinating array of trends and cycles, from realist *lunlipian* to action-adventure films, from pathos to suspense. During this immensely productive period in Hong Kong film history, filmmakers found inspiration in local pulp fiction and radio plays, but also in foreign cinema, especially from Europe and the US. Although this roughly twenty-year period from the late 1940s to the late 1960s witnessed substantial changes, it forms a relatively coherent era in Hong Kong film history. This coherence would be shattered in the late 1960s and early 1970s when a series of social, political and economic upheavals caused a dramatic break with the past, a genuine generational and cultural shift that would result in a new form of criminal realism and a new kind of Hong Kong crime film. The next chapter will begin to explore this sea change by looking at the role of film censorship, which, given colonial sensitivities surrounding crime, social problems and the rule of law, played a subtle but important role in shaping the Hong Kong crime film and Hong Kong cinema in general.

Intermezzo: Censorship of Cinematic Crime and Violence in Colonial Hong Kong

WHILE HISTORICAL CHANGE is often incremental, there occasionally are moments of rapid transformation – turning points and generational shifts that seem particularly abrupt and earth-shattering. In much of the world, the late 1960s was such a turning point, with culture, politics and society changing drastically as the baby-boomer generation came of age. In Hong Kong, this sea change was perhaps even more dramatic and complex than elsewhere, with the period from 1967 to 1979 witnessing various twists and turns. From New Territories' 'new towns' and public housing estates to mass transport systems and country parks, from Cantopop and Cantonese television to the growth of a distinct local identity, from civil society groups to the organisation of government institutions, much of what constitutes present-day Hong Kong can be traced back to this period. It is therefore no exaggeration to say that 'modern' Hong Kong was born at this time. Although television overtook cinema as the most influential medium during these years, filmmaking continued to reflect – and shape – the changing sociopolitical and cultural environment of Hong Kong. While historians have shown how the British colonial government actively encouraged the growth of a sense of belonging to the city following the profound challenge to its rule during the 1966–7 protests and riots (Jones and Vagg 2007, 409–25), it would likely not have succeeded in this effort were it not for the creative energy of local TV producers and filmmakers, who increasingly left film studios and period settings behind to explore everyday social realities and problems. However, where the leftist filmmakers of the early 1950s had attempted something similar with their realist *lunlipian*, the filmmakers of the late 1960s and beyond predominantly spoke the language of action. Man-fung Yip (2017, 2) has for instance argued that 'Hong Kong martial arts films of the period . . . are best conceptualised as a mass cultural expression of Hong Kong's colonial, urban-industrial modernity.' As he further explains:

Hong Kong in the 1960s and 1970s constituted an arena where different ideas, styles, experiences, and structures of feeling interacted and negotiated new forms and meanings of modern life . . . The martial arts film played an essential role in facilitating this process, reflecting and reinforcing the everyday experiences and discourses associated with a new modern social order. (Yip 2017, 2–3)

In his book Yip mainly focuses on period martial arts films, which seems somewhat counter-intuitive: wouldn't films set in present-day Hong Kong be more effective in negotiating Hong Kong modernity? This chapter proposes that one reason for the initial dominance of period films was colonial censorship, which, like so much else, underwent drastic changes from the late 1960s to the late 1970s. Indeed, as we shall see, the changes in censorship policy were also intricately linked to the gradual emergence of the modern Hong Kong crime film and a new form of criminal realism. Unlike the other chapters in this book, this chapter therefore temporarily shifts away from textual analysis to consider the era's fundamental shifts in genre filmmaking from the perspective of the censorship practised by the colonial government. I argue that, just like film genre itself, censorship is an evolving process constantly shaping and shaped by its contexts. Unlike in earlier decades, when censorship – like colonial governance in Hong Kong in general – was carried out predominantly in a walled-off, top-down manner, the government censors of the 1970s began to act increasingly as mediators between different social, economic and political forces and interests. In this they were influenced by the liberal and anti-colonial atmosphere of the times and by the changing nature of British governance in Hong Kong, but also by the specific (economic) interests of local film producers, theatre owners and distributors, the media and public opinion.

Over the last decade and a half, Hong Kong film censorship has increasingly come on the agenda of film scholars and historians (K. Ng 2008, 2009, 2021; Z. Lee 2013, 2017; H. Yau 2015; Du 2017, 2019; J. Chang 2019). With the partial exception of Z. Lee (2013, 2017), most of this scholarship has focused on political censorship in Cold War Hong Kong, especially from the late 1940s to the late 1960s. The current chapter builds on my own previous publications (Van den Troost 2014, 2017, 2020) to consider instead the role of moral censorship in the development of the Hong Kong crime film, in particular during the transformative period from the late 1960s to the late 1970s. According to Zardas Lee (2017), during this time Hong Kong's censors changed from 'Cold War warriors' into 'moral guardians'. While this is true in the sense that officials spent much more time debating and defending moral censorship than previously, it should not obfuscate the fact that politics remained an important concern for the censors until the early 1990s. Moreover, as previous chapters already indicated, moral and political concerns are not always so cleanly separated, with the crime genre a convenient vehicle for political and social criticism. Nevertheless, the broader shift of censorship focus is undeniable: Lee (2017, 156–7) links this to the government's desire to maintain legitimacy after the crises of 1966–7 and to the general easing of Cold War tensions. My own reading of the government archives confirms this interpretation, but also leads me to a view of the colonial authorities as having considerably less agency than Lee ascribes to them: the role of 'moral guardian' was one the government's censors were reluctant to exercise, leading to continuous controversies from the late 1960s into the 1980s. The main criticism the government received during this period was that its censorship was insufficiently strict, especially given the absence of an 'adults-only' film category. Critics – rather baselessly – argued that the government's permissiveness towards cinematic content contributed to the 'crime problem' that was a major public concern at the time. As we shall see in Chapter 3, this criticism was echoed in populist attacks against social work and rehabilitation policies, and in arguments in favour of the death sentence.

After a brief theoretical consideration of the genre-censorship nexus, this chapter will outline the history of Hong Kong's censorship apparatus from the 1910s to the 1970s. It will look more closely at the changes in censorship policy in the 1960s and 1970s, and how these were related to changes in Hong Kong cinema's generic landscape. From period swordplay and kung fu crime films to the modern Hong Kong crime film, major shifts in genre filmmaking can be linked to specific decisions by the censors. As we shall see, particularly crucial for the crime film and criminal realism in this regard was the censors' extra sensitivity towards depictions of crime and violence in contemporary Hong Kong. Next, I will further detail the censor's role as a mediator between various stakeholders, including film producers and distributors, theatre owners, the press and the public. While the censors' agency was rather limited overall, I will argue that in the 1970s the censors' approach can be described as one of 'liberal (de)colonisation': a paradoxical double process whereby strategically placed colonial officials imposed their comparatively liberal views on censorship despite persistent media criticism, while also overseeing an effort towards giving locals a greater say in how the city (and its film censorship) should be managed. All this confirms the 1970s as a transitional decade for both the Hong Kong crime film and Hong Kong identity, which were often in dynamic interaction and were mediated in an important way by the government's censorship.

Film Genre and Censorship

As described in the Introduction, film genre has been fundamentally reconceptualised in the last few decades so that what was originally seen as a relatively permanent and stable structure has come to be treated as a fluid, ever-changing process

(Altman 1998, 6). After Rick Altman (1999) and Steve Neale (2000) reoriented genre studies towards a more contextual and discursive approach, Jason Mittell (2004) went on to explicitly recognise the role of censorship in genre formation. Conceiving of genres as 'cultural categories', Mittell (2004, xii) treated genre as 'a process of categorization that is not found within media texts, but operates across the cultural realms of media industries, audiences, policy, critics, and historical contexts'. Within this framework, regulators (such as censors) are 'a facet of the institutional apparatus of media that can exert powerful discourses that shape genre categories' (46). Similarly drawing on Altman and Neale, Alexandra Naylor (2007) also asserts this connection between film genres and the censors' discursive power. Scrutinising 1930s discourses on the affects of horror as produced by film marketing, the trade press, spectators, censorship campaigners, censorship authorities and others, Naylor analyses the effects of censorship and the controversies surrounding it on the creation of horror as a genre. She notably highlights how the power between the many participants in this critical dialogue surrounding horror was not equally distributed, with censorship authorities such as the Studio Relations Committee (SRC) and its successor, the Production Code Administration (PCA), playing a relatively more central role (Naylor 2007, 8). Mittell and Naylor's arguments have, it should be noted, significant overlap with an earlier landmark study of film censorship that was not primarily interested in issues of genre: Annette Kuhn (1988, 7) already in the 1980s defined censorship as regulation, 'an ongoing and always provisional process of constituting objects from and for its own practices'. This effects for censorship studies something similar to what Altman's redefinition of genre as a 'process' would do for genre studies a few years later. Intent on shifting the focus of censorship studies away from its restrictive acts to its productive power, Kuhn further argues that a 1917 distinction made by the British Board of Film Censors between 'commercial' and 'propaganda' films led to the creation of the propaganda film as a genre (47–8).

Film scholars have rarely taken the genre-censorship link as a central concern, with only 1930s Hollywood censorship inspiring a considerable body of relevant research. Like Naylor, Alison Peirse (2013) has written extensively on the relationship between censorship and the 1930s horror film, while censorship's impact on the gangster film and the fallen woman film have been studied by Lea Jacobs (1997), Richard Maltby (1993) and Ruth Vasey (1997). It has long been popular belief that the end of the 'classical' Hollywood gangster cycle in the early 1930s was due to censorship pressure, even though scholars from Colin McArthur (1972, 38) onwards have argued that the cycle was already declining before censorship became an issue. Jonathan Munby (1999, 7), in a more recent study, posits that the change of the gangster formula was the result of many factors (such as formal exhaustion and the changing needs of the audience), but that 'censorship had always played a crucial role in determining the nature and meaning of the gangster's mutations'. Also moving beyond a strictly 'prohibitive' definition of censorship's import, Munby (10–11) argues that censorship caused responses that in turn influenced both censorship priorities and the form of the crime film itself. The studios for instance responded to censorship of the gangster film by producing so-called 'G-Men' films – such as *'G' Men* (1935) and *Bullets or Ballots* (1936) – focusing on law enforcement rather than criminal heroes. Leger Grindon's (1998) work on the 1930s boxing film further illustrates that the censorship of one genre can have unexpected knock-on effects on other genres as well. He argues that the censorship of the gangster film was one factor in the mutation of the boxing film, which absorbed conventions such as the gangster film's 'critique of the ethos of opportunity and the ambitions of the ethnic outsider' (360).

As the above scholarship indicates, censorship is never simply a one-way process. While this chapter shows how censorship policy shaped the emergence of the modern Hong Kong crime film, it will also consider the multiple forces the censors of the late 1960s and 1970s attempted to mediate, including different sectors of the local film industry, the media and public opinion, as well as the government's own interests and ideology. As the colonial government strived to be more responsive to the population to bolster its legitimacy, a transformation of previously top-down censorship practice was necessary. At the same time, colonial habits died hard: the 'localisation' of censorship was a gradual and often fraught process.

History of the Hong Kong Censorship Apparatus

The first piece of legislation that touched on film censorship was the Theatres Regulation Ordinance of 1908. Barely ten years after the first film screenings in Hong Kong, this Ordinance paid considerable attention to 'cinematograph displays', indicating that the new medium had quickly become of concern to the colonial government. Requiring written descriptions of each scene in a film to be submitted to the government prior to public screening, a permit was granted or refused based on these descriptions. The film itself, however, was not subjected to censorship until eleven years later, when the Places of Public Entertainment Regulation Ordinance of 1919 was introduced. This new law, applying to all kinds of public entertainment, devoted a great deal of attention to cinema, introducing censorship of the film itself and placing the authority over censorship with the Commissioner of Police and the Secretary for Chinese Affairs.[1] Unlike in the United Kingdom and the United

---

[1] In 1934, the Director of Education joined these two officials in the newly established 'Board of Censors'.

States, then, film censorship in Hong Kong was from the start carried out directly by the government.

Few relevant government documents are available from this period, so we mainly have to rely on laws, memoirs and sporadic newspaper reports to get an idea of the practice of censorship at the time. In the most comprehensive study of Hong Kong film censorship to date, Herman Yau (2015, 66–9) has argued that a prominent concern of colonial censors in these early years was to avoid offending friendly nations. This echoed the existing practice in the censorship of newspapers since the late nineteenth century (Michael Ng 2017) and would also be the last form of political film censorship to be removed from the law, in the 1990s.[2] In the first half of the twentieth century, the 'friendly nations' referred mainly to China and Japan. Herman Yau (2015, 68–9; 84–7) has found evidence of at least two locally produced films being banned for their 'national defence' and anti-Japanese themes: the Cantonese film *Lifeline* (命 *Saangming sin*, 1935) and the Mandarin film *March of the Guerrillas* (擊 曲 *Jaugik zeonhangkuk*, 1941). The censors nevertheless allowed dozens of similar films to be screened in Hong Kong in the late 1930s and early 1940s; they mainly just nudged filmmakers to make their criticisms of Japanese aggression less explicit. After occupying Hong Kong in December 1941, the Japanese implemented much stricter censorship. Due to the unwillingness of filmmakers to collaborate, however, only one propaganda film, *The Battle of Hong Kong* (攻 戰 *Hoenggong gungloekzin*, 1942), was made in Hong Kong during the war (H. Yau 2015, 93–100).

After the war, the British resumed authority over Hong Kong and it is from this point onwards that more detailed government records on censorship are available. At this time, film censorship, which before the war had been managed by the police, was assigned to the Public Relations Office (PRO), a new department created in 1946. A Panel of Censors was established in 1947, its membership of around twenty mostly drawn from the ranks of officials as well as other British and Chinese elites. The records from this period hint at a relatively casual approach to censorship – officials often had their wives join the Panel to stand in for them and there was no remuneration for the work. The intensifying Cold War soon increased the importance of censorship in the eyes of the colonial government, however, and led to the appointment of full-time censors and the legislation of the Film Censorship Regulations (1953). These Regulations described in more detail the procedures of censorship and created

---

[2] After almost thirty years, a form of political censorship has recently been reintroduced in Hong Kong as a result of new 'national security' legislation and an amendment of the Film Censorship Ordinance in 2021. See the Afterword for a further discussion of these recent changes.

an appellate body, the Board of Review, which could reconsider the decisions made by the Panel of Censors and guide overall censorship policy. The Board consisted of the Commissioner of Police, the Secretary for Chinese Affairs and the Director of Education. Aside from the addition of the Director of Social Welfare to the Board in 1963, the machinery of film censorship remained relatively unchanged until the early 1970s, when the growing contentiousness of censorship sparked significant reforms. The late 1960s and 1970s transformation of Hong Kong cinema thus coincided with the crisis and reform of local censorship practice. Indeed, as I argue in this chapter, these developments were related.

The key person behind the 1970s changes in censorship practice was Nigel J. V. Watt, a colonial official who had earlier been posted in Africa and in Aden. As part of his duties in the Public Relations Office – renamed the Information Services Department (ISD) in 1959 – Watt had joined the Panel of Censors in 1961 and was appointed as Director of the ISD in 1963. Heading the department responsible for the day-to-day operation of film censorship, Watt took charge more visibly in this area only in 1970, when film censorship came under repeated attack in the local press. The first salvo was launched by Henry Litton, Secretary of the Hong Kong Bar Association, who in a public speech lamented the lack of rules governing how a film should be censored ('Litton Deplores Absence of Rules', *South China Morning Post*, 24 April 1970). While this specific issue received limited further attention in the press, it would haunt the government for many years, especially after the absence of properly legislated censorship rules led some officials to question whether their practice of film censorship might in fact be technically illegal (Van den Troost 2020). More immediately pressing was the criticism that followed when the English-language press found out – only after directly asking the government – that Dennis Hopper's *Easy Rider* (1969) had been banned from release in Hong Kong a year earlier. After a week of media attacks on the censors' standards and their lack of transparency, Watt agreed to a lengthy interview with the *Hong Kong Standard* in which he – likely for the first time – revealed more information about the censors' backgrounds and their criteria for judging films (Bob Bennett, '"Generation Gap" May Hamper Film Censorship', *Hong Kong Standard*, 14 July 1970). Soon after, ISD started issuing monthly censorship reports in the hope that it would in the long run help to cool off the issue. In 1971, it also for the first time began to give distributors the reasons for the banning or cutting of their films and started discussing whether the government should be less secretive towards the general public about its censorship criteria ('Annual Report Film Censorship 1971', 4 January 1972, Hong Kong Records Series [HKRS] 1101-2-14, Public Records Office, Hong Kong [henceforth HKPRO]). Obviously, a shift towards greater transparency was underway.

Figure IM.1 Nigel Watt (third from left), Commissioner for Television and Films, attending a switching-on ceremony at Salon Films, 16 June 1978. Image provided by Getty Images.

These initial steps did not manage to pacify the government's critics, however, and it became clear that more drastic action was necessary. In late 1972, the Television Authority and Film Censorship Section were hived off from ISD and placed under the Secretariat for Home Affairs, where they became the 'Television and Films Branch'. Watt was appointed to lead this new department, as newly minted 'Commissioner for Television and Films'. Soon after taking up this new role, he launched a major reboot of film censorship and started talking to the press about his plans for the next four years. Two of his promised reforms were quickly accomplished: the censors' guidelines were updated and distributed to film producers, importers, exhibitors as well as the general public, and younger censors were appointed to replace the retirees previously responsible for censoring films. In a savvy public relations move, Watt presented both the freshly recruited censors and their new guidelines to the press on 2 May 1973, drawing considerable attention. Whereas all the new censors were young, local and predominantly female, the new Chief Film Censor, Pierre Lebrun, was a French-Canadian teacher newly arrived in Hong Kong, who did not speak Cantonese and had no experience in film – certainly an odd (and rather colonial) choice. As he had not yet received higher-level approval for his plans and appointments, Watt's frank interactions with the press were likely at least in part a strategy to push through his own vision: by going public, he ensured that his superiors would mostly let him have his way, especially when his actions received positive media coverage. People in the Colonial Secretariat were displeased with his tactics, expressing themselves as such in a memo on 25 May 1973 ('Memo: Film Censorship Standards', para. 3, HKRS 1101-2-15, HKPRO; 'Panel of Censors, 1945–1988', Item 65, HKRS 2139-2-1, HKPRO). Nevertheless, in December 1973, another restructuring gave Watt increased autonomy: his department was renamed the 'Television and Films Authority', and became independent from the Secretariat for Home Affairs.

In the following years, Watt further implemented his reform agenda under the mantra that the censors must 'try to reflect the attitudes of the community' ('Film Censorship in Hong Kong', 28 June 1978, par. 16, HKRS 313-7-3, HKPRO). His hiring of younger censors was part of this effort, as their average age was more representative of Hong Kong society at the time. Two other related initiatives were the engagement of an outside company to carry out a survey of public attitudes towards the standards of screened sex and violence, and the creation of a 'public advisory panel' composed of a representative sample of the population, of which the members would be invited to watch films with the censors and to express their opinions in a questionnaire. While the survey was completed and its results publicised in May 1974, the creation of the public advisory panel was more complicated, requiring legal changes. The drafting process lasted into 1976 and resulted in the first major update of the Film Censorship Regulations since 1953. Aside from paving the way for the establishment of the public advisory panel (in 1977), the new Regulations also allowed for the appointment of members of the public to the Board of Review, which had until then consisted solely of (mostly British) senior officials. In a final major administrative reshuffle, several licensing functions previously performed by the police were in 1977 transferred to Watt's department, which was renamed the 'Television and Entertainment Licensing Authority' (TELA). Watt's title was accordingly adjusted to 'Commissioner for Television and Entertainment Licensing'.

While TELA was in 2012 absorbed into the new Communications Authority and the responsibility for film censorship was moved to this new Authority's Office for Film, Newspaper and Article Administration (OFNAA), much of the practices and institutions created by Watt (such as the public advisory panel and the periodic public opinion surveys) remain in place to this day. As the first and longest-serving official in charge of film censorship, Watt oversaw the localisation of censorship administration, albeit with some apparent reservations, as the 1973 appointment of Pierre Lebrun as chief film censor indicated. The localisation of censorship, part of the broader transformation of British governance in Hong Kong (Steve Tsang 2004, 194), was completed when in 1983 Watt was succeeded as Commissioner for Television and Entertainment Licensing by Robert Sun 孫元 . All subsequent

Commissioners would be Hong Kong Chinese. Watt's tenure as the top censorship bureaucrat also coincided with key moments in the emergence of the modern Hong Kong crime film and a new form of criminal realism: his relatively liberal and hands-off attitude towards censorship, as gleaned from government records, arguably played an important role in the genre's emergence. The following section will explore how subtle shifts in censorship policy influenced genre evolution in late 1960s and 1970s Hong Kong.

Censorship Policy and the 'New Wuxia Century'

As noted at the beginning of this chapter, scholars have in recent years been delving more deeply into Hong Kong cinema during the Cold War, especially the period from the late 1940s to the 1960s. Much of this research has focused on political film censorship, drawing on government archives and other sources to explore what was clearly the predominant concern of the Hong Kong censors until the mid-1960s (K. Ng 2008, 2009, 2021; Z. Lee 2013, 2017; H. Yau 2015; Du 2017, 2019; J. Chang 2019). This scholarship generally confirms Du's (2017, 117) argument that political censorship happened along two axes:

> as a local response to both Chinese politics (the CCP vs. the KMT) and Cold War politics (the PRC vs. the United States-plus-Taiwan, the PRC vs. the United Kingdom-plus-Hong Kong) . . . and as a strategy of cultural governance vis-à-vis the vulnerability of Hong Kong and the control of internal stability during the 1950s and 1960s.

The popularity of the Cold War as a research framework has led to a relative neglect of the evolution of moral censorship in Hong Kong, despite its becoming both the public's and the censors' central concern from the mid-1960s to the late 1970s. To be sure, moral censorship was never really absent. The 1950 Directive for Film Censors for instance targeted depictions of crime, horror and violence, as well as 'matter which offends against or brings into contempt the accepted rules of morality or decency'. The latter included not only depictions of sex and physical passions, but also 'family quarrels, unhappy marriages, divorce, gambling, drunkenness, vice and depravity of any description, accidents, operations or hospital scenes' ('Film Censorship – Directive for Film Censors (1950)', HKRS 163-1-1159, HKPRO). Censorship of such subject matter was, and still is, common internationally, albeit to different degrees. There are some indications, however, that depictions of contemporary crime were under particularly careful scrutiny in Hong Kong. The 1950 Directive highlighted the following crime-related content for special attention:

1. Any incident which glorifies crime, or any incident in which the recognised authorities of the law are held up to contempt or ridicule, incidents where use of violence or criminal methods go unpunished.
2. Incidents capable of imitation which might encourage the use of firearms or other lethal weapons to commit crimes of violence.

The 1950 guidelines are vague and therefore adaptable to changes in society and politics. Almost no archival materials related to moral censorship are available for the 1950s and early 1960s, but there are indications that the censorship of crime, law enforcement and violence was relatively harsh. Anecdotally, Law Kar (1996, 57) has for instance noted that, even in the 1960s, crime thrillers and detective movies could only portray a positive image of law enforcers, and that the showing of officers not properly dressed could lead to a film being banned. Given that the Hong Kong Police Force was to a large extent the public face of the colonial government and that quite a number of officers in the 1950s and 1960s were Caucasian Britons, their depiction was undoubtedly politically sensitive.[3] Filmic violence or disrespect towards a police officer could easily be interpreted politically as an insult to the colonial government, or even as the incitement of rebellion, bringing the film into the dangerous orbit of political censorship. The presence of the Commissioner of Police in the Board of Review further ensured tight censorship of matters relating to crime and law enforcement, as the internal discussions in 1965 illustrate most clearly (see below).

In terms of censorship policy, the first half of the 1960s was a period of relative calm. The main development was the 1963 update of the Directive for Film Censors, the first such update in thirteen years. Much lengthier than the 1950 version, the 'General Principles for Guidance of Film Censors and the Film Censorship Board of Review' (hereafter referred to as the General Principles) are remarkable in that they devote much less space to politics and propaganda, and far more to the depiction of sex and violence – a good indication of how times had changed. Regarding violence, the General Principles reflect the growing concern with the 'youth problem', stating:

> It is generally undesirable to pass films which show an excessive amount of calculated and realistic violence, especially where impressionable youth may be encouraged to identify itself with and to imitate 'tough guys' on the screen. In particular, it is undesirable to allow scenes which persons may be encouraged to imitate by

---

[3] In a similar vein, David Newman (2013, 175) cites American consular documents from the 1920s that indicate 'pictures reflecting badly on the natives of India' were likely to be censored in Hong Kong, as at that time many police officers in the colony were of Indian ethnicity.

using firearms or other dangerous weapons to commit crimes of violence. ('General Principles for Guidance of Film Censors and the Film Censorship Board of Review', November 1963, HKRS 934-5-34, HKPRO)

The censors were now also asked to make a distinction between violence set in a much earlier age, and the less acceptable violence set 'in current surroundings'. Similar to the 1950 guidelines, images of violence against or by the forces of law and order were considered especially sensitive: 'It would be wrong to allow the impression that the Police can be knocked about with impunity; that crime pays.' Also noteworthy, in an earlier draft of the document, is the call to resist the 'whittling process': the 'progressive whittling away of earlier more rigid standards, largely under the pressure of box-office profits' (Memo from Secretary for Chinese Affairs to Board of Review: 'Film Censorship', 23 September 1963, HKRS 934-5-34, HKPRO). This specific warning was made in relation to sex, but the same 'whittling process' was certainly also underway in depictions of crime and violence. Despite the authorities' resolve to resist this trend, it would continue unabated over the next few years, leading directly to the censorship crisis of the early 1970s.

In the meantime, political censorship was further relaxed as well. A key turning point came in 1965, when the Communist-controlled press for several days attacked the restrictions on films made in the PRC. Around the same time, Southern Film Corporation, the main distributor of mainland films in Hong Kong, submitted two films to the censors – *A Glorious Festival* (光　　日 *Gwongfai dik zitjat*, 1964) and *The Red Detachment of Women* (　　娘子 *Hungsik noengzigwan*, 1961) – in the hope that they could be shown during the PRC National Day celebrations that year. The tense situation prompted Governor David Trench to write to the Foreign Secretary in London and led to an urgent meeting of the members of the Board of Review, at which a revision of the 1963 General Principles was launched. The Board eventually decided to reverse the censors' ban on *A Glorious Festival* but maintained the ban on *Red Detachment*. It simultaneously revised the General Principles so that similar films would not necessarily suffer the same fate in the future. Over the next few years, fewer films from the PRC were rejected, encountering more lenient censorship than films of a similar kind from Taiwan (Z. Lee 2013, 45–77; Du 2017, 125–38). The 1965 General Principles also reveal subtle changes in the attitude towards screen violence and crime. A new phrase was included, indicating the unsuitability of films bringing 'the impartial administration of justice in Hong Kong into disrepute'. In the detailed discussion of violence and crime, the most significant difference was the explicit differentiation between violence 'in conditions entirely alien to Hong Kong's' and (the more 'dangerous') violence 'in familiar surroundings' ('A Statement of the General Principles as Adopted on 20 November 1965 by the Film Censorship Board of Review', 20 November 1965, HKRS 1101-2-13, HKPRO). This implied that, in practice, non-Chinese crime and action films would be subject to less stringent censorship than local productions – something officials at the time adamantly denied to both the press and the film industry. In an illustration of the role of the Police in the censorship of crime and violence, the Deputy Commissioner of Police, Edward Tyrer, was the main voice to object to this policy relaxation, unsuccessfully pushing the Board of Review to continue banning scenes of 'urban violence' in any modern setting ('Censorship of Films: Policy', 23 September 1965, HKRS 1101-2-13, HKPRO).

After the confirmation of the new General Principles in November 1965, interdepartmental discussions about censorship quieted down almost completely, and for more than two and a half years little was done to change the existing system. Given the social unrest of 1966 and 1967, officials undoubtedly had other priorities during this period, although it is also possible that relevant archival documents from this still-controversial turning point in Hong Kong history have simply not been declassified or preserved. In any case, when (relative) stability returned in 1968, immediate changes were noticeable in the day-to-day operation of censorship, which was then attracting more and more public scrutiny. For one, the dramatic increase of archival records of this period indicates that officials were trying to improve accountability. From this point on, detailed reports on censorship decisions for specific films are available, especially those that seem to have had an impact on censorship policy more generally, as is some of the communication between censors and film producers/distributors. Starting from 1968, the Chief Film Censor also began submitting annual reports on film censorship. This extensive documentation allows for a closer look at the whittling process that had already alarmed certain officials in preceding years. The documents dealing with the 1968 Shaw Brothers period martial arts movie, *Death Valley* (斷　　*Tyunwan guk*), provide a good illustration of this process.

On 15 July 1968, the Chief Film Censor, William Hung 士, informed Shaw Brothers that *Death Valley* was approved for release, subject to a number of excisions: cuts were necessary in three scenes containing excessive violence, and in two scenes containing sex/nudity ('Death Valley' – Letter from Chief Film Censor William Hung to General Manager of Shaw Brothers H.K. Ltd, 15 July 1968, HKRS 394-23-12, HKPRO). In a lengthy written appeal to the Panel of Censors, Shaw Brothers' general manager, Laurence Ling 凌斯, asserted that the suggested excisions were not justified under the universal principle of freedom of speech, and went on to list several more specific reasons why the film should not be censored. Most significant among these was the argument that scenes of sex, nudity and violence similar to those that appeared in *Death Valley* were passed

Figure IM.2 Still from *Death Valley* (1968). © Celestial Pictures Ltd. All rights reserved 權 天映 娛樂有 公司全 擁有.

when they appeared in European and American films. Hence, censoring them in this movie would 'seem to indicate that there is partiality towards imported movie productions with unreasonable prejudice and discouragement for local producers'. Shaw Brothers, in other words, had not failed to notice the different standards to which local and overseas films were held by the censors since at least 1965, and was now using this discrepancy to push for a further relaxation of censorship for local films. Ling also pointed out that even similar Shaw Brothers films – such as the box office hit *One-Armed Swordsman* (1967) – had previously passed censorship without any cuts, and further argued that times had changed so sex had ceased to be taboo in public discussion ('re: Death Valley' – Letter from General Manager of Shaw Brothers H.K. Ltd to Panel of Censors, 1 August 1968, HKRS 394-23-12, HKPRO).

Aware that the appeal would have an impact on the then ongoing fad for bloody swordplay films launched by *One-Armed Swordsman*, the Board of Review decided to use it to establish a new standard for the guidance of the Panel of Censors. The report of the resulting meeting notes that censors had been passing scenes beyond the strict rules of the 1965 General Principles, which made it impossible to turn back the clock ('Death Valley' [Film Censorship – Board of Review]: Memo from the Acting Secretary for Chinese Affairs to the Board of Review, 22 August 1968, HKRS 1101-2-13, HKPRO). In the ensuing interdepartmental communication, most members of the Board of Review took a tolerant attitude towards sex and violence in films. Although *Death Valley* was eventually passed for exhibition with fewer cuts than originally prescribed, the Board still failed to come up with a consistent standard for moral censorship. Some members also expressed considerable apprehension that the predominantly British membership of the Board might possibly be more tolerant towards screen nudity and sex than the Chinese general population. In practice, the lack of a clear policy ensured that the erosion of censorship standards would continue unabated.

A full-blown censorship crisis was well underway at this point. In the 1968 annual report on film censorship, William Hung noted that 'local producers, especially those of Mandarin films, have been unusually lavish in turning out films with scenes of excessive sex, violence and bloodshed' ('Annual Report on Film Censorship (January–December 1968)', 10 January 1969, HKRS 1101-2-13, HKPRO). The censors did try to resist this general trend: while in 1966–7 only 49 films were cut and 31 banned (out of a total of 659 films submitted to the censors), by 1970–1 these numbers had risen to 144 films cut and 62 banned (out of a total of 762). Local producers and distributors meanwhile were unrelenting in their attempts to gain ground on the censors, as reflected in the increase in appeals to the Board of Review: between 1966 and 1971, this number grew from 22 to 50 per year ('Decisions of Panel of Film Censors during the Years 1966–1971' and 'Decisions of Board of Review during the Years 1966–1971', 27 August 1971, HKRS 1101-2-14, HKPRO). As noted earlier, criticism of censorship became more frequent in the media at this time as well, with some voices deploring the banning of certain films and others attacking the lax standards of the censors. Calls for the introduction of film classification became more frequent, with the matter raised repeatedly in the Legislative Council (on 7 and 9 October 1970, and again on 9 June 1971). The enduring controversy surrounding film censorship eventually resulted in the reforms launched by Watt in 1972–3, as discussed in the previous section.

From the perspective of Hong Kong genre history, the changes in censorship policy in the mid- and late 1960s were very consequential. When the 1963 General Principles allowed for a more relaxed approach towards violence set in the remote past (in contrast to violence 'in current surroundings'), they paved the way for Shaw Brothers' 'new *wuxia* century', launched in late 1965 and coming fully into its own with Chang Cheh's *One-Armed Swordsman*. The distinction the censors made between the remote past and the present was possibly a reaction to the global success and acclaim of Japan's samurai films, which in the wake of Kurosawa Akira 明's *Yojimbo* (心棒 *Yojinbo*, 1961) had taken a turn towards ever greater amounts of blood and gore. It was this same trend of samurai films that directly inspired Shaw's new-style martial arts films (K. Yau 2005). It appears then that Hong Kong's censors were playing catch-up, relaxing censorship in response primarily to overseas film trends, and then being caught unawares when local filmmakers started to make similar films in large numbers as well (which explains the Board of Review's 1968 debate about *Death Valley*). While in the case of sex and violence, the censors decided it was undesirable to 'turn back the clock', they were arguably more steadfast in curbing depictions of contemporary crime in Hong Kong. Even in December 1970, Chief Film Censor William Hung could still write that the censors felt that 'what is currently prohibited by the Police should not be permitted in a film which portrays the present-day Hong Kong' ('Notes and Comments on "A Statement of the General Principles as adopted on 20 November 1965 by the Film Censorship Board of Review"', 1 December 1970, HKRS 1101-2-13, HKPRO). In the same document, however, Hung also mentions that 'gangster films of usual pattern' were not particularly of concern, which indicates that there was space for escapist action-crime films, as long as they did not take too much of an interest in the actual realities of crime and punishment in Hong Kong. This certainly is reflected in most of the crime films discussed in Chapter 1, and it explains why 'realism' (*xieshi*) became such a common advertising term for crime films in the 1970s (see Chapter 3). The censors had turned realistic depictions of contemporary Hong Kong (crime) into a forbidden fruit, giving 'realism' commercial value by repressing it. In the five years following Hung's report, this remaining barrier would gradually be dismantled as well.

Censorship Policy and the Modern Hong Kong Crime Film

As Hung was writing down his reflections on the state of censorship in Hong Kong, a film had started playing in local theatres that inaugured not only a new generic cycle, but also a further erosion of censorship standards. Jimmy Wang 's *The Chinese Boxer* (*Lungfudau*, 1970) was an enormous box office hit, launching a trend of kung fu films that would soon be reaching audiences around the world. Whereas swordplay films are usually set in China's distant imperial past, kung fu as a genre takes as its setting the period from the late nineteenth century to the present. As such, kung fu challenged the censors' criteria for screen violence by pushing the bloody action familiar from late 1960s swordplay films much closer to the present, while also engaging more explicitly with themes relevant to contemporary Hong Kong, such as China's traumatic encounter with Western modernity (of which Hong Kong itself was an outcome) and anti-Japanese sentiment. Chang Cheh, for instance, pushed the boundaries of what was possible in terms of crime narratives by setting his kung fu films *The Duel* (大   *Daaikyutdau*, 1971) and *The Boxer from Shantung* (*Maa Wingzing*, 1972, co-directed with Pao Hsueh-li 學) in Republican-era China. Another strategy to avoid possible trouble with the Hong Kong censors was to set contemporary kung fu films in 'exotic' overseas locales: Chang set his *Duel of Fists* (拳擊 *Kyungik*, 1971) in present-day Thailand, which was also the setting for Bruce Lee's breakthrough film, *The Big Boss* (唐山大兄 *Tongsaan daaihing*, 1971). *The Way of the Dragon* (*Maanglong gwogong*, 1972) moved even farther afield, pitting Lee against mafia thugs in Italy. While there were commercial reasons for shooting movies overseas, censorship was certainly also a factor. Chang Cheh hinted at this in a 1972 interview, in which he criticised the Hong Kong censors for making social observation and critique nearly impossible in local films, and for encouraging the production of films that were removed from present-day reality in Hong Kong (H. S. Chow, 'Chang Lashes Out at Censorship', *China Mail*, 28 June 1972).

At this point, however, Chang was a relatively isolated voice calling for less censorship, as a moral panic surrounding violent crime was reaching fever pitch and compelled the government to take action on various fronts, including film censorship. The government's prioritising of the fight against crime was kicked off by then-outgoing Governor David Trench who addressed the issue in an October 1971 speech to the Legislative Council. Soon after, the order came down for all government departments to start a comprehensive investigation and analysis into the 'basic causes' of crime, as well as appropriate countermeasures ('Basic Causes of Crime' (Memo from Secretary for Home Affairs to all Department Heads), 15 November 1971, HKRS 160-3-57, HKPRO). Trench's successor, Murray MacLehose, who arrived in November that same year, continued these efforts. An initial report summarising media discussions on the 'crime problem' outlined many of the presumed causes that would largely be reiterated in more formal government investigations later. They included problems such as inequality, (police) corruption, influence of Western culture and of the triads, lack of healthy recreational activities, the indifferent attitude of the public, an inadequate education system, busy parents and excessively light punishment of offenders. One of the most mentioned causes was the flourishing of gambling, drugs and pornography, including the claim that 'the law . . . seems to tolerate all sorts of pornographic advertisements and publications, scenes of sex and violence on T.V. and in film shows which poison the mind of our youth' ('Causes of Crime', n.d. [likely December 1971], HKRS 160-3-57, HKPRO). As this last quote also indicates, this discourse clearly had a particular type of crime in mind: juvenile delinquency.

A lengthier and more formal report was circulated in May 1972, incorporating much of the earlier 'Causes of Crime' report, but also including crime statistics as well as analyses detailing how crime influenced public attitudes towards the government, the law, the courts and the police. Noting that concern with the 'crime wave' had reached the point where members of the public were forming patrol squads to protect themselves, the report also stated that, while crime statistics indicated a steady increase in crime in recent years as well as a sudden spike in the last twelve to eighteen months, the perception of Hong Kong being in the midst of a crime wave was 'a matter of subjective judgement'. Real or not, the perceived crime wave was in any case creating a lot of public dissatisfaction with the government, the law and the police, and therefore required urgent action. Among the long list of recommendations that concluded the report, one called for stricter censorship of television and cinema 'so as to reduce the display of scenes of violence, sex and perversion' ('Public Attitudes to Crime' (Memo from Colonial Secretariat to Attorney General, Commissioner of Police and Director of Information Services), 4 May 1972, HKRS 160-3-57, HKPRO). As the Civic Association, an influential semi-political party, also had started to publicly advocate for curbs on cinematic violence, censorship was tightened soon afterwards, even though the government publicly doubled down on taking the setting of a film into consideration ('Extract from Leg.Co. Meeting Held on 19.7.72: Violence in Chinese Language Films', 19 July 1972, HKRS 1101-2-14, HKPRO).

Filmmakers nevertheless continued to challenge the restrictions against crime films set in contemporary Hong Kong, with the censors beginning to give way in late 1972. A key film in this regard appears to have been John Law's *Back Street* (後 *Hyutsaa haugaai*), also known as *The Bodyguards* (女保 *Sanneoi boubiu*). While the film drew little attention at the time, the official correspondence surrounding it was preserved by the censors, hinting at its importance. With the plot involving violent conflict between two gangs of juvenile delinquents engaged in the prostitution racket, the film's cast also included Michael Chan 惠敏 and Alan Tang 光榮, who would soon become famous for their gangster roles and their alleged real-life triad connections. Given *Back Street*'s portrayal of the 'realistic violence of the present-day teen-aged delinquents', the censor in charge decided to ban it on 7 June 1972. However, after the filmmakers appealed, the Board of Review reversed this decision, agreeing to the release of the film subject to cuts in the fight scenes. It justified its overturning of the ban by arguing that the film 'did not show the Hong Kong under-

Figure IM.3 Poster of *Back Street*, also known as *The Bodyguards* (1973). Image provided by the Hong Kong Film Archive, Leisure and Cultural Services Department, with the permission of Kong Chiao Film Company.

world in any sort of a good light and . . . made a reasonable attempt to emphasise the sordidness of the activities portrayed' (Film: 'Back Street', 6 November 1972, HKRS 313-7-8, HKPRO). Given the long gap between the original ban in June and the Board's reversal in November, it seems likely that the film gave rise to a more substantial discussion not preserved in the archive, resulting in a policy shift that paved the way for more contemporary crime films to appear. Indeed, the following year saw the release of Kuei Chih-hung 桂 's *The Delinquent* (憤怒 年 *Fannou cingnin*, 1973, with Chang Cheh) and *Payment in Blood* (*Hyutzing*, 1973), Chang Cheh's *Police Force* (察 *Gingcaat*, 1973, with Tsai Yang-ming 揚名), as well as Ho Meng-hua 何夢 's *Kiss of Death* (毒女 *Dukneoi*, 1973) – the latter a violent rape-revenge film set in contemporary Hong Kong. Several of these films will be discussed in more detail in the next chapter.

Unsurprisingly, the public calls for more decisive action continued unabated. In February 1973, three unofficial members of the Legislative Council gave speeches criticising the violence in films and linking it to the increasing crime rate, especially violent crimes committed by youth. Responding to their calls for more censorship, the Secretary for Home Affairs, Donald C. C. Luddington, announced that the General Principles guiding the Panel of Film Censors were already under review, but also tempered expectations:

> Hong Kong cannot afford either to be out of touch with the rest of the world, or to have a lot of bored people . . . Thus if Government attempted to cut out all violence in films, public entertainment might be very severely reduced, for there are virtually no films made for the Hong Kong market alone. ('Guidelines for Film Censorship Under Review' (Press Release), 14 February 1973, HKRS 1101-2-14, HKPRO)

The censors' dilemma is reflected in the *Film Censorship Standards: A Note of Guidance*, presented to the public in May 1973 as part of Nigel Watt's reforms discussed earlier in this chapter. This booklet devotes more space to violence than to all other censorship categories combined – clearly an attempt to signal to the public that the government was taking the issue seriously. Actual policy changes were relatively limited, however. While the distinction between 'remote' and 'familiar' settings remained, it was added that 'not too much importance should be attached to this form of distance through time and make-believe' (Television and Films Division 1973, par. 9). Moreover, the guidelines acknowledged that violence could be used 'to make a substantial point about society and human relations' (Television and Films Division 1973, par. 13). This, along with other descriptions, reinforced the stricter censorship of gratuitous kung fu violence implemented since a year earlier but left the door somewhat open for crime films set in contemporary Hong Kong. A further distinction between a 'crudely made film' and one 'made with integrity and skill' – with the former singled out for more censorship than the latter (Television and Films Division 1973, par. 5) – meanwhile facilitated the removal of remaining restrictions, as its subjective nature was easily challenged by filmmakers.

This additional distinction based on the 'quality' of a film was likely made in consideration of the wave of acclaimed crime films then coming out of Hollywood, such as *Dirty Harry* (1971), *The French Connection* (1971) and *The Godfather* (1972). *The Godfather* in fact was passed by the censors with only a few cuts just several weeks before the *Note of Guidance* was presented to the public ('To Cut or Not To Cut: Censor's Job Is Hard Work', *Star*, 3 April 1973). Notably, this seminal gangster film's release in theatres was still hobbled by the continuing sensitivity surrounding the cinematic depiction of crime and violence, and the 'crime problem' more broadly. As 1973 was also the year of the government's first Fight Violent Crime Campaign (see Chapter 3), the censor asked all cinema managers and film distributors in Hong Kong to refrain from showing violent films during the campaign's duration, from 14 May to 14 July (Response to *Star*, 18 May 1973, HKRS 508-3-3, HKPRO). Although this was no more than a 'polite request' from the government, the distributor of *The Godfather* complied, postponing the film's release to October that

Figure IM.4 Subtly subverting the 1973 Fight Crime Campaign: *Payment in Blood* (1973). © Celestial Pictures Ltd. All rights reserved 權　天映娛樂有　公司全　擁有.

same year. As we will see in the next chapter, not every company was as considerate: Kuei Chih-hung's *Payment in Blood* – a film that directly undermined a central message of the Fight Violent Crime Campaign – was released during the campaign.

The preferential treatment of 'quality' films was as discriminatory towards local films as the long-standing distinction made between films in familiar and those in alien settings, but was harder to defend. Given the box office success of Hollywood crime films, local filmmakers had a strong incentive to follow suit with their own entries in the genre, and if they argued that they were dealing with important social issues in a serious way, it would be harder for the censors to stop them. Initially, however, the censors held firm, banning more locally made films in 1973 than at any time since at least 1965. Their main target was (kung fu) violence, but many of the films banned that year also involved crime, such as *One by One* (死對　 *Seideoitau*, 1973), *The Mandarin* (　人 *Munzaujan*, 1973) and *The Black Dragon* (　　 *Haklung*, 1973). Several of the banned films made explicit reference to *The Godfather* in their publicity, such as *The Mandarin* (released as *The Godfathers of Hong Kong* in the US) and *Chinese Godfather* (大　 *Daai gaaulung*, 1974, also known as *The Chivalrous Knight*). These banned films were all low-budget productions by small companies – likely these companies were willing to risk their films being banned in Hong Kong as the kung fu craze then sweeping the globe gave them a reasonable chance of recovering their investment in overseas markets. Upon being banned by the Panel of Censors then newly installed by Watt, many companies appealed to the Board of Review, usually without success. In the case of *The Black Dragon*, which was initially approved subject to certain excisions, the film's distributor appealed arguing that the film should be released without cuts because of its anti-crime, pro-police theme and its high-quality filmmaking ('Re: The Black Dragon' (Letter from Managing Director of Intercontinental Film Distributors (HK) Ltd to the Secretary of the Panel of Film Censors), 21 November 1973, HKRS 313-7-9, HKPRO). This particular appeal backfired, with the Board deciding to outright ban the film, at least in part because in its view the film depicted the Hong Kong Police Force as ineffectual and as resorting to all kinds of illegal methods in its operations against the criminals (Film: 'The Black Dragon' (Report by the Board of Review), 3 December 1973, HKRS 313-7-9, HKPRO). The distributor wrote back with a lengthy plea to allow the film to be released, with cuts if necessary, and referred to several similar Hollywood crime films allowed for release in Hong Kong, highlighting the censors' different standards for local films ('Re: The Black Dragon' (Letter from Managing Director of Intercontinental Film Distributors (HK) Ltd to the Secretary of the Panel of Film Censors), 19 December 1973, HKRS 313-7-9, HKPRO). It is unclear whether he ever received a reply.

The censors' campaign against (kung fu) violence seems to have eased somewhat in early 1974, with much fewer local films facing an outright ban that year compared to 1973. This might have been because, with the international kung fu film craze subsiding, fewer kung fu films were being produced and submitted to the censors, or simply because filmmakers reduced the violence in their films to avoid trouble. Announcing the results of the first professional survey of public views on film censorship in May 1974, Nigel Watt argued that they largely endorsed the censors' recent tightening of censorship. This survey indicated that over half of Hong Kong cinemagoers wished for stricter censorship, while one third wanted standards to be relaxed. Most considered the censorship of sex more of a priority than the censorship of violence and regarded the 'fantasy violence of the Mandarin movies' as more harmful than 'the realistic violence of most Western crime films' ('Film Censorship Too Lax: Survey – Stricter Control Urged', 1 May 1974, HKRS 70-6-579-1, HKPRO). It doesn't look like the censors tightened censorship following the survey: while between July and December 1973 45 per cent of all films submitted for censorship were cut and 5 per cent were banned, during the same period in 1974 only 42 per cent were cut and 3.6 per cent were banned. Nigel Watt claimed this was because there was a significant decrease in the number of films exploiting violence and sex in 1974 (Barry Choi, 'Excessive Screen Violence and Sex on the Way Out', *South China Morning Post*, 21 January 1975). While this may have been an attempt to put a positive spin on the declining censorship rates despite the recent survey results, there was likely some truth to this: the breakthrough Hong Kong crime films produced in 1974 and 1975 included very little action and focused more on drama.

The censors' action against excessive violence combined with their increasing tolerance for social and political criticism in films. About two weeks after the survey results were announced in May 1974, a short article in the *China Mail* hyperbolically spoke of a new trend of 'anti-government films', launched by *The House of 72 Tenants* (七十二家房客 *Catsapji gaa fonghak*, 1973), the Shaw Brothers comedy that revived Cantonese-language filmmaking. Several other Cantonese comedies 'taking side swipes at Government' followed in its wake: the article mentions *Hong Kong 73* (73 *Hoenggong 73*, 1974), *The Country Bumpkin* (大 *Daaihoengleoi*, 1974), *Gossip Street* (多咀 *Dozeoigaai*, 1974) and *The Tenants of Talkative Street* (巷 *Gaaizi hongman*, 1974) ('Now It's Anti-Govt Films', *China Mail*, 17 May 1974). Later that same year, the Hui brothers' *Games Gamblers Play* (星 *Gwaimaa soengsing*, 1974) was released and became a massive box office hit that further confirmed the trend noted by the *China Mail* reporter. Together with the move away from violent action, the popularity of social satire paved the way for the less action-focused, but socially and politically engaged crime films that dominated 1974 and 1975: *The Teahouse* (成 樓 *Singgei caalau*, 1974), *Kidnap* (天 *Tinmong*, 1974), *Big Brother Cheng* (大哥成 *Daaigo Sing*, 1975) and

Anti-Corruption (廉政暴 *Limzing fungbou*, 1975). Further facilitating the 'true crime' trend inaugurated by these films was the fact that many of the events they were based on were then daily reported in newspapers and on television, often in grisly detail. As we will see in the next chapter, filmmakers could further help their crime films pass the censors by including pro-government messages, by having their gangster heroes turn out to be undercover police officers or by staging the demise of the gangster at the end of the film.

In 1976 and 1977, several other developments gave further cover for the gradual relaxation of censorship of present-day crime and violence in Hong Kong, so that by the end of the decade Alan Tang's triad-glorifying 'Big Timer' films barely raised eyebrows anymore. These developments arguably stemmed from the crowning achievement of Nigel Watt's reform programme: the amendment of the Film Censorship Regulations, which came in force in August 1976. As discussed earlier, the amended Regulations allowed, among other things, for greater participation of members of the public in the Board of Review and for the creation of a public advisory panel. In September 1976, two members of the public joined the Board, Irene Cheung 張夫人 and Stephen Lau 劉文, with a third, Norman Leung 梁乃, replacing the Commissioner of Police in January 1977. The removal of the latter was significant, as the Police representative had in preceding years frequently been a voice for stricter censorship of crime and violence in films. On top of this, the public advisory panel, which started operating in February 1977, turned out to be slightly more liberal than the censors themselves ('Film Censorship in Hong Kong' (Memo from Assistant Director of Home Affairs Department to Directorate Members), 28 June 1978, HKRS 313-7-3, HKPRO). This more liberal attitude pertained especially to representations of sex and nudity, leading to a further relaxation of censorship in this area towards the end of 1977. Another public outcry followed, focusing on the wave of so-called '*maopian*' 毛 (*moupin*, 'hair films'), referring to the alleged decision by the censors to allow pubic hair to be seen in films. Throughout most of 1978, public attention remained focused on this issue, with the apparent relaxation in the censorship of crime and violence going largely unnoticed. As stated in a detailed government report on the state of film censorship in Hong Kong at the time, 'these critics seem to have entirely forgotten that scenes of excessive violence are being continuously churned out by producers, e.g. "Ironside 426" . . . which is basically a film on triads and gangland war' ('Film Censorship in Hong Kong' [Memo from Assistant Director of Home Affairs Department to Directorate Members], 28 June 1978, HKRS 313-7-3, HKPRO). The controversy surrounding sex and nudity, in other words, allowed for the increasingly relaxed censorship of crime and violence to go largely unchallenged.

The Complicated Dance of the Censors

From the above, it is clear that the censors had some influence on the direction of Hong Kong filmmaking in the late 1960s and 1970s, as seen in the shift from swordplay to kung fu, and from kung fu to crime. They were nevertheless constrained by various factors, so that they mainly served as mediators between different interests. In the following, I will consider the main actors shaping film censorship in 1960s and 1970s Hong Kong (and beyond): powerful local film studios and international film trends, local cinema operators and distributors, the press and the public, and the government.

We have already seen how Donald C. C. Luddington, the Secretary for Home Affairs, reminded the Legislative Council in 1973 that the censors' ability to aggressively cut or ban violence, sex and nudity in films was constrained by the fact that this would make it impossible to screen most of the films that were then circulating internationally. Hong Kong – as an increasingly important node in the capitalist camp located on the doorstep of the world's most populous Communist state – moreover had strong political and economic reasons to be liberal in this regard. Exerting strong control over the screening and production of films also wouldn't fit with how the British governed Hong Kong in general: as Mark Hampton (2011, 305) has argued for early Hong Kong television, the colonial government's approach 'favoured minimal regulation of oligopolistic commercial interests'. In the context of 1970s Hong Kong cinema, this meant that major studios like Shaw Brothers and later Golden Harvest had a certain sway with the censors. This, in fact, was a frequent complaint raised in appeals to the Board of Review, with the appeal against the censor's decision to request cuts in *Money Money Money* (仙杜拉偷搶 *Gwai maa Sindoulaai tau coeng pin*, 1975) offering perhaps the most elaborate example. In a lengthy and combative letter, the film's director Yu Tsong 于 accused the censors of favouritism and to prove it presented a detailed comparison of his film with a recent Shaw Brothers production, *Forbidden Tales of Two Cities* (傳奇 *Gong Ou cyunkei*, 1975), as well as a Golden Harvest one, *All in the Family* (城春 *Faa fei mun sing ceon*, 1975). In the concluding paragraph of the letter, Yu noted a more widespread perception of the censors' favouritism among independent filmmakers:

> Our film directors are already complaining that their hands have been considerably tied when working with small independent producers like ourselves hindering them from venturing into new horizons of creativity, stagnated permanently by the overcast of the censors' scissors. They also express their wish to join the more influential studios which can offer them a freer scope for their improvement

and expression of their art. ('Re: "Money, Money, Money": Appeal for Review' (Letter from Yu Tsong to Board of Review), 21 February 1975, HKRS 313-7-9, HKPRO)

A more spectacular anecdote involving the seminal gangster kung fu film *The Boxer from Shantung* further illustrates the special treatment given to the big movie moguls. Scheduled for release in Hong Kong on 10 February 1972, Shaw Brothers delivered a new copy of *The Boxer from Shantung* to the censors on 8 February, after earlier on having accidentally submitted the longer (and likely bloodier) international version. In a first indication of the VIP treatment Shaw Brothers could count on, the censors duly viewed the new version to meet the tight schedule, cutting a few hundred feet of violent footage and returning the film to the studio on 9 February. The next day, just hours before the film was scheduled to be shown in cinemas, studio head Run Run Shaw 夫 flew to the censors' offices by helicopter to personally complain to Chief Film Censor William Hung that the excised portions destroyed the continuity of the film's story, and to request permission to put back the missing links, guaranteeing that no blood or violence would be reinserted. Hung gave his permission, even though this would make it impossible for the censors to be sure that the version of the film shown in theatres conformed to their requirements ('Notes for Reference: "Boxer from Shantung"', no date [likely late February 1972], HKRS 394-23-12, HKPRO). Clearly, the local film industry's economic well-being – and especially that of the major studios – was an important consideration for the censors, which offers one explanation for the fact that many of the pathbreaking Hong Kong crime films in the mid-1970s were Shaw Brothers productions. The distinction based on quality introduced in the 1973 *Note of Guidance* arguably formalised this privileged treatment of the major studio(s), alongside that of foreign (especially Hollywood) films.

There are also indications that the government was quite susceptible to pressure from other sectors of the film industry: film distributors and theatre owners. The influence of the former was most obvious in the fate of the monthly censorship reports that were passed to the press starting from October 1970. When Doven Chow 周杜文 – a former production manager at Shaw Brothers and since 1968 manager of the local branch of Hollywood's United Artists – complained that the publicising of the titles of banned and cut films was hurting his business, the censors in October 1971 quietly replaced the monthly press releases with quarterly ones that no longer mentioned the specific films that were cut ('Note', 28 April 1972, HKRS 1101-2-14, HKPRO). The influence of theatre owners was meanwhile most felt in the long-delayed introduction of film classification in Hong Kong. Although the idea of classification had been discussed repeatedly by government officials since 1954, it took until 1988 for it to be actually introduced. While over the years various objections to classification were raised from different corners, a major roadblock appears to have been the opposition of theatre owners. Already in 1961, the government had approached members of the Cinema Managements' Association with the idea of introducing compulsory classification, but the latter were reportedly 'very far from enthusiastic' about it ('Film Censorship', 15 April 1961, par. 9, HKRS 934-5-34, HKPRO). As cinema was one of only few entertainment options available in Hong Kong and families tended to go to the movies together, theatre owners feared that not allowing children to watch certain films could cause severe economic losses. While public calls for classification were rare in the 1950s and 1960s, in the 1970s the idea was proposed many times in the Legislative Council and in the press as a way of dealing with the controversies then surrounding censorship. That classification was only introduced in 1988 had a lot to do with the persistent pressure from theatre owners, as Chief Film Censor Pierre Lebrun admitted in a 1978 interview ('Good Judgement Is His Best Guide', *Star*, 3 March 1978).[4]

Public opinion and the media also exerted influence on censorship policy in the 1970s. The censors paid close attention to newspaper reports and opinion pieces, and the government increasingly began to use surveys to get a better sense of public opinion. As the 1973 *Note of Guidance* put it, 'it is the aim of the censor to reflect in his work what he believes to be contemporary public attitudes' (par. 3). Nigel Watt's other reforms in that period – the adding of non-officials to the Board of Review and the establishment of the public advisory panel – reflected this objective as well. While opinion pieces and letters to the editor in newspapers give some indication of public sentiment, we should of course be careful not to see them as directly reflecting mainstream opinion. It seems likely that the frequent calls in the media for stricter censorship mainly came from the more educated local elite. When attempts were made to survey the general public's opinions on censorship, the result consistently tended towards more liberal attitudes. We have already seen an example of this when the opinions of the public advisory panel led to a relaxation in the censorship of sex and nudity in 1977. A similar conclusion about public attitudes was reached after an unusual experiment carried out by Radio Television Hong Kong (RTHK) in December 1977: the public broadcaster created a short film with various sex scenes

---

[4] Further contributing to the government's tardiness was its realisation in the early 1970s that its censorship might in fact be illegal, as it had legislated the *manner* of censorship but never the *principles*, despite the Places of Public Entertainment Ordinance indicating that both should be legislated. It feared that its decades-long, potentially illegal censorship would be revealed if it suddenly legislated the principles of censorship by introducing film classification (for a detailed discussion of the legal issues involved and the 1987 scandal that followed the leaking of this information, see Chan 1988, 212–3; Van den Troost 2020).

and forms of nudity and screened it to an audience of several hundred people. This was then followed by a survey to collect the audience members' opinions on what they considered acceptable and what not, which showed differences based on viewers' sex, occupation and age. As the head of the team conducting this experiment later said in an interview with *The Star*, aside from a viewer's sex (with men more accepting of screened sex and nudity than women) and age (with the young more tolerant than the old), occupation played a major part in influencing attitudes ('The RTHK "Blue Movie" Could Lead to More Sex on Screen', *Star*, 27 January 1978). While only a summary of the RTHK research findings is available in the government archives, it appears that working- and middle-class citizens were more tolerant than the more educated elites. This had also been one of the conclusions of the first survey on censorship carried out in 1974 ('Film Censorship Too Lax: Survey – Stricter Control Urged', 1 May 1974, HKRS 70-6-579-1, HKPRO).

Even though all the above forces constrained the censors' power and censors insistently claimed to merely reflect public attitudes, the archival records give hints as to how a powerful and seasoned official like Nigel Watt could still push through his own vision in key instances. This is best illustrated through an episode that played out in 1976–7, right after the coming into force of the Film Censorship (Amendment) Regulations in the summer of 1976. As we have seen, two non-officials joined the Board of Review in September that year, which, as the result of another change in the law, was now chaired by the Commissioner for Television and Films, Nigel Watt. The first appeal brought before this newly constituted Board involved Martin Scorsese's *Taxi Driver* (1976), which the Panel of Censors had earlier subjected to certain excisions. In a rare but certainly not unprecedented outcome (as in *The Black Dragon* case in 1973, discussed above), the Board came to a harsher conclusion, demanding the removal of the film's final sequence, which shows how the vigilante taxi driver is rehabilitated in society and celebrated as a hero in the newspapers ('Decision of Film Board of Review on the Film "Taxi Driver" Screened on 23rd September, 1976', 23 September 1976, HKRS 313-7-10, HKPRO). As the archival records indicate, Watt objected to this extra excision and argued that many films with similar endings had been passed by the censors previously, but he was overruled by the rest of the Board. In an unprecedented move, Watt refused to pass this decision to the film's distributor and forced the Board to reconsider the cuts in a new meeting. He justified this action arguing that *Taxi Driver* had already received many awards, and that by cutting the film's ending the new Board would come in for criticism in the press ('Watt's letter to Katherine Fok, Assistant Director of Home Affairs', 4 October 1976, HKRS 313-7-10, HKPRO).

Apparently unable to reach a compromise, the Board then deferred a decision for six months, during which Watt wrote to *Taxi Driver*'s distributor to ask how the film had been received by other censors in the region, apparently hoping to find support for his stance. At the same time, Watt also moved to limit the powers of the Board to get his way. Requesting legal advice from Senior Crown Counsel regarding the Board's statutory powers, he obtained an interpretation that implied that the Board only could reconsider the cuts already made by the Panel of Censors and could not make additional cuts of its own – even though it had done so multiple times in the past ('Letter from Nigel Watt, Chairman of the Board of Review, to Katherine Fok, Assistant Director of Home Affairs', 2 November 1976, HKRS 313-7-3, HKPRO). Basically, the new, more 'Chinese' Board suddenly found itself less powerful than the Panel of Censors, which was led by Pierre Lebrun and controlled by Watt. Clearly, despite all the apparent progress towards greater public participation and openness in government, the deck was still stacked in favour of British colonial officials throughout the 1970s.

It is somewhat ironic, however, that Watt in 1976 used his power as a high-ranking colonial official to press for a more liberal standard of censorship, arguably aligning him more with mainstream opinion than the Board of Review, which was now dominated by local elites. This dynamic of what I call 'liberal (de)colonisation' was typical for the transitional decade of the 1970s, with the impulse towards greater localisation and autonomy accelerating in subsequent decades. As we have seen, Watt was the last expatriate official to occupy – until 1983 – the post of Commissioner for Television and Entertainment Licensing. Pierre Lebrun, for his part, continued to serve as Chief Film Censor until 1989. Although the information we have about Nigel Watt as a person is fairly limited – aside from his official communications in government archives, he comes up a number of times in journalist Peter Moss's (2006) memoir – he seems to have been a fairly open-minded and cosmopolitan individual. At this crucial turning point in the late 1960s and 1970s, the world view of this powerful censorship chief likely influenced Hong Kong's cinematic decade of 'fists and pillows', as well as the film industry's astonishing commercial success from the 1970s to the 1990s. Regardless of Watt's world view, however, it may just have been the general governing philosophy of late colonial Hong Kong that predetermined the evolution of film censorship. The economic and financial policy of 'positive non-intervention' initiated by Financial Secretary John Cowperthwaite in the 1960s and continued by his successor Philip Haddon-Cave in the 1970s (Steve Tsang 2004, 171–2) finds its counterpart in the relatively hands-off way in which film censorship was conducted at this time. While the censors claimed to be reflecting public attitudes in their work, the economic success of Hong Kong's film industry was at least as important to them, leading them to engage in a complicated dance with public and private interests throughout the 1970s, with significant repercussions for the Hong Kong crime film, and Hong Kong cinema in general.

PART II

THE MODERN HONG KONG CRIME FILM, CRIMINAL REALISM AND HONG KONG IDENTITY, 1969–1986

3   A New Form of Criminal Realism

THE INTERMEZZO ZEROED in on the rapid transformation of colonial censorship as a crucial factor in the generic changes taking place in 1970s Hong Kong cinema, especially the rise of what I have called the modern Hong Kong crime film. This chapter will deal with roughly the same historical period as the Intermezzo, but returns to the film texts themselves, linking the gradual appearance of the modern crime film not only to changes in censorship but also to specific social trends and debates, and to the popularity of crime films internationally. As the 'crime problem' sparked a moral panic in late 1960s and 1970s Hong Kong and the corruption of the police force as well as its collusion with crime groups often made for sensational headlines, filmmakers had a clear incentive to tell crime stories, especially when New Hollywood successes such as *Dirty Harry* (1971) and *The Godfather* (1972) proved the genre's commercial viability. It was the first time in Hong Kong film history that actual local crime problems – such as violent robberies, juvenile delinquency, prostitution and the drug trade – were frequently and realistically explored on the silver screen. Indeed, in no other decade has the local crime film been so closely tied to real-life crime and criminal justice as in the 1970s.

The period under study in this chapter unsurprisingly also saw the emergence of a new form of criminal realism. If Hong Kong crime films in the 1950s and 1960s typically could be placed in either the realistic *lunlipian* tradition or that of pulp fiction action-adventure, 1970s crime films in a sense more fully merged these two traditions to create something new, with films pursuing an increasing degree of realism in depicting Hong Kong society and its urban spaces while also being unabashedly sensationalist and action-driven, with crime plots offering a handy excuse to include as much nudity and violence as the censors would permit. This trend coalesced in the mid-1970s in what some critics have called *shehui qiqingpian*. These are films characterised by their focus on sensational crimes and the underbelly of society, as well as their ripped-from-the-headlines plots. Crucially, they usually include scenes of violence and sex to attract audiences. A typical example are cinematic exposés of the local sex industry, a not insignificant subgenre in Hong Kong cinema that first appeared in the 1970s and survives up to the present.

I will start this chapter by outlining some of the broader historical and film industry contexts to situate the rise of the modern Hong Kong crime film and the new form of criminal realism. The 1960s and 1970s were a period in which crime and policing occupied a central position in the public mind, with the police force proving itself crucial to the maintenance of British rule in the face of social unrest, and with questions surrounding the colonial government's legitimacy at least in part deflected to the issue of (youth) crime. After considering the new form of criminal realism that appeared in the late 1960s and 1970s, this chapter will chronicle the gradual appearance of various types of pioneering crime films, often highlighting the role of censorship in this process. Starting from the problem youth films produced by the then-declining Cantonese-language film industry of the late 1960s, we will next look at the rise of kung fu gangster films, spearheaded by the work of Chang Cheh and Kuei Chih-hung at the Shaw Brothers studio. Contrary to the frequent characterisation of the dominant Shaw Brothers studio as out of sync with the localisation of Hong Kong cinema, the studio in fact played a pathbreaking role in the emergence of the modern Hong Kong crime film until around 1976–7, after which it indeed became increasingly irrelevant, with its film production winding down by the mid-1980s. Alongside other companies, Shaw Brothers for instance contributed important films to both the *shehui qiqingpian* trend that flourished in the mid-1970s and to the triad and police films that followed soon after. Overall, my account here illustrates how the foundation for the 'golden age' of Hong Kong crime cinema in the 1980s and 1990s was already laid in the critically often neglected decade of the 1970s. In this period, a new form of criminal realism helped to make sense of life in a city that became something of an anomaly in the history of colonialism – a colonial enclave in a decolonising world that would soon outstrip the imperial metropole in terms of its economic success, modernisation and vertiginous urban development.

A Tumultuous Era

Most historians agree that the 1966 and 1967 riots caused tectonic shifts in Hong Kong society and politics, giving impetus, amongst others, to the government's major reforms in the late 1960s and 1970s, and to the growth of a distinct Hong Kong identity (for example, Bickers and Yep 2009). The Star Ferry riots, which lasted from 6 to 8 April 1966, are so named because the trigger for them was a slight increase in the price for cross-harbour ferry tickets, with the ferry at the time the only way to get from Kowloon to Hong Kong Island. Clearly, social and political tensions ran high in the colony, fully bursting into the open during the much longer-lasting civil unrest of 1967. While the events of 1967 are often attributed to the instigation and coordination of Beijing-supported leftists in Hong Kong (Steve Tsang 2004, 183–90), the scale of events indicated that, at least initially, the leftists could count on substantial support amongst the general population (J. Carroll 2007, 153). The tumult started in early May when a strike at a plastic-flower factory evolved into clashes between workers and the police. Demonstrations and strikes continued for weeks after, with the situation further escalating in late June and July, when there were deadly clashes at the border with mainland China, as well as several days of violent confrontations between rioters and police in Kowloon and on Hong Kong Island. The government imposed a curfew and the police started to aggressively raid suspected leftist bases, seizing weapons, bombs and propaganda materials. The leftists then launched a bombing campaign, which continued until the end of the year. The resulting terror and casualties among police officers and civilians, including children, turned public opinion firmly against the leftists, who by September also started to lose support from Beijing (J. Carroll 2007, 156).

The riots apparently woke the Hong Kong government up to the need of shoring up public support, something it would be repeatedly reminded of during various social movements in the 1970s, such as the campaigns for the recognition of Chinese as an official language (1970) and against corruption (1973). The government's actions were multifaceted and far-reaching, involving a combination of targeted repression, deflection, public relations efforts, and actual improvements in governance. Crime and policing, and in particular their popular perception, were central to the government's agenda during this decade. As Jones and Vagg (2007, 412–3) note, the riots made the government especially concerned about rising crime and about young people, who had been the main participants in the riots. In the area of criminal justice, this resulted in a five-fold response:

> (1) the arrest, cautioning and locking up young offenders on an unprecedented scale; (2) the mass mobilisation of the population – but especially youth – in community action against crime; (3) the increased deployment of youth-oriented social work programmes; (4) a focus on a de-politicised pro-government education and the development of civic values in the school curriculum; and (5) the development of social science research into the 'youth problem'. (Jones and Vagg 2007, 413)

A perhaps unintended consequence of the mobilisation of the population in crime prevention was a growing public interest in the 'crime problem' – in one week in

1972 alone, there were twenty-five newspaper editorials on the subject (Jones and Vagg 2007, 418). Hence, even though crime statistics in the late 1960s and early 1970s showed only a limited increase in crime, Jones and Vagg (2007, 452) argue that official attention to crime created a 'self-fulfilling spiral': the government's focus on the problem led to more intensive policing and efforts to increase the public's reporting of crime; this in turn produced higher crime figures, resulting in a public outcry, a further increase in police activity, and so on. One noteworthy outgrowth of this was the launching of annual Fight Crime campaigns from 1973 onwards, which involved massive publicity efforts to mobilise the population in the fight against crime (430–3).

The government's focus on crime was partly also aimed at repairing the police force's reputation, which, although briefly boosted by the force's performance during the 1967 Riots, was heavily tarnished due to the problem of police corruption (Lethbridge 1985, 54–81). The government had undertaken anti-corruption efforts in the past, but the sensational escape to England of Peter Godber, a high-ranking police officer suspected of corruption, sparked a public outcry and demonstrations that finally paved the way for the establishment of the Independent Commission Against Corruption (ICAC) in 1974 (Steve Tsang 2004, 203–4). Over the next few years, so many policemen were brought to justice that in 1977 thousands of officers staged a protest against the ICAC, with some even charging into the ICAC headquarters and injuring ICAC staff. The government quickly moved to appease the force by granting a partial amnesty, promising that offences committed before 1977 would not be prosecuted anymore (Lethbridge 1985, 126–58). While this inevitably tarnished the image of the ICAC, the organisation was able to recover its prestige over the ensuing years (J. Carroll 2007, 174–5). The anti-corruption effort meanwhile also improved the reputation of the police, which was further consolidated through various public relations efforts, the introduction of neighbourhood policing (in 1974), and the growing professionalisation of the force (Jones and Vagg 2007, 409–49). By the late 1980s, the police force so widely reviled in the early 1970s had become a source of pride for many Hongkongers.

Changes in the Hong Kong film industry were equally dramatic. Whereas in the post-war decades the Mandarin and Cantonese cinemas had both thrived, Cantonese filmmaking began to decline rapidly in the late 1960s, with no pictures made in the dominant local language in 1972. At the end of that same decade, however, the tables had been turned, with Mandarin-language cinema close to extinction. A variety of factors contributed to these twists of fortune, the most important arguably the rise of television. With cinema moving towards greater spectacle in response to television's challenge, the financially powerful Shaw Brothers studio, which focused mainly on Mandarin-language films, was better prepared for this transition than the many small and low-budget Cantonese companies. After 1972, it was ironically also the Shaw Brothers who brought back Cantonese-language filmmaking, by producing the box office success *The House of 72 Tenants* (1973). This film's cast included many TV actors from Television Broadcasts Limited (TVB), which had been co-founded by Shaw Brothers studio head Run Run Shaw in 1967 and produced content in Cantonese (Law K. 2018, 46). Television would continue to be an important source of talent and ideas for the local film industry throughout the 1970s (Kung and Zhang 2002). The adverse turn for Mandarin-language cinema after 1973 meanwhile was linked to the decline of the classic studio mode of production so successfully applied by Shaw Brothers in the 1960s. Even as in the early 1970s Shaw Brothers nearly monopolised local film production, the return of Bruce Lee to Hong Kong and his employment by Golden Harvest, a company established in 1970 by former top Shaw executives, heralded a new era. The astonishing success of Lee's films gave Golden Harvest a powerful boost, and it soon took its place beside Shaw Brothers as the industry's other leading studio (Teo 1997, 94–7). Co-producing films with small semi-independent companies and giving filmmakers more creative freedom and higher salaries, Golden Harvest's business model was less centralised and eventually proved more flexible and durable than the rigid, classical mode of Shaw Brothers (Po 2013b, 8–25).

In terms of genre, the post-1967 years were dominated by the fad for masculine martial arts films set off by Shaw director Chang Cheh's *One-Armed Swordsman* (1967). While kung fu films were dominant from 1970 onwards, swordplay (or *wuxia* 武俠) movies continued to be made throughout the decade, experiencing a brief revival between 1976 and 1978 with Chor Yuen's adaptations of Gu Long 古 's martial arts novels. Kung fu reasserted its dominance soon after in the form of kung fu comedies, launching both Sammo Hung 寶 and Jackie Chan to stardom in the final years of the decade. This new kung fu-comedy hybrid was a logical development, as comedy was the other major genre of this period, with the films of the Hui brothers topping box office charts in almost every year between 1974 and 1978. The theme songs of their films, performed by Sam Hui 冠傑, moreover helped to establish Cantopop as the dominant form of local pop music (Chu 2017, 48–52). While the humour in 1970s comedies was often broad, there was a strong element of social satire in them as well, making them the other major genre alongside the crime film to deal with the realities of life in modern Hong Kong. A final genre of note during this decade was softcore pornography, most prominently the cynical 'cheating' films by director Li Han-hsiang 李 at Shaw Brothers. Sex and nudity were, like action and comedy, not limited to one genre of course, and their presence in, for example, mainstream martial arts films make for a striking contrast with more recent Hong Kong cinema, which is generally much more chaste. As a result, commentators today frequently refer to Hong Kong 1970s cinema as the era of 'fists and pillows' (May Ng 2018b, 4–7). It is in this environment that the modern Hong Kong crime film and a new form of criminal realism appeared and increasingly flourished.

A New Form of Criminal Realism

In the course of the 1970s, the relationship between Hong Kong film and society became increasingly direct. As we have seen in the previous chapter, this was at least in part due to the relaxation of censorship, as up until the early 1970s censors were especially sensitive towards realistic depictions of contemporary Hong Kong's less savoury aspects. This arguably turned locally oriented 'realism' into something of a forbidden fruit, and as a result the term was frequently used for film marketing purposes throughout the decade.[1] A typical example is the first of the Shaw Brothers' landmark *The Criminals* (奇案 *Hoenggong keingon*) series of omnibus films (1976–7), which was promoted as a '*true* record based on *real* people and *real* events'. Whereas in the 1950s 'realism' often connoted a serious, perhaps even politically engaged treatment of social problems, in the 1970s it was mostly used to strengthen a film's sensationalist appeal. Although 1970s crime films frequently commented on real social problems and, through location-shooting and other techniques, became 'realistic' to an unprecedented degree, they were therefore generally reviled by young local critics as vulgar works of exploitation – posited almost in diametric opposition to the realist works of the 1950s then being canonised by these same critics. Rather than simply dismissing these films for their lack of taste, however, I will here take them seriously. Given that an important part of the appeal of these films derived from their engagement with the local realities of crime and criminal justice, I will in this and the following chapters frequently connect films with specific crime-related events and social debates to shed further light on the modern Hong Kong crime film's appearance, as well as the new form of criminal realism that accompanied it. It is important to stress (again) that this sociopolitical context was not simply reflected in films: as indicated by Jones and Vagg (2007, 452), the 'crime problem' of the 1970s had a lot to do with contemporary governmental and social discourse, which consolidated around the belief – not necessarily the reality – that violent (youth) crime was a serious problem in Hong Kong. As we shall see, many late 1960s and 1970s films mirrored this belief and thereby reinforced it. By increasingly representing local problems and engaging contemporary debates, Hong Kong cinema in these years also helped to consolidate the discourse of a distinct

---

[1] In Chinese, the term most often used for 'realism' was *xieshi*, but other terms were occasionally used as well, such as *xianshi* 實 (*jinsat*) and *zhenshi* 實 (*zansat*).

Hong Kong identity and belonging, a process the crime film was central to, as will be further explored in Chapter 4.

The criminal realism of the 1970s can be better understood by considering the term used for an important subset of this decade's crime movies: the *shehui qiqingpian*. This is how a 1978 article in the Shaw Brothers magazine *Hong Kong Movie News* (影 *Xianggang yinghua*) describes the trend of true crime films then exerting a strong influence on local film production (Ngaan 1978). The term can be roughly translated as 'society marvellous/strange situations film' or more loosely as 'sensational society film', but *qiqing* 奇情 (*keicing*) has various, broad connotations that cannot be directly translated into English. Recently, Tan See Kam (2021) has brought the term to wider attention: he translates *qiqingpian* 奇情 (*keicingpin*) as 'strange or queer films' and places them primarily within the romance genre, in particular the tradition of *caizi jiaren* 才子佳人 (*coizi gaaijan*, 'talented man and beautiful lady') love stories. He also argues that *qiqingpian* 'chiefly draw on Chinese legends and traditional folklore' (86). Tan's dissection of the term *qiqing* is worth quoting at length:

> The term *qiqing* is an adjective-noun composite, with *qi* [奇] variously signifying odd, strange and surprising (as in *qiguai* [奇怪]); amazing, astonishing and astounding (as in *jingqi* [奇]); marvellous, wonderful and miraculous (as in *qiji* [奇]); fantastical, bizarre and odd (as in *qiyi* [奇]); and finally, peculiar, extraordinary, special and queer (as in *qite* [奇]). The noun component, *qing* [情], generally refers to affective matter, and in the context of *qiqing* films characteristically encompasses sentimental love and romantic passion of the transcendental kind. (Tan 2021, 86–7)

While Tan's definition captures one important meaning of *qing*, the term could also refer to a strange/amazing/marvellous 'plot', as in *qingjie* 情 (*cingzit*), or simply featuring strange/amazing/marvellous 'situations', as in *qingkuang* 情 (*cingfong*). As such, the term *qiqing* was also often associated with fantasy, detective and adventure stories. The way it was used in numerous ads for crime films from the 1930s to the 1970s attests to this. Similar to the practice in Hollywood at that time (Altman 1998, 7–15), Hong Kong film promotion often tried to increase a film's appeal by connecting it to multiple genres and/or sentiments, with *qiqing* one of the terms often thrown in for various types of crime films. *Qiqing* for instance is used in the promotional materials for Lee Tit's pioneering crime film of 1936, *House Number Sixty-Six*, along with other words such as *zhentan* 偵探 (*zingtaam*, 'detective'), *kongbu* 恐怖 (*hungbou*, 'horror'), *jinzhang* 張 (*ganzoeng*, 'suspenseful'), *ciji* 刺 (*cigik*, 'exciting'), *xiangyan* (*hoengjim*, 'erotic'), *zhuangguan* 壯 (*zonggun*, 'spectacular') and, interestingly, *xieshi* ('realist'). *Qiqing* also appears in the posters for many of the 1950s and 1960s unofficial justice fighter films, detective films and suspense thrillers discussed in Chapters 1 and 2. *Qiqing*'s connotations are therefore broader than romance, promising an 'amazing' or 'sensational' story in general. Reinforcing this interpretation is the fact that it is often placed next to the word *quzhe* 曲折 (*kukzit*), which indicates a plot with many twists and turns.

When *qiqingpian* is then preceded by *shehui* 會 (*sewui*, 'society'), as in the 1978 *Hong Kong Movie News* article, it indicates a film that will tell a shocking/strange tale pulled from real life. According to this same article, *shehui qiqingpian* are characterised by their focus on sensational crimes and the underbelly of society, as well as their ripped-from-the-headlines plots. They also usually include scenes of violence and sex to attract audiences (Ngaan 1978). As Ng Ho (2005, 209) further details, the *shehui qiqingpian* of the mid-1970s were very heterogeneous in terms of narrative content, comprising stories of gang warfare, the drug trade, prison life, swindlers and gamblers, horrific murders, cops and robbers, people smugglers, undercover agents and informers, vigilantes and sex clubs. This narrative reach makes it comparable in scope to the crime film, and arguably similar also to the social problem film. The latter has been defined by Landy (1991, 432) as a type of film 'directed toward the dramatization of topical social issues'. Various scholars (Roffman and Purdy 1981; Maltby 1983) have identified populism as one central element in Hollywood social problem films – an observation we will see similarly applies to many of the Hong Kong films here discussed as crime films. Ng (2005, 210) further pinpointed a few additional traits of the *shehui qiqingpian* of the mid-1970s: the use of location-shooting; convoluted and chaotic plots designed to include violent fights, sex scenes and nudity; a palpable sense of distrust towards the government; a view of the police as powerless and of the city as rife with crime, thereby encouraging vigilante behaviour; realistic and vivid dialogues, including triad slang and even triad hand gestures; and, finally, frequent problems with the censors.

It is at this point useful to recall that the dominant genre of the 1950s, the *lunlipian*, also often appeared together with the word *shehui*, as in *shehui lunlipian*. This further indicates that 1970s criminal realism was in a sense a synthesis of the realist *lunli* melodrama and the pulp fiction action-adventure tradition of the 1950s and 1960s – the latter type as mentioned often associated with the term *qiqing* in promotional materials. Despite critics' canonisation of 1950s *lunlipian* and their condemnation and/or neglect of 1970s *qiqingpian*, the main difference between the two is arguably that the former assumed an ethical and pedagogical mission, while the latter were driven by the profit imperative. These seemingly opposed objectives were never completely absent in either period of course: the makers of *shehui lunlipian* had to keep the market in mind to ensure their survival, while some *shehui qiqingpian* engaged in sharp social criticism and spoke up for the oppressed. Both objectives most obviously coexisted in the output of Patrick Lung, for instance, and he is deservedly considered one of this period's most important directors. We turn now to the problem youth film, one genre in which Lung made his mark and which embodied the transition between the two periods in Hong Kong film history here delineated.

Problem Youth Films

As already mentioned, perceptions of a serious youth crime problem were likely the result of a self-fulfilling spiral, when the government's increased anxiety about youth after the 1966 and 1967 riots led to more police attention to youth crime, resulting in higher youth crime figures, which then inspired calls for even more police efforts. The concern about youth crime, however, predated 1966 and it can also be linked to the changing police discourse regarding organised crime. After a major campaign against the triads in the late 1950s, the police had claimed that conventional triads were defeated, with only fragmented gangs of young hoodlums remaining (Jones and Vagg 2007, 459). When increased police action against these supposedly fragmented youth gangs resulted in the dramatic growth in arrests of young men aged between 16 and 21 from 1969 to 1974, the police therefore tended to frame this as a problem of youth crime, not of organised crime. This was despite the fact that organised crime was clearly flourishing at this time. It was only around 1975 – when the ICAC had taken decisive action against police corruption (often by organised crime groups) – that the police shifted its discourse again to focus on the problem of the triads as 'organised criminal syndicates' (Jones and Vagg 2007, 459–63). Suggestive of a link between official and popular discourse, this was also when triad films came to be produced in increasing numbers.

The moral panic surrounding juvenile delinquency in part also occurred because police discourse in the 1960s tapped into the broader generational conflicts of this era, which saw the post-war baby boomers come of age. Raised in Hong Kong, these youngsters regarded the city as their home and were more critical of the colonial system than their elders, many of whom had arrived as refugees. To their parents, however, they seemed 'spoiled, restless, and dangerously westernized, turning their backs on traditional codes of behaviour (especially filial piety and discipline) and thereby posing a menace to the social order' (Fu 2000, 71). The riots and young people's involvement in them raised even more alarm about juvenile delinquency, resulting in heated debates and calls for action in the news media. With local youth films produced since the late 1950s (Yung 2003, 221–35), local cinema contributed to this discourse with a remarkable wave of problem youth films in 1969.²

Having launched the Jane Bond cycle in 1965 (see Chapter 1), Chor Yuen once again proved to have his finger on society's pulse, kicking off the problem youth cycle with *The Joys and Sorrows of Youth* (冷暖　春 *Laangnyun cingceon*, 1969). About a dozen similar films were produced in 1969 and 1970, all much more pessimistic than earlier youth films. As Fu (2000) has argued, the films in this cycle were in fact somewhat schizophrenic in nature: on the one hand, they appear designed to attract a young audience by depicting alluring aspects of youth culture (parties, nightclubs, luxurious homes, Western fashions, dating, fighting and so on), while, on the other, they do all this in a highly moralising narrative that indicated that all these 'fun' activities easily made youngsters turn to crime and become 'Ah Fei'　　(problem youth). As Fu (2000) also shows, the films in the 1969–70 cycle were self-consciously contributing to the public discourse of the time, which was preoccupied with finding the causes of youth crime and proposing possible solutions.

To fulfil the goal of social analysis, most of the films in this cycle feature large casts of young actors, allowing for the elaboration of various 'pitfalls' for young people (drugs, alcohol, nightclubs, lack of adult supervision and anti-establishment sentiment), with at least one character providing the desired alternative of a 'virtuous' young person (who respects his/her elders, works hard, is honest and so on). The films also engage directly with the question of youth crime in their dialogues. For instance, in a direct address to the camera at the beginning of *The Joys and Sorrows of Youth*, Chor Yuen gravely announces that his film will talk about 'youngsters in our society'. Later in the same film, a young man and his older sister argue about the value of hard work and a university education, with the rebellious youth

---

² The earliest surviving film touching on the problem of juvenile delinquency is Fung Fung 峰's *The Kid* (　　 *Sailou Coeng*, 1950). The film was adapted from a comic book by Yuen Po-wan 步 , touted at the time as a Southern Chinese equivalent to the famous Sanmao 三毛 comics from Shanghai. In the film, the Kid, played by a very young Bruce Lee, is enthralled by a resourceful rogue who operates according to the rules of the *jianghu*, displaying loyalty, honour and courage. Although the Kid becomes a member of this rogue's gang, the socially subversive nature of this criminal is (very implausibly) neutralised when, at the end of the film, he renounces his criminal ways after a picketing female worker reminds him of the need for class solidarity. Further strengthening the film's leftist inclination, the Kid eventually leaves the corrupting city with his siblings and uncle to settle in 'the countryside' – a veiled reference to the recently established People's Republic of China. Notwithstanding its comic book roots, *The Kid* can be seen as an example of the realist *lunlipian* discussed in Chapter 1. Remarkably, Bruce Lee would ten years later star in another pioneering realist *lunlipian* dealing with juvenile delinquency, *The Orphan* (人 孤　 *Janhoi gu hung*, 1960).

claiming it is all useless and he has no responsibility to a society that has never cared for him. Chor then abruptly cuts to another conversation between a pair of young lovers in a different location, in which another young man, as if in response, states his belief in the value of hard work and his desire to contribute to the country and the people. Heavy-handedly juxtaposed in this way, the latter youth's viewpoint is subsequently endorsed by the film, with the first young man ending up under arrest for murder. In another example, Chan Wan's *Social Characters* (　　　女 *Feinaam feineoi*, 1969) does its social analysis in the form of an almost randomly inserted, documentary-like montage of interviews with various (fictional) authority figures, each giving their view on the causes for juvenile delinquency: a businessman blames the schools, a school principal blames society in general (including pornography, wild music, dance halls and bars), while a police inspector puts the main responsibility with parents.

There are certainly differences in the social analyses and remedies proposed in these films. Whereas most agree on the responsibility of the family to keep youth on the right path, some films focus exclusively on this factor. Chiang Wai-kwong's *Boys and Girls* (七彩　　　女 *Catcoi hungnaam lukneoi*, 1969) places the blame solely on the parents: it is the lust and complete abdication of parental responsibility of two fathers that causes the young protagonists to fall under the control of a criminal gang. Consistent with the Robin Hood-like populism we earlier encountered in his *Black Rose*, Chor Yuen for his part mainly blames social inequality and excessive materialism in both *The Joys and Sorrows of Youth* and his *The Prodigal* (　子 *Longzi*, 1969).

Figure 3.1 Director Chor Yuen addresses the camera at the beginning of *The Joys and Sorrows of Youth* (1969).

Early on in *The Joys and Sorrows of Youth*, for instance, the poor protagonist accidentally scratches a fellow student's Rolls Royce with his bike. While the accident is clearly caused by the rich student, a friend convinces the poor man to take in stride the undeserved abuse he receives. As the friend points out, 'In a court of law, a bike will certainly lose against a Rolls Royce.' Chor's distrust of the government and a rule of law that favours the rich is obvious here. Both of his films are amongst the darkest of the problem youth cycle, ending with tragic deaths and wrongs not righted. Set in a church, the conclusion of *The Joys and Sorrows of Youth* even involves an explicit assertion of the non-existence – or at least indifference – of God himself, as a prayer of a devoutly Christian woman to save the life of her wounded friend is immediately followed by a shot of the friend breathing his last. The subsequent close-up of the woman's deeply disillusioned look up towards the image of God that dominates the church ensures the film ends on a very desolate note indeed.

The most accomplished film of the problem youth cycle was undoubtedly Patrick Lung's *Teddy Girls* (1969). While it shares many of the characteristics of the cycle discussed so far (an ensemble cast of young actors, explicit analysis of the problem of youth crime, a pessimistic conclusion), Lung's film is distinguished by a more sophisticated script, co-written with young film critics Lam Nin-tung 林年同 and Kam Ping-hing   . Lung was rewarded for his efforts with another box office success and enthusiastic reviews. In a contemporary review of *Teddy Girls*, Law Kar (1969) praised the film's sophisticated editing, seriousness, and – most importantly – its realist aesthetic, noting the research the filmmakers had done prior to shooting (such as visiting a reformatory for young female offenders and interviewing some of the young women, as well as consulting with experts) and praising their naturalistic use of colloquial language and slang. In the film's end credits, Lung moreover prominently acknowledges the assistance received from 'the personnel of Probation and Corrections Division, Social Welfare Department, Hong Kong', and, as we shall see below, the solution to the problem of juvenile delinquency the film proposes is very much in line with the ideas at the Social Welfare Department at the time. This in fact sets *Teddy Girls* apart from the other films in the youth crime cycle. Put alongside his *Story of a Discharged Prisoner* (1967, discussed in Chapter 1) and *The Window* (1968), which features a school for blind girls run by nuns, Patrick Lung was rather unique in the late 1960s as a filmmaker consistently promoting social work by government and civil society. In this regard, his work prefigured a view of government-society relations that would increasingly mark Hong Kong life from the 1970s onwards. His sociology-like research prior to filming and the praise it received from young critics at the time also reflect this fundamental shift.

As Jones and Vagg (2007, 249–67) note, under the influence of ideas popular in the UK, the Hong Kong government already in the 1950s had shifted towards

Figure 3.2 Newspaper ad for *Teddy Girls* (1969). Image provided by the Hong Kong Film Archive, Leisure and Cultural Services Department, with the permission of Eng Wah & Company.

stressing rehabilitation rather than punishment of offenders, especially young ones. The Social Welfare Department worked hard to 'engage young people generally in positive activities that would encourage them to grow into good citizens' (249). This philosophy is represented in *Teddy Girls* primarily by the head of the Girls' Home, Mr To (Kenneth Tsang), who sees juvenile crime primarily as caused by society and who in his institution promotes a more tolerant and understanding approach focused on skill training and humanistic care for the girls. While he repeatedly argues against taking excessive disciplinary action, it should be noted that he does not disavow punishment entirely: when at one point the main protagonist, Josephine Tsui (Josephine Siao   ) releases an elderly neighbour's pigeons, To punishes her with fifteen days of solitary confinement. Hence, even this representative of a more 'enlightened' stance in the context of the film resorts to measures that would be considered excessively authoritarian and inhuman by many today.[3] The film nevertheless indicates that To's comparatively softer touch is under attack from an even more disciplinarian philosophy, requiring him to constantly defend his beliefs against the people he works with, the reporters who interview him, and the police. The police view is

---

[3] Similarly, the film also exhibits a fundamental patriarchal bias, with Josephine's neglect by her mother highlighted as the primary reason for her delinquent behaviour.

briefly aired towards the end of the film, when in response to reporters' questions a police officer suggests arresting more offenders is the sole way to fight juvenile crime. The reporters' subsequent exchange with To is much lengthier, with To giving an overview of all the various causes of youth crime, mainly blaming parents and society, and again restating his belief in reform rather than punishment. This final contrast between the head of the Girls' Home and the police officer recalls the ending of *Story of a Discharged Prisoner* as discussed in Chapter 1, which also put the punitive mindset of the police in a negative light and endorsed a more compassionate approach instead.

While these problem youth films engaged in often lengthy analyses of the causes of youth crime, political dissatisfaction was glaringly absent in them as a cause for youthful rebellion, despite the recent memory of the 1966 and 1967 riots. Only *Social Characters* passingly refers to these events, when early on one of the leaders of a youth club says that she suspects that some mysterious forces are trying to turn the club's members into delinquents, inviting them to join dance parties as well as protests at the Tsim Sha Tsui ferry pier. In this way, the film casually suggests that protests and riots are the work of criminal groups intent on disturbing the stability of the colony, a message that Hong Kong's government censors apparently found agreeable enough to leave uncut. Although Chor Yuen's very pessimistic youth films most effectively hint at a very profound social discontent and anger with the status quo, he refrains from directly criticising or even mentioning the government. Patrick Lung's *Teddy Girls* engages the function of government most directly, not in a confrontational manner, but more with a reformer's mindset – criticising the authoritarian impulse (the police) while endorsing authorities that listen to the people and deal with their problems (the Girls' Home run by the comparatively enlightened To). If in the film To and the police officer stand in for the government in general, it is noteworthy that both are locals, and not Caucasian Brits. The major expansion in social welfare provision and the rapid localisation of the government that marked the 1970s are in this way prefigured in Patrick Lung's late 1960s films. While his films offer only indirect and 'constructive' criticism, only a few short years later such caution became less necessary, as we shall see in the following sections.

Chang Cheh and Kuei Chih-hung: Pioneers

Chapters 1 and 2 indicated how in the 1950s and 1960s gangster films and police thrillers were rarely produced in Hong Kong. This situation changed rapidly in the 1970s and by the end of the decade both had become major genres in local cinema. While the early 1970s works of low-budget directors such as John Law and Cheung Sum 張森 paralleled or even prefigured some of these changes, we have to look at the then-dominant Shaw Brothers studio for the most important breakthroughs. Two of the studio's directors, Chang Cheh and Kuei Chih-hung, led the way by exploring new subject matter and filmmaking styles in several of their hit films of this period. Shaw Brothers – today still mostly associated with period films – in fact played an important role in the rise of the modern Hong Kong crime film and the localisation of Hong Kong cinema. While the studio's decline in the late 1970s and early 1980s was related to its inability to keep abreast of broader societal and industrial changes, this should not lead us to overlook the studio's pioneering crime films of the mid-1970s. Indeed, my account in this chapter in part aims to bring more nuance to the common narrative that Shaw Brothers was out of touch with contemporary Hong Kong society. Poshek Fu, for example, mentions a 1970s localisation strategy at Shaw Brothers, but describes this strategy as 'limited' and 'half-hearted' (2008, 17). This overall judgement is not entirely unjustified, but his reading of *The Teahouse* (1974) significantly understates the importance of the film in terms of localisation (Fu 2008, 19–20). As will become clear in this chapter and the next, moreover, *The Teahouse* was not the only localised Shaw Brothers crime film that broke new ground in the genre, with other young directors at the company – such as Sun Chung 孫仲, Hua Shan 山 and Mou Tun-fei 敦 – making noteworthy crime films between 1976 and 1979.

Chang Cheh was an unlikely figure to be a catalyst for change in the 1970s. Born in 1924 in Hangzhou, he had been shooting films in Hong Kong since 1958 and had – after the runaway success of his swordplay film *One-Armed Swordsman* (1967) – become one of Shaw Brothers' leading directors. Despite his films' premodern settings, Chang was clearly attuned to the sentiments of the younger generation – he has for instance claimed that his period swordplay film *The Assassin* (大刺客 *Daai cihaak*, 1967) was infused with the 'fervour, violence and rebelliousness' of the 1967 riots then taking place (C. Chang 2004, 99; White 2015). Less noted, but even more relevant, are several of the youth films he made in this period. He contributed *Dead End* (死 *Seigok*, 1969) to the 1969–70 problem youth cycle and returned repeatedly to the genre in the next few years, with films such as *Young People* (年 人 *Ninhingjan*, 1972), *Generation Gap* (叛 *Bunjik*, 1973) and *Friends* (朋友 *Pangjau*, 1974). Over these same five years, Chang also produced several landmark gangster and police films. As mentioned in the previous chapter, the first two of these – *The Duel* (1971) and *The Boxer from Shantung* (1972) – were set in mainland China during the Republican period (1911–49), possibly due to the government's censorship standards. While still at a remove from contemporary Hong Kong, these films marked a significant edging closer to the present compared to earlier martial arts films, which were usually set centuries ago, or simply in an undefined, semi-mythical ancient China.

In its focus on internecine gang warfare, *The Duel* is similar to the handful of 1950s and 1960s gangster films discussed in Chapter 1: *Tradition* (1954), *Bloodshed on Wedding Day* (1965) and *Adventure in Fishing Harbor* (1967). Like these films, *The Duel* refers to familiar *jianghu* values, especially *yi* (*ji*, 'brotherhood, righteousness, and chivalry'): in one scene the character for *yi* is shown written on a large calligraphic scroll hanging behind the 'good' gang leader. This same scroll is later dramatically torn up by the young gangster protagonist when the leadership position has been usurped by the villain. Much more than in the earlier films (but typical for Chang's output), the main value celebrated in *The Duel* is the horizontal tie of brotherhood. In a scenario replayed numerous times in later Hong Kong gangster films, *The Duel*'s two heroes are initially on opposing sides but, through the appreciation of one another's righteous behaviour, end up fighting and dying together. Coming out the following year, *The Boxer from Shantung*, which Chang co-directed with Pao Hsueh-li, is the first Hong Kong film that adopts the rise-and-fall narrative of Hollywood's 'classical' gangster films of the 1930s. It uses 1930s Shanghai as a setting for this narrative – the first of many movies and TV series since to do so. In the film, Ma Yongzhen, a rural migrant from Shandong province, starts as an honest poor man standing up for the downtrodden, but gradually loses himself to the lure of wealth and power, which spark his desire to fight his way to the top of the Shanghai underworld. It is worth noting here that the perceived celebration of the gangster hero in early 1930s Hollywood films famously led to a tightening of American film censorship (Munby 1999, 5). Despite his eventual comeuppance, some people at the time interpreted the gangster's rise to glory and its similarities to the myth of capitalist success as subversive of the status quo and as encouraging criminal behaviour. By adopting this rise-and-fall narrative in the Hong Kong context, *The Boxer from Shantung* was clearly pushing the envelope, which might have been an unspoken factor in the film's censorship troubles discussed in the last chapter.

Indeed, *The Duel* still goes out of its way to depict its two gangster heroes as unwilling participants in the gangster world: one claims to be in this line of work only due to the loyalty he owes to the benevolent gang boss who adopted him as a child, while the other is in fact acting as an undercover agent for the Nationalist government in South China. Their final battle together is explicitly framed as a noble self-sacrifice to the Nationalist cause, and when they lie dying after annihilating a whole gang together, one of them notes that they have succeeded in cleansing society from scoundrels – including themselves! While such attempts to condemn gangster-like behaviour are present in *The Boxer from Shantung* as well, this film has a more subversive edge. In a lengthy analysis, Yip Man-fung (2017, 45) for instance has argued that the film is 'a trenchant critique of the popular capitalist myth that sees Hong Kong as an open society, a place of open opportunities where individual pursuit of success is not only possible but highly desirable'. Most telling in this regard is the film's conclusion: when Ma has single-handedly annihilated a rival gang, he seemingly loses his mind and starts to laugh madly, allowing his one surviving enemy to inflict a mortal wound. Ma's laughter is ambiguous, and one can wonder whether he has simply gone mad from all the bloodshed, or whether he has finally realised the ultimate meaninglessness of his fight for wealth and power.

Chang was involved in two other crime films that were landmarks in the depiction of crime and policing in contemporary Hong Kong. Both released in 1973, *The Delinquent* and *Police Force* were made in collaboration with other directors – the former with Kuei Chih-hung and the latter with Tsai Yang-ming. As its title suggests, *The Delinquent* is an update of the 1969–70 problem youth films, albeit in a kung fu film format. Its story of a young man seduced into a life of crime highlights poverty and inequality as the main forces pushing the protagonist in this direction. The film's particular strength is its highly realistic depiction of the life of Hong Kong's working poor, through plenty of location shooting in working-class neighbourhoods and public housing blocks. Rather than simply having characters talk about poverty as a cause of crime like most of the 1969 films did, the same argument is here made visually, through the use of location. The gritty realism betrays Kuei's hand, as Chang mostly remained confined to the convenient Shaw Brothers studio sets throughout the 1970s. More important from a genre perspective is Chang and Tsai's *Police Force*, Hong Kong's first modern police thriller. The film was made with generous police assistance – including in the scriptwriting process (Ng 2005, 244–6) – and was released in June 1973 to coincide with the first 'Fight Violent Crime' campaign, the earlier-mentioned massive public relations effort to encourage people to report crime and cooperate with the police. This close association of the

Figure 3.3 Location shooting in a working-class neighbourhood in *The Delinquent* (1973), with onlookers visible in the background.

first Hong Kong police film with a government and police agenda is telling. Hong Kong filmmakers would continue to play a role in shaping the police image in subsequent decades, while the Hong Kong Police Force would on occasion borrow from the world of film for its own public relations efforts.

Police Force's significance becomes more obvious when compared to a similar film that was released two months earlier, Chu Mu 朱 's *Police Woman* (女 察 *Neoi gingcaat*, 1973). A low-budget film produced by Chu's short-lived independent company, *Police Woman* is not a police thriller in the strict sense of the word. By focusing mainly on an innocent taxi driver (Charlie Chin 林) who finds himself harassed by a gang, *Police Woman* in fact resembles some of the suspense/detective films of the 1950s and 1960s in that the police mainly appear to make arrests at the end of the film. While the taxi driver gets important help from the titular policewoman (Yuen Qiu 元) in the film's second half, she is never in uniform and acts independently from the real police force, which throughout the film is shown to be rather ineffective and even unhelpful. This policewoman moreover gets involved because the gang has murdered her sister, signalling a personal rather than a professional commitment. Chu's film is still significant in that the filmmakers clearly realised they were exploring new material, with one advertisement claiming the film contained 'the newest subject matter never before seen on the silver screen' – subject matter that would moreover be *xianshi* 實 (*jinsat*, 'realist'). Like *Police Force*, it aligned itself with contemporary police discourse, with the same ad stating that the film 'promotes the spirit of cooperation between the people and the police'.

Although *Police Woman* is a typical low-budget action flick with barely any break between the fighting and chase scenes, it also contains a jarring but clearly significant piece of dialogue in the middle of the film. This scene has the protagonist taking a break at a restaurant with his fellow taxi drivers, when one of them looks up from his newspaper and loudly complains about the crime problem in Hong Kong. This leads to a monologue from the protagonist, who starts by linking crime to urban life and inequality ('It's a rat race: the rich get richer, and the poor get poorer!'), but the cause of crime that gets most attention – without a hint of irony – is the amount of sex and violence young people can see in films and magazines. The protagonist's hotheaded friend interjects: 'If I were the government, I'd just ban the whole lot: the books, the films. Then I'd improve the social services and give the crooks a chance: those who didn't accept the chance, the die-hard crooks, I'd get them, I'd take them out and shoot them!' Despite its clumsiness, this scene encapsulates many of the issues featured in the films discussed in the rest of this chapter, which I argue are central to the criminal realism of the 1970s: censorship, the crime problem (and the populist response to it), as well as films' increased interest in sociopolitical commentary.

Figure 3.4 Poster for *Police Force* (1973). © Celestial Pictures Ltd. All rights reserved 權 天映娛
樂有 公司全 擁有.

In contrast, Chang and Tsai's *Police Force* is interesting for its subversion of standard kung fu film tropes, which the film does in a highly self-conscious manner. As is common in Chang's work, a young man's best friend is murdered, so he sets out to take revenge. Unconventionally, he decides to do this by becoming a policeman. When after several years he finally locates the murderer, he is faced with a dilemma: should he execute his vengeance as he had originally sworn to, or should he uphold the law and the reputation of the police force as his training and career have taught him? His eventual foregoing of personal vengeance in favour of judicial justice breaks with the conventional morality of the kung fu universe, moving *Police Force* deeper into crime film territory. Unsurprisingly given the official backing it received, the film affirms the ability of the police force and the law to fight crime and achieve justice for all. Given the prominence of this theme, the film's focus on a police protagonist, and its comparatively realistic portrayal of the Hong Kong Police Force, the film can be considered the first real local police thriller. Wong Chung, who played the police protagonist, would become a famous local movie cop later in the decade and into the 1980s.

For a much more critical contemporary vision of the Hong Kong Police Force, one must only look at a Kuei Chi-hung film that appeared in Hong Kong theatres about four weeks after *Police Force*. *Payment in Blood* (1973) tells the story of an upright citizen (Yueh Hua 岳) who witnesses a murder, reports the crime to the police, and agrees to testify in court, despite serious triad intimidation and violence against his family. The police repeatedly prove incapable of protecting their witness, however: this model citizen's child is kidnapped, his wife is murdered, and he himself eventually is forced to kill various criminals in self-defence. An angry letter from a City District Officer to the Assistant Secretary for Home Affairs two weeks after the release of the film confirms its subversiveness, with the officer questioning the work of the censors as the film's message 'is unacceptable both in theme and in timing (of its release) at the height of the Fight Violent Crime Campaign', the main aim of which after all was to encourage citizens to report crimes and cooperate with the police (Memo from City District Officer [Yau Ma Tei] Helen Yu to Assistant Secretary for Home Affairs, 31 July 1973, HKRS313-7-8, HKPRO).

No action was taken in response to this letter, but Kuei would run into trouble with the censors throughout the rest of his career, as he repeatedly set out to break established boundaries in the depiction of violence, crime, sex and politics. This was true for what are arguably his most important crime films, *The Teahouse* (1974) and its sequel *Big Brother Cheng* (1975). Both films were big hits at the box office and together launched the modern triad film. The term 'triad film' is most appropriate here because although earlier gangster films had engaged to some degree with triad lore and culture, none had depicted the triads with a lot of realistic detail.

The Teahouse is the first Hong Kong film to represent triad rituals, hand gestures and slang in a contemporary setting. On Kuei's insistence, the film was also shot primarily in Cantonese, undoubtedly to increase its realism (Chan and Tse 2011, 38). Adapted from Kong Chi-nam 之南's popular novel *The Heroic Deeds of a Villain* (1973), the film focuses on a teahouse opened by recent immigrants from mainland China, who are led by Big Brother Cheng (Chan Koon-tai   ). Episodic in structure, the film shows how the teahouse community – a microcosm of Hong Kong society – encounters various public security problems: robbery, rape, forced prostitution and, connected to it all, juvenile delinquency. In what can be read as a populist response to Patrick Lung's liberal/elitist perspective in *Teddy Girls*, the various episodes of *The Teahouse* and *Big Brother Cheng* repeat one consistent message: that the Hong Kong courts are much too soft on criminals, especially juveniles, resulting in rampant crime. Confirming this populist positioning is a sequence in *The Teahouse* making fun of the Social Welfare Department – the very department celebrated by *Teddy Girls* – as out-of-touch bureaucrats easily duped by cunning common folk.

Given the constant threats to their safety, Brother Cheng and his friends gradually take the law into their own hands, becoming vigilantes. Kuei himself in fact saw *The Teahouse* primarily as a 'vigilante film', describing it as the first Mandarin film on vigilantism and mentioning *Death Wish* (1974) with Charles Bronson as a direct inspiration (*The Star*, 'Director Raps Film Censors', 12 June 1976). What distinguishes Kuei's film from the Bronson vehicle, however, is the involvement of triad societies: as Brother Cheng and the teahouse community start to punish wrongdoers themselves, they quickly run into trouble with two triad groups. As the conflict with one of these groups escalates and requires violent countermeasures, Brother Cheng and his friends become virtually indistinguishable from the second, largely benign triad society that is also present in the film – one that still adheres to 'traditional' triad values, such as an understanding that there are certain criminal activities one should not engage in, no matter how profitable they are. Recalling the imagery in Chang Cheh's *The Duel*, one promotional poster of *Big Brother Cheng* even shows the hero in front of a huge *yi* character, further associating him with triad heroism. This presence of a 'good' triad group that upholds traditional values is perhaps the ultimate signifier of a deep distrust of a modern rule-of-law type society and embodies a desire to return to an imagined older, less impersonal, and more 'Chinese' form of social order and justice (Berry and Farquhar 2006, 138–55). It would soon become a genre convention, and while it recalls the 'family myth' in Coppola's *The Godfather* (Man 2000, 116), it also has local precedents in the 1950s and 1960s gangster films discussed earlier. Even though Brother Cheng is eventually – in an implausible twist clearly meant to placate the censors – revealed to be an undercover police officer, Kuei's two films paved the way for a spate of modern-day triad films that became

Figure 3.5 Poster for *Big Brother Cheng* (1975), showing the eponymous protagonist in front of a giant *yi* 義, indicating the values of righteousness, brotherhood, loyalty. © Celestial Pictures Ltd. All rights reserved 權 天映娛樂有 公司全 擁有.

an important cycle later in the decade. This cycle would initially start as part of a broader trend for 'true crime' films.

True Crime

According to Sek Kei (2018, 69), this 'true crime' cycle was kicked off by Cheng Kang 剛's *Kidnap* (1974). An earlier and arguably more important film, however, was Patrick Lung's *The Call Girls* (應召女 *Jingziu neoilong*, 1973). Establishing a particular local subgenre that has seen occasional entries up to the present, Lung's film was the first serious exploration of the local sex industry. Somewhat like his *Teddy Girls* a few years earlier but with more sex and nudity thrown in, *The Call Girls* has an ensemble cast that allows for the development of several characters' individual stories, which together aim to paint a comprehensive picture of the world of prostitution. Fictional interviews conducted for a TV programme aptly named 'Society and You' are interspersed throughout the film, presenting different views on the sex trade, including arguments in favour of and against its legalisation. In terms of local censorship policy, the film was a significant breakthrough. The Panel of Censors initially banned it for its long sequences 'showing the operation of the call-girl system and widespread scenes of nudity, love-making, drug taking and gang fighting' and because they felt it 'smear[ed] the image of Hong Kong and paint[ed] a great part of it as a sink of inequity'. A scene showing police corruption was another reason given for the ban ('Call-Girls', 1 December 1972, HKRS 313-7-8, HKPRO). After an appeal by the film's production company, however, the Board of Review passed the film for release subject to certain cuts, justifying its decision by arguing that 'there was sufficient social comment in the film to show that it was not made merely for prurient motive' (Film: 'Call-Girls', 23 January 1973, HKRS 313-7-8, HKPRO). Subsequently becoming a great critical and commercial success, the film effectively paved the way for the blossoming of 'true crime' films.

One of the highest-grossing films in the following year, *Kidnap* further reinforced this trend. The film was based on the sensational murders and kidnappings by the local 'Wild Wolf' gang that took place between 1959 and 1961, with the Shaw Brothers magazine *Hong Kong Movie News* claiming director Cheng Kang tracked down and interviewed the one surviving convicted criminal in the case, and received generous police support to make the film as realistic as possible (*Hong Kong Movie News* 1973a). Three members of the gang were sentenced to death by hanging in 1962 – one of the last times the death sentence was executed in Hong Kong. It was *Kidnap*'s attention to the criminals' execution that most directly linked the film to the public discourse of its day, as the abolition of the death penalty was then a hot-button topic. Executions had been halted in Hong Kong since 1966, after opposition to the death penalty in the UK led to the Governor being instructed to commute all death sentences in the colony to sentences of life imprisonment (Vagg 1997, 393). This became particularly controversial in 1973, when Governor Murray MacLehose decided not to commute the death sentence of a convicted murderer. This decision responded to the public calls for harsher punishment of criminals, of which the Brother Cheng films were one expression.[4] In an appeal letter to the authorities in London, however, seventy-one prominent Hong Kong lawyers, university heads, journalists, church leaders and businessmen criticised the Governor's decision and questioned its motivation, linking it to the authorities' desire to appear tough given the launch of the 'Fight Violent Crime' campaign (Baker et al., 'A Plea for the Life of Tsoi Kwok-cheong', *South China Morning Post*, 27 April 1973). The Queen's subsequent commutation of the man's death sentence caused further controversy in Hong Kong and kept the debate alive for many more weeks on the city's opinion pages.

In his film, Cheng Kang does not take a clear position in the debate surrounding the death sentence. The focus of *Kidnap* is on the three gang members who are eventually executed, and, although they commit horrendous crimes in the course of the narrative, they still appear as ordinary individuals we can empathise with. The final quarter of the film is devoted to their execution, amplifying the melodrama by cross-cutting their deaths with the near simultaneous deaths of the gang leader's unborn child, his girlfriend and another kidnapper's heartbroken mother. By going into melodramatic overdrive, *Kidnap* largely sidesteps difficult questions surrounding the death sentence, turning the film into a cautionary tale. As a third-person narrator puts it at the beginning of the film: 'The purpose of this film is to stress the moral of the story, so that on the path these men once walked no new footprints are left.' On the one hand, then, the film presents the death sentence as a punishment that could deter others from making the same mistakes, dovetailing with a common argument in favour of the death sentence one can find in numerous opinion pieces at the time. On the other hand, *Kidnap*'s sympathetic portrayal of the kidnappers and – conversely – the largely negative impression we are given of their victims can also lead one to question the justice of the punishment they receive, especially as their execution is shown to have very negative repercussions for the innocent people close to them. Similar to Lung's approach in *The Call Girls*, Cheng clearly capitalised on the topicality of the death sentence in Hong Kong, while avoiding a clear stance on the issue that would risk alienating a section of the audience or run afoul of government censors. Unsurprisingly, this would be the approach of most of the

---

[4] *Big Brother Cheng* in fact refers directly and approvingly to the Governor's decision not to commute this murderer's death sentence.

filmmakers who started making 'true crime' films in the following years – few shared Kuei Chih-hung's appetite for controversy and boundary-breaking.

The commercial potential of ripped-from-the-headlines films was definitively confirmed the following year, when Ng See-yuen 吳思 's *Anti-Corruption* (1975) became the second-highest grossing film at the local box office. A sensationalised account of the events leading up to the establishment of the ICAC, Ng's film was daring in that it focused mainly on the corruption of a British cop, Hunter (based on the real case of Ernest 'Taffy' Hunt). In a lengthy flashback, the film narrates Hunter's arrival in Hong Kong and his gradual induction into local police practices, showing how a culture of corruption left new cops with two options – participate, get rich and have a successful career, or not participate, remain poor and face dismissal (or at least a lack of career prospects). *Anti-Corruption* relishes in depicting the often very inventive ways in which cops received kickbacks and how such money was distributed institutionally, in the process showing how corruption had reached into very high levels of the police hierarchy. Hunter's role model in the film is a senior police officer, Peter Gosper (based on the most well-known corrupt cop at the time, Peter Godber), whose successful escape from Hong Kong leads to a public outcry – represented in the film with fragments of black-and-white documentary footage of student protests – and to the establishment of the ICAC. *Anti-Corruption* finally goes on to detail the ways in which this new organisation took down corrupt officers – through investigation of their assets, surveillance and interrogations. Over the mugshots of several arrested corrupt cops and gangsters, and then shots of Wan Chai and the Hong Kong harbour, a third-person voice-over concludes the film by noting that the anti-corruption campaign cleaned up the police and that henceforth the anti-corruption spirit penetrates every corner of Hong Kong society. Hong Kong, the narrator grandly proclaims, 'can now stride forward with a whole new appearance'. With the film coming out just a year and a half after the establishment of the ICAC, this seems an overly optimistic claim. Although it to some extent truthfully reflected the real change the ICAC brought to local governance and its public perception, the film's relegating the problem of corruption unambiguously to the past was most likely intended to placate the censors, whom we have already seen were sensitive to portrayals of local police corruption.

Just weeks before *Anti-Corruption* hit the theatres, a spectacular bank robbery took place that would prove further fodder for filmmakers eager to explore 'true crime' filmmaking. In early August 1975, a gang ambushed a Hang Seng bank escort as it came out of the new Cross-Harbour Tunnel in Hung Hom, shooting two guards and a bank employee, and making off with over HK$7 million in cash, making it the largest robbery of its kind in Hong Kong history (Kenneth Ko, 'Bank Cars Ambushed; $7.2m Stolen', *South China Morning Post*, 6 August 1975). A massive manhunt ensued, the money was recovered, and a series of arrests were made about six weeks later. Even before the police closed the case, a film inspired by the robbery had already hit the theatres: Chor Yuen's *The Big Holdup* (大劫案 *Daai gip ngon*, 1975) quite faithfully restaged the robbery at the location where it had taken place. Coming out before the culprits were arrested and more details of the case were made public, the rest of the film is fictional and remarkably old-fashioned, harking back to the model set by Lee Tit's *We Want to Live* (1960, discussed in Chapter 1): after an action-heavy opening act, it mainly focuses on the melodramatic backstories of the robbers themselves. Based on the same robbery and providing a striking contrast with Chor's film was Ng See-yuen's *Million Dollars Snatch* (七　元大劫案 *Catbaakmaan jyun daai gip ngon*, 1976), which came out a year later. Masterfully combining truthful details from the case with the conventions of Hollywood heist and cops-and-robbers films, it clearly foreshadows the Hong Kong action-crime films of the 1980s and 1990s. It could be considered on a par with Leong Po-chih 梁普智 and Josephine Siao's *Jumping Ash* (　　 *Tiufui*, 1976, discussed in the next chapter), a film often touted as a precursor to the Hong Kong New Wave of the late 1970s and early 1980s.

Much of the freshness of *Million Dollars Snatch* derives from its use of real locations, its avoidance of highly recognisable film stars, as well as its realistic depiction of police work (such as forensic ballistics) and criminal activities. As in *Anti-Corruption*, documentary footage is used occasionally in the film, seemingly taken from news reports about the police manhunt. Following a typical cops-and-robbers format, the film starts by setting up the two main characters: Chan (Lin Wen-wei 林文偉), the brooding bank robber, and Inspector Li (Chang Kung 張弓), the tough overworked cop on his tail. Several other participants in the robbery are introduced before the hit on the Hang Seng money transport is planned and executed about halfway into the film. The film then details the robbers' efforts to escape capture, the progressing police investigation, and, finally, the successful round-up of the whole gang. While this generic format was new to Hong Kong cinema, it must have been familiar to local audiences from numerous foreign films. In its ending, however, the film defies expectations. As Inspector Li and his men have cornered Chan, the last remaining robber still on the run, Li manages to approach Chan unseen from behind and shoots him. This, however, is then shown to be only Li's imagination: instead, he jumps down, disarms the robber and arrests him. The reason for these two alternative endings is unclear: it might have been due to censorship (a police officer shooting a suspect from behind without warning would not reflect well on the police force), or simply due to a desire to include a more cathartic showdown while staying close to the facts of the case (no robber was shot during arrest). What is even more puzzling, however, is the film's coda, which has Li – shown throughout the film as a dedicated, professional detective – arrested by the ICAC. The implications of this odd ending are puzzling: does Ng simply want to remind his viewers that the police are not all-powerful anymore, and have to answer to the ICAC? Or, given Li's exemplary behaviour throughout the film, does he actually intend to criticise the ICAC for going too far and for hindering the important crime-fighting work of the police? This latter interpretation, which hints at the bureaucratic hurdles faced by the streetwise cop, would soon become a well-established trope in local police thrillers.

That the topic of the film remained somewhat sensitive in the eyes of the authorities was confirmed by its entanglement in a minor censorship controversy prior to its release. Although the Panel of Censors passed *Million Dollars Snatch*, the government's Legal Department applied for an injunction order against the screening of the film, because it feared the film would prejudice the appeals of several people convicted for the robbery. Even though this injunction was dropped a week later after someone from the Legal Department watched the film ('Crown Drops Objection to $7m Robbery Film', *South China Morning Post*, 30 July 1976), the incident indicated the risks involved in making 'true crime' films. The authorities' lingering touchiness on the topic of crime explains why filmmakers often included messages that supported the government's agenda, as we have seen with *Anti-Corruption*, and as will be even more obvious in *The Drug Queen* (大毒后 *Daai dukhau*, 1976, discussed in the next chapter). In any case, the lure of profits began to outweigh the risks at this point and more and more crime exposés started to appear, both on TV and in cinemas. In 1976 and 1977, Shaw Brothers for instance released the *The Criminals* series: five films containing two to four short films each, all based on true crimes. The main contributors to this series included Kuei Chih-hung, as well as three other young Shaw directors who made a mark on the late 1970s crime film; Sun Chung, Hua Shan and Mou Tun-fei. Even earlier, on television, Rediffusion Television (RTV) released 'Ten Sensational Cases' (十大奇案 *Sap daai kei ngon*, 1975), while TVB made the anthology series *CID* (1976) with help from the police (Law K. 2018, 47). In the next chapter we will see that, as a result of these developments, the modern Hong Kong triad film and police thriller began to take shape as distinct local genres.

Films such as *The Call Girls*, *Anti-Corruption*, *Big Brother Cheng* and others discussed above show that a wide range of philosophies and views regarding justice, law and (police) authority started to be explored in 1970s Hong Kong crime films. Rather than treating these films as inferior knock-offs of Hollywood hits, this chapter has aimed to show how they were deeply connected to pressing social and political concerns surrounding local crime and policing. As a corollary to this, the term 'realism' was used more than ever to promote crime films. Aside from the example of *The Criminals* series mentioned earlier, even *Police Force* was promoted in *Hong Kong Movie News* as 'extremely realistic [*zhenshi* 實 (*zansat*)], to the point of being documentary-like', a description it earned merely because of the shots it included of an actual police parade and of a graduation ceremony at a police school (Dungzi 1973). In Shaw magazines, directors such as Kuei Chih-hung, Sun Chung and Hua Shan were often described as shooting their crime films in a 'social realist [*shehui xieshi* 會寫實 (*sewui sesat*)]' style (*Hong Kong Movie News* 1973b; Ngaan 1976; Wong 1978). So were Chung Kwok-yan 國仁's numbers films and Alan Tang's Big Timer series – both discussed in the next chapter (Coengzi 1978) – and films like *Anti-Corruption*, *Million Dollars Snatch* and *Jumping Ash* (Po 2018). One aspect of this was the touting of the bona fide gangster or police credentials of certain film personnel. Shaw Brothers indirectly hinted at Chung Kwok-yan's underworld connections in its promotional materials (Coengzi 1978), and to this day it is widely believed that Alan Tang had triad connections. *Jumping Ash* meanwhile launched the film career of its scriptwriter Philip Chan 欣健, who for years had worked as a police officer. Stylistically speaking, the 'realism' of these films varied greatly, but the persistent use of 'realism' as a promotional term indicates that throughout the decade there was a strong demand for films that engaged with the realities of present-day Hong Kong. The fact that this pursuit of realism found expression in crime films speaks to the function of the genre in Hong Kong cinema and its role in the articulation of Hong Kong identity, a topic that will be further explored in the next chapter.

4   Crime Films and Hong Kong Identity

THE PREVIOUS CHAPTER has indicated that the relaxation of government censorship in the 1970s, along with other factors, allowed the modern Hong Kong crime film to become an important discursive space to reflect on crime and criminal justice-related topics that were then major issues of local concern. As part of a broader public sphere, crime films – defined by a new form of criminal realism – took their stories mainly from the newspaper pages and were as a result highly varied, at least initially. The *The Criminals* series of omnibus films produced by the Shaw Brothers in 1976 and 1977 best exemplified this diversity: while supposedly all based on true stories, the genres covered by the short films in this series included true crime horror, police procedural, triad film, and even courtroom drama. Very soon, however, crime films mainly started to coalesce around the figures of the (triad) gangster and the cop, which have continued to dominate Hong Kong crime cinema until the present. What happened was clearly not a typical process of 'genrification' whereby a new genre (or genres) gradually took shape (Altman 1998): Shaws' *The Criminals* series and other films covered in the previous chapter indicate that filmmakers were already familiar with a broad range of both local and foreign crime film genres. This chapter will therefore explore some of the reasons why triad films and police thrillers came to dominate local crime cinema, such as the global success of action films and the well-established reputation of Hong Kong in this area by the mid-1970s, as well as the continued relevance of real triads and police to Hong Kong life. Crucially important, I argue, were the rich narrative possibilities offered by triads and cops, with each group having a distinctive culture as well as intricate internal hierarchies, rules and power dynamics that could be fruitfully explored in a nearly infinite number of films.

This final reason in particular has made stories about triad gangsters and police officers excellent vehicles to allegorically explore broader cultural and political issues beyond the more immediate concern with the 'crime problem' that preoccupied the crime films covered in Chapter 3. The awareness and assertion of Hong Kong as a place with its own culture and its own way of life – in other words, the awareness of a distinctive Hong Kong identity – became one of the genre's implicit themes. In this regard, the Royal Hong Kong Police could feature in films as a shorthand for Hong Kong's colonial status, connoting repression and the unwanted intrusion of Western values and power structures, or alternatively, as a positive symbol of what made Hong Kong different – more modern, prosperous and cosmopolitan – than mainland China. Triad gangsters similarly could carry both positive and negative connotations in films: as representatives of 'Chinese traditional values', they could evoke nostalgia for a simpler time when words such as loyalty, righteousness and brotherhood still meant something, or in contrast, they could highlight the emptiness or patriarchal oppressiveness of these same values. Beyond these tradition/modernity-related themes – of which I have just scratched the surface – the figures of the Hong Kong cop and gangster could be used to reflect on various other cultural and sociopolitical tensions, as many examples in this and other chapters indicate. This flexibility was undoubtedly a reason for the long-lasting popularity of the modern Hong Kong crime film.

This chapter will start by expanding on the enduring connection between the crime film and Hong Kong identity. Next, it will look at the increasing stabilisation of the genre around the figures of the triad gangster and the cop in the late 1970s. The triad film was the more productive genre during these years with three main strands of triad film developing: films about famous real-life gangster bosses; sensationalised explorations of Hong Kong's criminal underbelly; and action-filled tales of rank-and-file triad members with a heavy focus on the value of brotherhood. The first two of these strands are clearly related to the 'true crime' trend discussed in the previous chapter, while the last one was less well developed but would turn out to be a crucial link to the type of heroic bloodshed crime film later popularised by John Woo's *A Better Tomorrow* (1986). The police thriller remained relatively underdeveloped during this period and was also more obviously indebted to foreign (especially American) models. Nevertheless, the police films discussed here show how a conscious effort was made to translate the genre to local circumstances, attesting to the dominance of criminal realism throughout the 1970s. The next and final section of this chapter looks at how the figure of the immigrant gangster from mainland China appeared in gangster films from the late 1970s to the late 1980s. As many other scholars have argued, this figure has often been used to allegorically comment on Hong Kong and mainland China relations, especially in view of the approaching 1997 Handover. My account here draws attention to several earlier films in this subgenre that have so far slipped under the radar and that highlight the role of colonial censorship and immigration policy in shaping this figure's representation. A closer look at the *Long Arm of the Law* (旗兵 *Saang Gong kei bing*, 1984–90) series further shows how the four films in the series became increasingly direct in their politics, a development that can be linked both to the further relaxation of political censorship and to the increasing pessimism about Hong Kong's future in the late 1980s, especially in the wake of the June Fourth massacre in 1989. The Self/Other dynamic in films about immigrant gangsters is but one way in which the crime film contributed to the discourse of Hong Kong identity. The next chapter will deal with two other genres – problem youth films and cop thrillers – that served a similar function.

Crime Films and Hong Kong Identity

As we have seen, crime films in late 1960s and 1970s Hong Kong took part more than ever before in a public sphere in which violent crime was a major concern. By realistically depicting crime in Hong Kong, filmmakers satisfied a popular demand for sensational details (whether real or fictional) about the crimes that prominently featured in the local news at this time. The rise of location-shooting during the 1970s added to films' realist credentials, with the intended aesthetic effect likely one of shock at, and morbid fascination with, the awful crimes and colourful underworld that existed at the periphery of one's daily life – an underworld which had for a long time been kept from view by the censors. Intentionally or not, these films through their location-shooting also brought into view parts of the city that had in the past rarely, if ever, been shown in local films. In a context where self-awareness of, and pride in, a distinctive local identity and way of life was on the rise, crime films were part of a process by which the city, as it were, looked at itself in the mirror – sometimes admiringly, sometimes self-critically – and tried to understand itself. While criminal realism was a tendency within the Hong Kong crime film throughout its history, it is this particular context that made criminal realism dominant in local crime cinema from the late 1960s to the early 1980s.

Two interesting questions to consider are, first, why the crime film in this period so quickly organised itself around the figures of the local cop and the triad gangster, and, second, why this configuration has been so enduring. Beyond commercial cinema's tendency towards standardisation, a few likely reasons suggest themselves. First, as the last chapter has already indicated, gangsters and the police frequently made the news during the 1970s, providing plenty of fresh material for filmmakers to work with. Real life continued to offer much inspiration throughout the 1980s and 1990s, but arguably less so since the turn of the century, when the nature of (organised) crime and policing changed to less spectacular forms – even if the occasional triad attack still makes the news.[1] Second, from the 1970s to the 1990s the action-crime film was one of the dominant forms of action cinema throughout the world, so Hong Kong filmmakers, by the early 1970s already known for their outstanding skills in action cinema, logically were attracted to the genre. Throughout this period, major Hollywood crime films – similarly organised around the figures of the cop and the gangster – influenced Hong Kong directors, and sometimes the other way around as well. While Hollywood action since the 2000s has been dominated by science fiction and superhero films, however, Hong Kong action filmmakers have largely stuck to contemporary crime and period martial arts films – lack of access to massive budgets for special effects is a likely reason for this, as is, perhaps, a certain nostalgia for Hong Kong cinema's 'golden age' of the 1980s and 1990s.

Practical, commercial and sentimental reasons aside, Hong Kong triad gangsters and the Hong Kong Police Force simply make for fascinating subject matter for filmmakers interested in going beyond these figures' suitability for staging spectacular action scenes. As organisations with their own hierarchies, power dynamics, rules and culture, both the police force and triad societies provide ample opportunity for drama, and also exude a somewhat mysterious, sometimes even glamorous appeal to outsiders, both locally and internationally. In overseas markets, this has been one way to make Hong Kong (action-)crime films stand out among the competition. In police thrillers, this fascination has taken the form of exploring different branches of the police force, the details of their work, and the various rivalries between departments, or between senior officers and the rank and file. Given the triads' secretive nature, films about them have tended a bit more towards fantasy, or have focused more often on particular individuals, both fictional and real. Somewhat like the police thriller, inter- and intra-group rivalry often takes centre stage in triad films, while sometimes the details of specific illicit trades (especially in drugs and sex) provide major narrative interest. The similarities between triads and police have in some films become a major theme in themselves.

Finally, and perhaps most importantly, the fact that triads and the police are both social groups involved in transgressing or enforcing the Law and that both are involved in asserting authority and power over a certain territory makes them useful subjects to allegorically explore broader cultural and sociopolitical tensions, especially in an environment in which it is risky – for commercial and/or political reasons – to broach such topics directly. As detailed later in this chapter in the section on mainland gangsters in Hong Kong, Hong Kong-mainland China relations have

---

[1] The most noteworthy triad attack in recent years happened during the 2019 protests, when white-shirted men with suspected triad links and possibly with police backing attacked protesters returning home at the Yuen Long train station.

been one such topic. Over the years, many variations on this theme have appeared in Hong Kong crime films, featuring for instance mainland police in Hong Kong – as in the *Her Fatal Ways* (姐，你好 ! *Biuze, nei hou je!*) series (1990–4) – or Hong Kong cops and gangsters in the mainland – as in *Rock N' Roll Cop* (一 *Saang Gong jat hou tungcapfaan*, 1994) and *Drug War* (毒戰 *Dukzin*, 2013). One earlier film, *Banana Cop* (偷 *Jing Leon peipaa*, 1984), even featured a British Chinese cop whose investigation leads him from London to Hong Kong and back.[2] The most sophisticated political allegories of this kind have arguably been Johnnie To's *Election* (2005) and its sequel (2006). Both films use the plot device of a triad election to comment on Hong Kong's then semi-democratic system, and the role of the mainland authorities in it.

The allegorical dimension of crime films goes beyond the self-consciously political. Taking John Woo's gangster films as one of their case studies, Berry and Farquhar (2006) have for instance argued for the importance of premodern codes to a wide variety of Chinese-language films. These codes 'were fundamental to Confucian notions of ruling the nation through virtue, rather than to modern concepts of rule by or of law' (Berry and Farquhar 2006, 135–6). Although now long gone as law, the codes 'persist as mythic symbols of national identity, ideal masculine behavior, and institutional governance' (136). It is specifically the code of brotherhood that they see as central to Woo's gangster films. As discussed in earlier chapters, Woo was certainly not the first to associate gangster heroes with traditional values that are disappearing due to the advance of capitalist modernity – the trope can be traced back at least to *Tradition* (1954, discussed in Chapter 1). As *Brotherhood* (子弟 *Gongwu zidai*, 1976, discussed below) also attests, this has been an enduring theme in Hong Kong gangster films – one that has in more recent decades often been deconstructed by filmmakers as well. One can find a variation on this theme in 1980s and 1990s police films, in the frequent appearance of streetwise cops who resist the impersonal professionalism and individualistic career-mindedness of their younger, often Western-educated superiors. Again, the great diversity of narratives and attitudes should be stressed here. The Alan Tang 'Big Timer' films discussed below, for instance, link their gangster protagonists' business success to their adherence to traditional values such as brotherhood and loyalty, in a way prefiguring more recent celebrations of a 'Confucian capitalism'. Police films since the 1990s meanwhile have frequently celebrated the teamwork and professionalism of the police force, seemingly as a stand-in for the achievements and modern civic values of Hong Kong people in general.

---

[2] It should be added here that both *Banana Cop* and the *Her Fatal Ways* series are crime comedies. Comedy offers a light-hearted way to tackle politically sensitive topics, defusing real-life tensions through laughter.

In short, Hong Kong crime films have certainly never spoken in just one voice. This probably does not come as a surprise, but it bears highlighting as accounts of genre films tend to essentialise the meaning(s) of a particular genre. Instead, as in the public sphere in general, multiple views are expressed in crime films and neither triad gangsters nor the police are fixed in their signification. As some of the above examples already hint at, certain broad value changes can be discerned in crime films from the 1970s to the present, but this is a topic beyond the scope of this book. What is certain is that the criminal realism of the 1970s made crime films a prominent venue in which various ideas on Hong Kong culture, politics and identity could be explored. The growing dominance of triad films and police thrillers in the late 1970s was a crucial step towards this.

Triad Films and Police Thrillers

In 1976 and 1977, both the triad film and the local police thriller took on the form they would roughly maintain for the next three decades. In the case of the triad film, three major strands can be discerned at this time: films about famous real-life gangsters, or what Teo (1997, 230–42) has called the 'Big Timers'; action-heavy tales of fictional rank-and-file triad heroes usually focused on the value of brotherhood; and gritty, sensationalised explorations of actual organised crime. The first and the last of these strands are clearly connected to the 'true crime' trend discussed in the previous chapter. Yeung Kuen 楊權's *The Drug Queen* (1976), the first film based on a contemporary 'Big Timer', was in fact an unofficial spin-off from Ng See-yuen's *Anti-Corruption* (1975), sharing much of the earlier film's cast and picking up its side plot involving Ng Sik-ho 吳　, a real-life drug lord with several corrupt cops on his payroll. *Anti-Corruption* had shown how Ng was arrested in 1974, and how his wife and partner-in-crime, Cheng Yuet-ying 　月　, escaped. *The Drug Queen* starts where *Anti-Corruption* ended this subplot – with Cheng getting away during a police raid – and goes on to chronicle Cheng's life on the run, her failed attempts to leave Hong Kong and her eventual capture. More interesting, however, are the difficulties the film had in making it to the theatres: just as with *Million Dollars Snatch* a few months later, the government's Legal Department applied for an injunction to prohibit screenings of *The Drug Queen*, because it feared it would prejudice the final determination of the criminal charge against Cheng Yuet-ying ('Court Bars Showing of Drug Film', *South China Morning Post*, 28 December 1975). The film's release was eventually delayed by two months until after the trial had taken place, coming out in March 1976. Even then, its fate seemed uncertain: a newspaper report noted that the entire staff of the narcotics division of the Colonial Secretariat attended the film's gala opening 'to check out the facts' ('Just Checking

Out the Facts', *The Standard*, 5 March 1976). That the narcotics division didn't raise any objections to the film can likely be attributed to the extraordinary lengths the filmmakers went to please the authorities. The film repeatedly stresses how the establishment of the ICAC has completely changed the Hong Kong Police Force. For instance, it shows how corrupt cops are terrified by the mere mention of the organisation's name and dare no longer to accept any bribes, and how the police force is now very professional and focused on fighting crime. A voice-over narration at the end of the film claims that 'everyone in Hong Kong praised the police for their efforts and success [in capturing Cheng]' and calls on all citizens to assist the police in combating crime. 'If everyone cooperates', the film exhorts, 'Hong Kong will not only be a beautiful city, it will also become a prosperous and stable paradise for living.' The government's legal actions and filmmakers' ham-fisted attempts to please the authorities indicate the precariousness of the crime film as a viable local genre at the time.

Similar uncertainties also surrounded Hua Shan's *Brotherhood* (1976), which can be considered the first contemporary triad film in a romanticised vein. The film follows the travails of a courageous young gangster who upholds the traditional values of loyalty, righteousness and brotherhood in a contemporary *jianghu* where such values are only window dressing for the naked pursuit of wealth and power. With elaborate depictions of triad initiation rites and the execution of the *jiafa* ('family law'), and with the protagonist unambiguously a triad member, this Shaw Brothers picture clearly went a step further than *The Teahouse* and *Big Brother Cheng*. It was almost certainly the success of these two earlier films that led to the production of *Brotherhood*: promotional materials highlighted how the film was adapted from the work of Kong Chi-nam, the same author who had originally penned the Big Brother Cheng stories. In an article published in *Southern Screen* (南國 影 *Nanguo dianying*), one of the Shaw Brothers' movie magazines, it was anticipated that *Brotherhood* would encounter 'significant regional restrictions' but would fare well in the Hong Kong market (Laan 1976, 35). This hints at the often-stricter censorship policies in the important Southeast Asian and Taiwanese markets, as well as the increasing significance of the Hong Kong market itself, where clearly the studio discerned an appetite for triad films. While *Brotherhood* performed fairly well at the box office, it nevertheless did not equal the success of the Brother Cheng films. Neither did two other films inspired by Kuei Chih-hung's hits, Sun Chung's *The Drug Connection* (毒后 史 *Dukhau beisi*, 1976) and *Big Bad Sis* (*Saadaam Jing*, 1976), both featuring – in a throwback to the late 1960s – a female anti-crime vigilante. This possibly led Shaw Brothers to reduce its investment in this type of film: in the following years, it was mainly Golden Harvest and several small independent companies that took the lead in producing triad and police thrillers.

The third strand of triad films that arose in the late 1970s were the so-called 'numbers films', which used numbers with special triad meanings as their titles. Attracting audiences by offering an insider's perspective on actual triad activities and rituals, the key figure behind this group of films was a man named Chung Kwok-yan, a homophone for the word meaning 'a Chinese'. While approximately five numbers films were produced by different companies and helmed by different directors between 1977 and 1979, Chung's involvement was a constant, whether as a production manager, scriptwriter, actor or director. The film that set off this series was Lam Kwok-cheung 林國 's *Ironside 426* (四二六 *Sei ji luk*, 1977), produced for Golden Harvest and with Chung credited for the story. To help the film's highly realistic depiction of triad activities pass the censors, several precautions were taken. First, *Ironside 426*'s protagonist is revealed from the beginning to be an undercover agent tasked with infiltrating the triads and he successfully brings down the whole gang by the end of the film. Second, promotional materials claimed the story took place in 1973, just before the sea change brought by the ICAC. Finally, the use in the title of '426' – which is code for the rank of 'military commander' or 'Red Pole' in a triad society – evaded the censors' policy against triad slang and names in film titles by also making it the undercover cop's police identification number. In a sign of the continuing relaxation of censorship, however, the main attraction of the film remains unmistakable: exposing the ins and outs of the triad world. Hence, the cop starts his undercover career with a minor scam – joining an old friend in roasting and selling discarded dead ducks as fresh ones. Hawking their goods on the street, they soon are asked to pay protection fees by a local gang, seek help from a martial arts club when their stall is destroyed, and are introduced to a gang boss who agrees to protect them. This then leads to the friends' ritual initiation as members of a triad society, to their being put in charge of a numbers racket, and so forth. As the undercover cop's criminal career progresses, a convincingly realistic picture of the triad world is established.

While the numbers films took an interest in the triads' 'business' activities, another series of films that appeared around the same time more actively blurred the distinction between successful businessmen and successful triad leaders. Unlike the numbers films, these films were the work of one company, Wing-Scope. Its founder Alan Tang, at that time known mainly for playing the lead in numerous Taiwanese romantic melodramas, starred in the company's films and left the directing mostly to Stanley Siu 榮. In the late 1970s and early 1980s, Wing-Scope found its niche by shooting almost exclusively 'Big Timer' films, such as *The Discharged* (出冊 *Ceotcaak*, 1977), *The Rascal Billionaire* (*Baakfan soenghung*, 1978), *Law Don* (家 *Gaafaat*, 1979) and *Absolute Monarch* (手 天 *Zeksau ze tin*, 1980). The first two of these films, *The Discharged* and *The Rascal Billionaire* were loosely based on well-known and recognisable underworld figures, respectively Lee Choi-fat

李　　 and the Ma brothers – Ma Sik-yu 惜如 and Ma Sik-chun 惜　. Lee reportedly was an associate of the famous 1930s Shanghai gangster Du Yuesheng 杜月　 and had been an important figure in Hong Kong's entertainment and nightlife circles in the late 1940s and early 1950s, until the colonial government forced him to leave the territory in 1951. The Ma brothers belonged to a later generation of gangsters: associates of Ng Sik-ho, they made their fortune in the drug trade in the late 1960s and early 1970s, but were also involved in other businesses, establishing the still extant *Oriental Daily* newspaper in 1969. What is remarkable about Wing-Scope's Big Timer films is that they focus on the glamour of their protagonists: while *The Discharged* and *The Rascal Billionaire* still roughly follow a typical rise-and-fall narrative, *Law Don* and *Absolute Monarch* start with men already at the top, who after a crisis reassert their supremacy. All these films focus on the glamour of success in such a way that there is no moral questioning of the illicit ways by which this success is achieved, whether it is through trafficking drugs, murdering competitors, gambling fraud or other dubious business practices. In the process, the boundaries between regular businessmen and gangsters are almost completely erased: the successful tycoons of today are shown to have started out as ordinary criminals, and even after moving into respectable businesses their behaviour remains subject to the same codes that rule the triad underworld. These narratives certainly

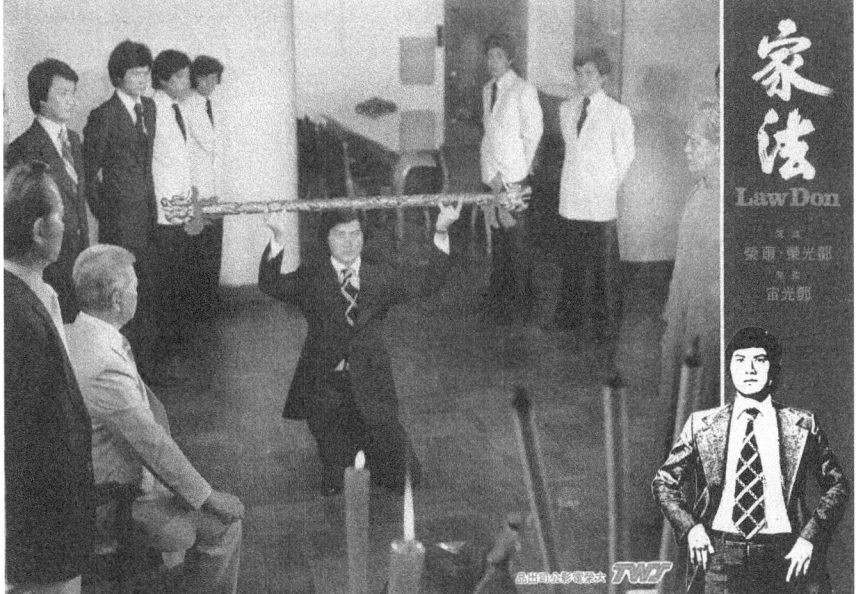

Figure 4.1 Hung Ying (Alan Tang) accepts the dragon baton in *Law Don* (1977). Image provided by the Hong Kong Film Archive, Leisure and Cultural Services Department, with the permission of Media Asia Film Distribution (HK) Limited.

have a basis in fact, as the Ma brothers' life story suggests, but the almost untrammelled glorification of such men is still somewhat surprising and may be taken as a testament to Hong Kong's freewheeling economy and rampant materialism in this period. It also attests to the rapid changes in the censorship of crime films over just a few years' time.

Of Wing-Scope's films in the late 1970s and early 1980s, it is *Law Don* that is most unambiguously a triad movie and provides the clearest contrast with Chung Kwok-yan's numbers films and the action-heavy, romanticised tales of ordinary gang brothers. In *Law Don*, Alan Tang is Hung Ying, the eldest son who succeeds his triad leader father after the latter's retirement. As a newcomer, Ying must prove himself both internally (vis-à-vis his three brothers) and externally (against several rival gangs). Much of the film is devoted to the power struggles and intrigues that would become the staple of countless later triad films. What sets the film apart is its highlighting of the *jiafa* or 'family law', which also gives the film its Chinese title. Ying's leadership is shown to be based on his strict adherence to these traditional rules of the triads and the film includes several punishment scenes as illustration, including the cutting off of a man's ear for disloyalty and another man being beaten thirty-six times for a lesser violation. While the *jiafa* is a culturally specific tradition, the film's narrative and depiction of the gangster world are clearly influenced by *The Godfather* films, albeit without the moral questions those films raise. At the end of *Law Don*, Ying saves his 'family' from annihilation by rival gangs, eliminates the competition and is about to cripple two of his brothers for their betrayal (they save him the effort by committing ritual suicide in front of the Hung family altar). Throughout the whole film, Ying remains a heroic figure and a model of efficient business management: he is strategic, entrepreneurial and decisive. Not insignificantly, his outfit throughout the film is a Western-style business suit – in a sense, the triad leader has become a model of Chinese- (or Hong Kong-) style capitalism. A final point worth noting about *Law Don* and Tang's other Big Timer films is that they are stunningly misogynist. As Shu Kei (1979) wrote in a review article on Tang's first three Big Timer films, the world of the triads in these films is entirely a man's world, and it is invariably the treachery, greed and/or jealousy of wives and girlfriends that lead to the (near) downfall of the male triad hero. This is an attitude often associated with triad films nowadays, but in the context of the late 1970s this was somewhat unusual: several earlier triad films, including *The Drug Queen* and *Brotherhood*, had prominently featured powerful female gangsters and gang leaders.

Compared to the productivity and variety of the triad film, the local police thriller developed more slowly. Riding high on the kung fu wave from earlier in the decade, Hong Kong filmmakers participated in international co-productions, some of which featured police protagonists involved in the fight against the international drug trade. Several such films were produced in the middle of the decade, including most famously *The Man from Hong Kong* (搗   *Zikdou wonglung*, 1975) and *Cleopatra Jones and the Casino of Gold* (1975). These films were action-focused and not particularly interested in exploring the realities of policing in Hong Kong. It was only in 1976, three years after Chang Cheh and Tsai Yang-ming's *Police Force*, that the local police thriller really took root, with Leong Po-chi and Josephine Siao's *Jumping Ash* becoming the second-highest grossing film at the local box office. In a detailed analysis of the film, Po Fung (2018, 81) goes as far as to call it 'the first cop film in Hong Kong cinema'. As with the triad film, the modern police thriller came out of the fad for true crime in 1975–6. Although *Million Dollars Snatch* had already signalled an interest in the exploration of local policing in Hollywood-influenced genre formats, its cops-and-robbers narrative was skewed more towards the activities of the criminals. *Jumping Ash*, coming out less than two weeks later, shifted the balance towards the police. Like the 'international' action films that preceded it, Leong and Siao's film starts overseas, with an assassin from Hong Kong executing a Chinatown gang leader in Amsterdam. The gang leader's son and his lieutenant travel to Hong Kong to seek revenge against the drug lord who ordered the hit and who is also under investigation by a tough and upright police sergeant, Callan Leong (Ga Lun 嘉倫). After a setback in his investigation, Leong is suspended from duty, but he extralegally teams up with one of the gangsters from Amsterdam to bring down the drug lord. He eventually manages to capture this villain along with the evidence necessary to bring him to justice: the film concludes with Leong walking off while his superior talks to reporters, taking all the credit.

As this brief outline indicates, *Jumping Ash* draws on tropes established by American cop films of the late 1960s and early 1970s, such as *Bullitt* (1968), *Dirty Harry* (1971) and *The French Connection* (1971). These films popularised the figure of the cop-turned-vigilante, a hard-bitten character who executes a 'higher' moral justice beyond the restrictions of judicial law. In the process, he (or she) must break free from bureaucracy and the constraints imposed by career-minded superiors. Often praised for its realism and authentic depiction of local crime and policing, *Jumping Ash* thus also introduced a form of 'police populism' in Hong Kong crime cinema, in which sympathy is elicited for street cops who risk their lives to keep society safe, despite facing constant complaints and criticism from the general population and the existence of various civil rights and rules of conduct that they perceive as hindering their job.[3] Once again, censorship is a likely reason for why it took so long for vigilante cops to take root in Hong Kong, as illustrated by the clash among the censors about Scorsese's *Taxi Driver* (discussed in the Intermezzo) and the odd

---

[3] I borrow the term 'police populism' from Wilson (2000).

double ending of *Million Dollars Snatch* (discussed in Chapter 3). Indeed, while 1973's *Police Force* can be considered the actual first local cop film, it was noteworthy for having its hero forego personal vengeance in deference to the legal process – a sharp break with the kung fu film conventions that the film also drew on, but one that undoubtedly made the film more palatable to a police force that wanted to burnish its public image. Ironically, the commercial success of *Jumping Ash* and its numerous successors would do much more to help improve the force's image, even if these films mostly reserved their sympathy for grassroots vigilante cops, not the judicial system in general. Conversely, the film's box office success in 1976 can also be read as a sign of the improving reputation of the police following the establishment of the ICAC in 1974.

While *Hot Blood* (入冊 *Japcaak*, 1977) is artistically less accomplished than *Jumping Ash*, it goes further than Leong and Siao's film in its pro-law enforcement attitudes and police populism. Directed by Yeung Kuen, who earlier included heavy-handed pro-police messages in his portrait of a real-life gangster in *The Drug Queen*, *Hot Blood* includes scenes of police heroes beating up and torturing suspects, as well as arresting them under false pretences, all tactics that the film seems to endorse. Early in the film, for instance, one of the protagonists threatens to drop a suspect from a high-rise window to get a confession. For this, he merely gets scolded by his superior, who moreover goes on to say that this method of questioning is actually quite effective. *Hot Blood* also refers repeatedly to the police force's efforts to improve relations with the public. On the one hand, these efforts are questioned, as when the two heroes are unjustly forced to apologise to a prominent doctor who filed a complaint against them. On the other, a subsequent scene has one cop reminding his colleague and friend not to behave like 'a bad guy with a badge', as this reflects poorly on the force. Later, this more responsible cop protagonist – portrayed by an early-career Chow Yun-fat – is murdered by a pair of hoodlums, and the film shows long lines of ordinary people lining up to pay their respects at the deceased cop's grave in what can be considered the film's strongest emotional appeal to support a beleaguered but righteous police force. In a final reference to contemporary concerns, the film also brings up the death penalty, the absence of which, two cops complain, merely serves to encourage gangsters. As an interesting counterpoint to this, the murdered cop's partner in the end explicitly refuses to kill the murderer, even when the latter taunts him that he will not face the death penalty. Instead, the cop laconically responds that 'life imprisonment is worse – no hope forever'.

As should be clear from the above, the early police thrillers and triad films of this period remained closely related to the mid-1970s trend of 'true crime' stories but were also influenced by the generic conventions of predominantly American police and gangster films. It is their strong interest in the realities of local crime and crime fighting that makes them very different from the films about triads or police detectives that appeared in earlier years. The next section will zoom in on a rather unique subgenre that also has its roots in this period: films about mainland gangsters in Hong Kong. With their complex depiction of these 'intruders' as both Self and Other, the films in this subgenre became a popular way for filmmakers to comment on Hong Kong identity and on the relationship between Hong Kong and mainland China, especially in the run-up to the 1997 Handover.

Illegal Immigrants as Self and Other

The filmic representation of mainland gangsters in Hong Kong has been a topic of enduring interest in studies of Hong Kong cinema. Much of this scholarship has focused on Johnny Mak's *Long Arm of the Law* (1984).[4] Rather than simply revisiting these analyses, this section will expand the corpus of films under consideration and in this way shed light on previously ignored histories and dimensions of the immigrant gangster figure in the 1970s and 1980s. Given the figure's potential for political allegory, it should come as no surprise that once again government censors tried to control and regulate it. I will show that, with the further relaxation of censorship, later entries in the *Long Arm of the Law* series became more explicit in their politics, highlighting local anxieties in the run-up to 1997 while also illustrating how the rule of law came to be seen by many as an important part of Hong Kong identity.

The motif of the immigrant gangster can in fact be traced back to two of the triad genre's seminal works, Kuei Chi-hung's *The Teahouse* and its sequel *Big Brother Cheng*. Two thirds into the first film, a New Territories farmer seeks Brother Cheng's help: a real estate developer has burned down his house and is trying to force him to sell his land. In a flashback, we learn that Brother Cheng illegally sneaked into Hong Kong about a year earlier and that this farmer helped him avoid capture by the authorities. Together with other fresh mainland immigrants, Cheng first worked as a hawker and then opened his teahouse. As discussed in Chapter 3, the way in which these (illegal) immigrants support one another and gradually are forced to take the law into their own hands makes them nearly indistinguishable from a triad society. But what is also interesting about the film is that Kuei Chih-hung treats Brother Cheng and his friends as locals: as a group of people running a typical Hong Kong

---

[4] For a short overview of representations of illegal immigrants in Hong Kong films and television in the late 1970s and 1980s, see Cheng (1990). Some representative analyses of *Long Arm of the Law* can be found in Li (1994), Yau (1994), Fang (2001), and Chu (2003).

teahouse, they in effect stand in for the Hong Kong community at large. The mutual help between them and the farmer, who in the Hong Kong context represents a 'true' native, further strengthens the idea of Hong Kong as a community where recent immigrants and locals live in harmony as fellow Chinese. This aspect of the film can be seen as Kuei taking a stand on yet another of the social issues of the day: the government's policy towards legal and illegal immigrants from mainland China. Due to a spike in immigration from mainland China in 1973, growing awareness of a Hong Kong identity, as well as the onset of a global economic recession and increasing unemployment, local anti-immigrant sentiment was on the rise, eventually prompting the Hong Kong government to introduce the 'Touch Base' policy in November 1974 (just a month after *The Teahouse*'s release). This policy, which authorised the repatriation of illegal immigrants from China unless they were able to reach the urban areas of Kowloon or Hong Kong Island, was aimed at reducing the influx of immigrants.

Agnes S. Ku (2004) has argued that the growth of a distinct Hong Kong identity was closely interrelated with the changing public and official discourses surrounding immigration policy, with the notion of 'settled residence' in the 1960s and the introduction of the legal category of 'Hong Kong belonger' in 1971 feeding into the articulation of a local consciousness. Parallel to this, public attitudes towards Chinese illegal immigrants shifted from tolerance in the 1950s to anti-immigrant sentiment in the 1970s (Mok 2021). *The Teahouse* appeared at a tipping point in this transition and is likely one of the last films that does not treat recent immigrants from the mainland as, in some way, 'Other'. In the following years, sentiment against illegal immigration further intensified, with illegal immigrants' involvement in criminal activities especially highlighted in the media. Mok (2021, 354), for instance, mentions a 1973 article in *The Standard* that attributed several hold-ups to mainland immigrants, and notes that many locals believed immigrants were involved in the spectacular Hang Seng robbery of 1975 (358). Although Ng See-yuen's film on this robbery, *Million Dollars Snatch* (see Chapter 3), did not depict the robbers as coming from the mainland, other heist films would soon highlight bank robbers' mainland origin. The first film to do so was Mou Tun-fei's *Bank Busters* (撈　　Lou gwo gaai, 1978), a Shaw Brothers production.[5] The plot of Mou's film clearly set the mould for this type of film, including the much better-known *Long Arm of the Law* series: a group of mainland youths illegally sneak into Hong Kong and – motivated by greed – resort to committing robberies. As in later films, the gang members are

---

[5] Unfortunately, no copy of Mou's film is in circulation. The following details are based on information available in the *Hong Kong Filmography Vol. VIII* (2014) and in contemporary film reviews.

Figure 4.2 Still from *Bank Busters* (1978). © Celestial Pictures Ltd. All rights reserved 權 天映娛樂有 公司全 擁有.

depicted as fierce and loyal to each other, and all die by the film's end. What sets the film apart from later works is that the gang obtains a notebook containing evidence of police corruption, which the last remaining member of the gang manages to pass to the ICAC before getting killed.

The combination of the robbery and police corruption plotlines led contemporary reviewers to compare the film to *Million Dollars Snatch*, which, as we have seen in Chapter 3, concludes with the cop protagonist taken away by ICAC officers. In a review in *Ming Pao*, critic Cauzi noted the similarities between the two films, including their combination of fact and fiction, as well as their use of unknown actors and real locations (quoted in Hong Kong Film Archive 2014, 233). *Bank Busters* was thus clearly a product of the mid-1970s trend towards true crime. Even more interesting, however, is that Mou himself claimed that the government's banning of Tang Shu-shuen 唐書's *China Behind* (再 中國 *Zoigin Zunggwok*, 1974) inspired him to make this film (Hong Kong Film Archive 2014, 233). Tang's film was the first film by an ethnically Chinese director to focus on the ravages of the Cultural Revolution and followed four students as they fled China to Hong Kong. Once the students make it to Hong Kong, they find that life in a capitalist society is not all that wonderful either. The banning of Tang's film illustrates how the border-crossing plot and the focus on harsh conditions in the mainland remained a sensitive area for the censors, despite their growing openness to criticism of the Hong Kong government. Herman Yau (2015, 166) has noted the mainland authorities' direct involvement in censoring *China Behind*: Xinhua News Agency, the PRC's unofficial representative office in the city, invited Tang for a 'chat' after the film had been submitted for censorship but had not yet been shown publicly, indicating that the Hong Kong censors had passed a copy to them for comment. Likely under mainland pressure, these censors eventually banned *China Behind*, only lifting this ban in the 1980s (K. Ng 2020, 171–5). The practice of mainland authorities pressuring the Hong Kong censors to ban certain films continued into the 1990s, as we shall see below.

That *Bank Busters* was screened in Hong Kong only four years after the banning of *China Behind* can be attributed to the post-Cultural Revolution liberalisation and ideological relaxation accompanying Deng Xiaoping 小平's rise to power in the late 1970s. While the censorship records of *Bank Busters* are not available, those for a very similar film submitted to the censors around the same time are. Advising to ban *The Stowaways* (偷 來客 *Taudou loihaak*, 1979), chief film censor Pierre Lebrun noted that the former Political Adviser would never have passed such a film a few years earlier, 'in the climate of the politics of those days' (Additional Comments by Pierre Lebrun on Censorship Report of 'The Big Circle Boys', December 1978, HKRS313-7-10, HKPRO). Lebrun was eventually overruled by officers from the Special Branch invited to offer their opinion: *The Stowaways* was allowed to screen after some cuts involving violence, sex and triad symbols, as well as the change of its original title, 'The Big Circle Boys' (大'O'仔) (Second Censorship Report on 'The Big Circle Boys', January 1979, HKRS313-7-10, HKPRO).[6] In his objections to the film, Lebrun argued that it shed too sympathetic a light on the mainland gangsters: for him, the 'message' of the film was that 'the H.K. community should receive the refugees from China in order to "protect" them from resorting to crime' and that they only turn to crime 'due to the attitude of the Government and the community' (Additional Comments by Pierre Lebrun on Censorship Report of 'The Big Circle Boys', December 1978, HKRS313-7-10, HKPRO). At a time when the government was attempting to stem a new wave of immigrants from China, a film that portrayed these immigrants sympathetically would, in Lebrun's view, send the wrong message. Lebrun's report on *The Stowaways* suggests that *Bank Busters* was not banned in part because it did not sympathise too much with the mainland gangsters it portrayed. His comments also attest to the colonial government's long-term involvement in shaping the discourse surrounding immigration from mainland China (see also Ku 2004; Mok 2021). Soon after, in 1980, the increasing anti-immigrant sentiment would result in the end of the 'Touch Base' policy. From then on, every resident of Hong Kong was expected to always carry their Hong Kong ID, which, among other things, made it easier to identify illegal immigrants from the mainland and send them back across the border.

[6] As already noted, censors at this time did not allow triad names in film titles, even though the gangs of mainland immigrants in Hong Kong were widely known as Big Circle gangs.

Given the period's many headlines about mainland immigrants and immigration policy, one can find references to the problems of people smuggling and discrimination against new immigrants in several 1980–1 crime films. Prominent examples include Mou Tun-fei's exploitation flick on people smuggling, *Lost Souls* (打 *Daa se*, 1980), and Wong Chung's cop film *Mobfix Patrol* (*Cungfungce*, 1981), which touched on the selling of fake IDs to illegal mainland immigrants and featured a mainland gang. More relevant however to the evolution of the immigrant gangster motif in the Hong Kong crime film was the Alan Tang vehicle *Don't Kill Me, Brother!* (毒不丈夫 *Mouduk bat zoengfu*, 1981). The film recycles Tang's by then very familiar 'Big Timer' formula of a man attaining wealth and power through his ingenuity, daring and scant regard for the law, but with a twist: the hero is an illegal immigrant from China spurred on in his quest for success by a desire to take revenge on his Hong Kong-raised brother, who refuses to acknowledge their kinship and does not provide help when it is most needed. As the feud between the two brothers results in their deaths as well as that of their families, *Don't Kill Me, Brother!* can be read as a call for reconciliation between the two long-separated 'brothers', Hong Kong and mainland China. The film was not a great success commercially or critically but marked a shift towards using the mainland immigrant gangster figure for social/political allegory.

Most consequential at the time were two films dealing with another large group of immigrants in Hong Kong. Vietnamese refugees had been arriving in the colony since 1975, but their number increased dramatically in 1978–9 because of rising Sino-Vietnamese tensions, which in 1979 culminated in a brief war. Many of the refugees from Vietnam during these years were ethnically Chinese. Ann Hui , who already in 1978 had shot a TV movie about this issue, returned to the subject in two films that made an impact both commercially and critically. The second of these, *Boat People* (投奔怒 *Tauban nou hoi*, 1982), received the greatest acclaim and was also one of the first Hong Kong films shot on location in mainland China, on Hainan Island. Given this use of location and the film's focus on the plight of the Vietnamese following the communist takeover, the film was widely read as expressing fears for the future of Hong Kong upon the territory's expected change to PRC sovereignty (Teo 1997, 214–5). While these fears became much more widespread during the two years of negotiations preceding the 1984 Sino-British Joint Declaration about Hong Kong's future, the association of the sufferings of the Vietnamese with the possible future fate of Hongkongers is already present in Hui's *The Story of Woo Viet* (故事 *Wu Jyut dik gusi*, 1981), which – unlike *Boat People* – adopted a crime film format. The film starts with Woo Viet (Chow Yun-fat) arriving in Hong Kong on a refugee boat. Settled in a camp, he soon kills two Vietcong agents in self-defence, escapes, and sets out to flee to the United States with a fake passport. Preparing for the journey, he gets involved with Sum Ching (Cherie Chung 楚), a fellow Vietnamese hoping for a new life in the US. To save her from the brothel she gets sold to during a stopover in the Philippines, Woo ends up stranded in Manila working as an assassin for an underworld boss. Betrayed by this boss, Woo manages to fight his way to a boat, but loses Sum Ching in the process. The film thus ends in the bleak way it started, with Woo Viet in a boat, trying to find a better life in another country.

The Story of Woo Viet encourages an allegorical reading in (at least) two places. The first time Woo Viet leaves the refugee camp in Hong Kong to meet with his pen pal, the social worker Lee Lap-quan (Cora Miao 人), he looks around the teahouse they are meeting in and pointedly comments 'It's really like Vietnam here.' Later, when Woo and Sum start to date and visit a flower market, they are interrupted by the police chasing and catching two illegal immigrants from mainland China. As he later writes to Lap-quan, it is at this moment he realises that his and Sum's fates are intertwined: they are 'two Chinese condemned to exile'. In this way, the film connects the travails of illegal immigrants from Vietnam and mainland China to those Hongkongers themselves might face in the future. As such, Hui's Vietnam films encourage sympathy with the plight of Vietnamese refugees and rather straightforwardly invite the audience to identify with them. The film's casting facilitates this identification: the roles of Woo Viet and Sum Ching are played by two Hong Kong stars, Chow Yun-fat and Cherie Chung. This treatment provides an interesting contrast to the portrayal of illegal border crossers from mainland China in the influential *Long Arm of the Law* series. In this series, mainland Chinese characters are simultaneously sociopolitically and culturally 'Othered' and identified

Figure 4.3 A Vietnamese refugee compares Hong Kong and Vietnam in *The Story of Woo Viet* (1981).

with. Unlike in Hui's films, most of the lead characters in the *Long Arm of the Law* series are portrayed by relatively unknown actors, which further reinforces these films' ambiguity by making identification less straightforward.

The first film in this series was directed by Johnny Mak and came out in 1984, just months before the signing of the Joint Declaration. Although *Long Arm of the Law* is his sole directorial credit, Johnny Mak was an important film producer in the 1980s and 1990s and was involved as a scriptwriter in all subsequent entries in the series, which were helmed by his brother Michael Mak 傑. In the 1970s already, Johnny Mak had been a pioneer of the true crime trend on television, producing the seminal 1975 series 'Ten Sensational Cases' (Cheuk 2008, 34). *Long Arm of the Law* basically follows the same formula that brought Mak success on television and combines gritty realism with sensational action. Although the film was initially rumoured to have encountered some difficulties with the censors (Jing 1984), it eventually seems to have passed without major cuts in what can be considered a sign of the further relaxation of political censorship. The film follows the same basic plot we have already seen in *Bank Busters* and *The Stowaways*: a group of mainland Chinese sneak into Hong Kong and commit various violent crimes, including a heist on a jewellery shop. Although the basic plot of the film was not new, Chu (2003, 99) has noted that *Long Arm of the Law* drew on several incidents involving violent crime that had made the headlines in the preceding year: the increasing number of robberies by mainland immigrants in late 1983, police firing their guns on the streets in early 1984, and several fierce confrontations between the police and local triads soon after. What really made the film a topic of discussion, however, was its perceived commentary on Hongkongers' predicament of having their city's fate determined by the British and Chinese governments, without any real voice in the process. In the film, this situation is (imperfectly) mirrored in a triangular relationship between mainland gangsters (PRC), Hong Kong triads (Hongkongers) and Royal Hong Kong Police (UK).

As the film primarily follows the mainland gangsters, their portrayal is the most complex. In several ways, Mak paints them as inferior Others: motivated by greed and lust, their Red Guard past has made them both adept at using various weapons and completely ruthless in the pursuit of their interests. The film repeatedly highlights their lack of urban sophistication for comic effect, drawing on the country bumpkin ('Ah Chaan') stereotype that had become common in local comedies since the 1970s (Cheng 1990, 98). As Mak indicated in an interview, however, he also wanted to highlight how 'we are all Chinese' (Li 1984, 9). Indeed, the mainland gangsters are arguably the most sympathetic characters in the film: details on their families or lovers serve to humanise them, while their strong group loyalty partly redeems them. It is this group loyalty that makes them a more fearsome force than the local triads, who are depicted as treacherous, weak and self-interested. The main differences between mainland Chinese and Hongkonger, the film seems to imply, relate to political system, class and level of economic development, which are in the end rather superficial and easily overcome. The depiction of the Royal Hong Kong Police, on the other hand, is very scathing: after the gang has been tricked by local gangster Ah Tai (Shum Wai 威) into killing a plain-clothes officer, the police force pulls out all the stops to avenge the death of 'one of their own'. Later, when Ah Tai is held hostage by the mainland gang, the police show no compunction in treating him as collateral damage. That the rule of law is just a façade is further confirmed by the film's famous final shoot-out in the Kowloon Walled City. Originally a Chinese garrison, the Walled City technically fell outside of British jurisdiction in Hong Kong and over time became an urban enclave rife with vice and crime (Lai and Chua 2018). When in the film the gangsters seek refuge here, however, the police don't hesitate to follow them into what is technically Chinese territory, eventually spraying the attic in which the gangsters are trapped with bullets and simply walking away when silence and blood dripping down from cracks in the ceiling confirm the gang's demise.

The three sequels that followed *Long Arm of the Law* were each stand-alone stories but retained the elements that had made the first film a success, such as spectacular violence, political allegories involving the triangle of Hongkongers, the PRC and the British (colonial) government, a cynical attitude and gritty realism. *Long Arm of the Law II* (旗兵 *Saang Gong kei bing zuk zaap*, 1987) retained the same screenwriter, former police officer Philip Chan. It therefore showed a lot of continuity with the first film, while also taking inspiration from the success earlier that year of Ringo Lam 林嶺東's undercover cop film *City on Fire* (*Lung fu fungwan*, 1987). It follows three former cops from China who 'fled to freedom' in Hong Kong but were arrested and are awaiting repatriation. To deal with a new wave of robberies by the Big Circle gangs, the Hong Kong Police Force offers the ex-cops citizenship if they agree to work as moles and infiltrate these gangs. The three are teamed up with a local undercover cop who first treats them condescendingly but gradually comes to respect and befriend them. Following both the undercover cop film convention and the pattern established by the first *Long Arm of the Law* film, their in-between position eventually turns out to be unsustainable, with the moles killed either by the Big Circle gangs or by the Hong Kong Police.

The third and fourth films took the series in a slightly different direction and made their politics more overt. This likely had much to do with an important change in local film censorship legislation: the 1988 Film Censorship Ordinance. This Ordinance introduced film categorisation and followed much public criticism of the government's political censorship. While the 1988 law still protected the government's ability to censor films that 'might affect good relations with other countries', the very contentiousness of political censorship in this period pushed the Hong Kong government to use this power very sparingly.[7]

Scripted by Stephen Shiu 元 and Johnny Mak, *Long Arm of the Law III* (旗兵 三 *Saang Gong kei bing dai saam zaap*, 1989) is probably the first film to imagine the vulnerability of Hong Kong's autonomy under the 'One Country, Two Systems' arrangement proposed by the PRC.[8] In the film, an ex-People's Liberation Army soldier (Andy Lau 劉德) flees to Hong Kong to escape an unwarranted death sentence after his forced confession to a crime. Once there, a Big Circle gang coerces him to work for them by keeping his fellow illegal immigrant lover hostage. He is also pursued into the territory by a cop surnamed Mao (Elvis Tsui 徐) who repeatedly shows his ID and a picture of him shaking hands with PRC leader Deng Xiaoping. This cop carries out his investigation with utter disregard for Hong Kong law and the British authorities, who prove unable to hold him to account. Given the breakdown of the rule of law in Hong Kong that the cop's incursion signifies, the fugitive and his lover try to escape from the city. In an unusual happy ending, they eventually succeed in getting to Panama, chosen for its lack of an extradition treaty with the PRC.[9] Noteworthy is that the film borrowed much of its plot from *The Story of Woo Viet*, with two mainland Chinese refugees replacing Hui's Vietnamese couple (Shu 1990). As such, it also makes a clearer political distinction between 'good' ordinary Chinese and 'bad' CCP government. Its overt anti-CCP messaging shows that the filmmakers felt comfortable enough to test the new censorship boundaries in Hong Kong, indicating a greater trust in the local rule of law and free speech protections than the film's narrative itself suggests.

Underground Express (旗兵 四 地下 *Saang Gong kei bing dai sei zaap: Deihaa tungdou*, 1990), the final entry in the series, came out the next year and made rather opportunistic use of the 1989 Tiananmen protests. Reprising the basic plot of the third film but drawing on these recent events (with the film's opening showing news footage of the protests and the June Fourth crackdown), it purports

---

[7] For a detailed discussion of the circumstances surrounding this law's introduction, see Van den Troost (2020).

[8] Shiu's participation in the scripting of the third and fourth entries in the series is another likely reason for the increased explicitness of their politics: aside from his involvement in the film industry and other businesses, he in more recent years has become a prominent political commentator.

[9] The film thus uncannily deals with fears that came to a head thirty years later, when the Hong Kong government's attempt to amend legislation that would make possible the extradition of fugitives to mainland China led to the 2019 protests.

Figure 4.4 A cop surnamed Mao shows his identification, and a picture of himself with Chinese leader Deng Xiaoping in *Long Arm of the Law III* (1989).

to show the real-life efforts to extricate student leaders from mainland China following June Fourth. This effort is initiated by a democratic activist/schoolmaster clearly modelled on Hong Kong activist and politician Szeto Wah 司徒 . In the film, this character hires Big Circle gangsters to help smuggle the students into Hong Kong. A rabid mainland cop follows the fugitives into the colony with a group of agents and in one scene even ends up in an armed conflict with the Hong Kong Police. Recently released archival documents reveal that the Xinhua News Agency pressured the local authorities to ban the film, but that the latter rebuffed this effort, arguing that '*Underground Express* has no pretentions to being a serious film' and that 'all parties were portrayed in the same unfavourable light'. They further pointed out that to ban the film would give it 'unnecessary publicity and make a laughingstock' of Hong Kong, and that they perceived no public interest in the film ('Film Censorship: Underground Express', 17 July 1990, Foreign and Commonwealth Office 40-2932, National Archives, UK).[10] Unlike a Taiwanese documentary about June Fourth a year earlier, the film thus escaped censorship. The Hong Kong authorities' judgement turned out to be accurate, as the film barely attracted attention. *Film Biweekly* devoted only one article to *Underground Express*, which acknowledged the film's low quality but was rather positive about its depiction of Hong Kong politics and the local democracy movement, praising it for being the first film to directly deal with these topics (Ho 1990). Indeed, what the film illustrates is not just the dramatic change in political censorship in just one

---

[10] I thank Sebastian Veg for alerting me to this document.

decade, but also the Hong Kong crime film's ability to speak powerfully to social and political issues.

The discussion of *The Story of Woo Viet* and the *Long Arm of the Law* series has brought us into what is widely considered a new era in Hong Kong cinema, heralded by the appearance of the Hong Kong New Wave in the late 1970s and early 1980s. Both Ann Hui and, less frequently, Johnny Mak are considered members of the New Wave. In the next chapter, we will look at the way the New Wave filmmakers and sympathetic film critics promoted a generational shift in local filmmaking. In the process, they deepened the localisation of Hong Kong cinema, with films on topics such as problem youth and local police culture. With censorship further challenged by these young filmmakers and finally reduced to a minimum for crime-related topics, gritty realism began to lose some of its commercial appeal. The dominance of criminal realism came to an end, setting the stage for the golden age of Hong Kong crime cinema.

5 The New Wave, Critical Discourse and Deepening Localisation

MUCH ACADEMIC AND critical writing postulates a turning point or even a clean break in Hong Kong cinema in the late 1970s and early 1980s. Referring to the group of young, often Western-educated directors entering the film industry at this time as the 'Hong Kong New Wave', an impression is created of a veritable revolution taking place in local filmmaking. The history of the modern Hong Kong crime film outlined so far indicates that the newness of the 'New Wave' has been somewhat overstated, since many of the innovations often attributed to these Young Turks – such as the exploration of the 'real' Hong Kong, as well as stylistic and narrative experimentation – built on the breakthroughs of the preceding decade or so. This is not to say that no important changes in Hong Kong cinema took place during these years: the young generation did indeed popularise certain technical improvements and production methods. As Cheuk (2008, 238–40) has pointed out, these filmmakers benefited from the rise of independent production companies, which gave them more freedom to innovate. They put more stress on art direction, largely abandoned 'canned music', and made greater use of on-location sound recording. Born around 1950, they were also mostly raised in Hong Kong, which translated into a strong local consciousness infusing their films.

While many commentators have pointed out how the young filmmakers operated within existing genres, the prominence of the crime film in the New Wave has remained somewhat underexplored. This is partly because critics and scholars have used narrower genre categories to discuss New Wave films, analysing, for instance, Alex Cheung 國明's cop thrillers *Cops and Robbers* (指兵兵 *Dim zi bingbing*, 1979) and *Man on the Brink* (人 *Binjyunjan*, 1981), Ann Hui's murder mystery *The Secret* (劫 *Funggip*, 1979), or Kirk Wong 志強's action/triad film *The Club* (廳 *Mouteng*, 1981). Ng Ho is one of the few critics to have appreciated the importance of crime as an overarching theme for the New Wave, linking it to the period's renewed concern with juvenile delinquency and the films' 'anti-establishment, anarchist sentiments' (Ng H. 1999, 55). 'The main theme of the Hong Kong New Wave', Ng argues, 'was exactly that of the young people feeling like caged animals in a colonialist society' (55). Ng here is pointing towards the political dimension of crime in Hong Kong cinema. The dominance of the crime film in New Wave output confirms how the depiction of crime was a major way by which a strong local consciousness in Hong Kong cinema took shape. As already touched upon in the previous chapter, the existential crisis sparked by the 1997 Handover linked the issues of crime, local identity and politics even more tightly together in the 1980s.

Following a brief sketch of the social, political and economic changes taking place in Hong Kong during the 1980s, this chapter will revisit the discourse surrounding the Hong Kong New Wave to indicate why the term was used and what it referred to. Drawing on Hector Rodriguez (2001), I will show how the Hong Kong New Wave in a sense was willed into existence by both critics and filmmakers, and how some of its putative characteristics were prefigured in the commercial cinema of the preceding years – a fact that was however stubbornly disavowed as a condition for the New Wave's very existence. To acknowledge the increased importance of film critics in Hong Kong film culture in this period, I will frequently refer to their writings about the films under analysis. I will also argue that in this period the crime film further deepened the localisation of Hong Kong cinema by telling local crime stories – not only about mainland gangsters in Hong Kong (as discussed in the previous chapter), but also about juvenile delinquents. As in the late 1960s, these problem youth films reveal an important aspect of Hong Kong's colonial governmentality, one in which youth's political discontent was disavowed and displaced onto anxiety about (youth) crime, to be dealt with through social work, education and/or parental care. Unlike in the late 1960s, however, some of the New Wave filmmakers began to deconstruct and even directly challenge this governmentality, leading to a very public clash with the censors. A second dimension of the New Wave explored in this chapter is its ambivalent association with the police thriller. In this genre, local police culture was documented to an unprecedented degree, thereby offering yet another channel for exploring Hong Kong specificity and identity. The popularity of the cop thriller invites us to think about perceptions of the Hong Kong police at a time when these perceptions were in rapid flux and the police force was actively trying to improve its public image. While the focus in this chapter is mainly the New Wave 'moment' (1979–82), I will occasionally consider films made later in the decade to indicate the continuity of criminal realism, even as it gradually became displaced as the central mode of the Hong Kong crime film. To indicate this broader shift, this chapter concludes with an analysis of several films that prefigured John Woo's *A*

Better Tomorrow (1986), the film that sounded the death knell for criminal realism's local dominance even as it brought Hong Kong crime cinema to global attention.

Boom Times

The 1980s is often considered a golden era for Hong Kong, both economically and culturally. Following decades of astonishing growth in the manufacturing sector, Hong Kong now started to turn itself into an international financial centre, while Deng Xiaoping's policy of reform and opening also allowed it to resume its old role as 'the premier entrepot of China'. Local manufacturing meanwhile continued to expand significantly until the early 1990s, even though it declined as a contributor to GDP overall (Steve Tsang 2004, 176–7). In the same period, Hong Kong entrepreneurs began to move their factories across the border, mainly to Guangdong province, where labour was cheap and abundant. Even as the economy of Hong Kong and the mainland became increasingly interlinked, however, the giant neighbour to the north began to give rise to great anxiety in the colony. With the British lease of the New Territories approaching its end date, Governor MacLehose had approached Beijing in 1979 in the hope of extending British sovereignty over the colony beyond 1997. Deng Xiaoping however insisted Hong Kong should return to the PRC, leading to several rounds of Sino-British negotiations between 1982 and 1984 – a process in which Hong Kong people themselves had no part. This resulted in the 1984 Sino-British Joint Declaration, which confirmed the Handover would take place in 1997 under the 'One Country, Two Systems' framework that promised Hong Kong a high degree of autonomy as a 'Special Administrative Region' of the PRC (Steve Tsang 2004, 211–27). With the memory of the Cultural Revolution still fresh, however, fears in the colony ran high, peaking in 1989 and the years after because of the Chinese authorities' violent crackdown on pro-democracy protesters in Beijing and other cities. Throughout the 1980s and 1990s, the '1997 factor' made itself felt in various aspects of life, including cinema.

In terms of crime, Jones and Vagg (2007, 483) note three main themes in discussions on the subject in 1980s Hong Kong: a continued preoccupation with juvenile delinquency; the worry that 'get rich quick' crimes would multiply in the run-up to 1997; and the fear of violent crimes committed by illegal immigrants from mainland China. All three themes found their way into local crime films. Both in the rapidly growing field of local criminology and in government policy, juvenile delinquency was by far the predominant concern. Jones and Vagg (2007, 483–4) attribute this to the tendency of the local youth towards political activism since the late 1960s, a trend the government feared could complicate the transfer of sovereignty in 1997. Echoing Governor Trench's speech in 1971, Governor MacLehose in his 1980 policy address for instance expressed alarm at the 'disturbing and bewildering' increase in youth crime (Hong Kong Government Information Services 1980, 11). More studies were commissioned and several of the 1980s 'Fight Crime' campaigns targeted youth crime, sometimes in combination with anti-triad campaigns. As in the 1970s, crime thus remained an important social concern (Jones and Vagg 2007, 479). This general context certainly was fertile ground for a continued flourishing of local crime films.

This flourishing took place at a time when the local film industry was moving from strength to strength, making its impact felt regionally and even globally. Stimulated by demand in the Southeast Asian and Taiwanese markets in the mid- to late 1970s, independent companies, often backed by conglomerates, had started to appear (Lent 1990, 101). Although these new players proved willing to support young filmmakers' cinematic debuts, few of them became a lasting presence. In the 1980s, only one company seriously challenged the dominance of Golden Harvest, which by this time had displaced the rapidly declining Shaw Brothers. This company, Cinema City, was established in 1980 by three movie comedians – Dean Shek 天, Karl Maka 嘉 and Raymond Wong – and carefully 'packaged' its films (with upgraded production values, special effects, stunts, shooting in international locations, as well as aggressive publicity campaigns), resulting in a series of box office successes (Bordwell 2010, 44; Ng and Wong 2016). Like Golden Harvest, it allowed its key talents to set up their own branch companies – the most successful example being Tsui Hark 徐克's Film Workshop established in 1984 (Zhang 2004, 251). The commercial success of the 1980s was accompanied by rapid developments in genre filmmaking. Despite the widespread practice of genre-mixing, certain trends can be discerned. Kung fu films often left period settings behind to take in modern urban backgrounds, usually as action-adventure films (Sek 1992, 55; Bordwell 2010, 131). Horror films gained more prominence following the box office successes of Sammo Hung's *Encounter of the Spooky Kind* (打 *Gwai daa gwai*, 1980) and *The Dead and the Deadly* (人嚇人 *Jan haak jan*, 1982), which mixed horror with comedy and kung fu (Cheng 1989, 20). The decade's most significant development, however, was the crime film's arrival as a major genre alongside comedy and martial arts films.

The Hong Kong New Wave and New Hong Kong Cinema

When describing what the New Wave brought to Hong Kong cinema in the late 1970s, most commentators would agree with Marchetti (2012, 97), who writes: 'Taking up location filmmaking and local stories, comfortable with new editing techniques and synchronized sound, these filmmakers brought a fresh, more personal approach to the commercial genres popular at the time.' Some accounts also acknowledge the New Wave's roots in social and cultural developments in Hong Kong since the late

1960s, as well as the pioneering efforts of certain directors. Law Kar (2001, 32–3), for instance, argues that the political ferment and social activism of the late 1960s and 1970s stimulated local film culture, leading to the blossoming of cine clubs, film and culture magazines, and experimental filmmaking. He highlights three precursors to the New Wave who, in his words, 'modernized Cantonese films': they were Chor Yuen and Patrick Lung (some of whose crime films were discussed in earlier chapters), and the female director Tang Shu-shuen, whose debut – the period drama *The Arch* (夫人 *Dung fujan*, 1970) – became the first Hong Kong film to receive broader international acclaim (Law K. 2001, 33–8). In 1976, Tang launched the film and television magazine *Close-Up* (大寫 *Datexie*), which played a crucial role in lionising the young New Wave directors (Marchetti 2012, 98). This, it should be noted, was done purely on the basis of these directors' work in television – the magazine folded in 1979, around the time the New Wave directors' first films started to appear.[1] The young directors' TV work has remained an important part of the New Wave myth (see, for instance, Cheuk 1999; Teo 1999), with some local critics even arguing that only their efforts in TV – and not in cinema – really deserved the 'New Wave' label (Li 1981, 13–14).

A striking absence in almost all accounts of the Hong Kong New Wave's origins are the crime films discussed in Chapters 3 and 4 of this book. This is odd, given that these films prefigured several of the innovations often attributed to the New Wave. As we have seen, for instance, crime films from around 1973–4 onward increasingly relied on location shooting, told local (crime) stories, and occasionally exhibited real visual flair: it is for instance fair to say that a director like Kuei Chih-hung also brought, to borrow Marchetti's phrasing, 'a fresh, more personal approach to the commercial genres popular at the time'.[2] So why was the work of Kuei and others not acknowledged in accounts of the New Wave's origins, to the extent that, until fairly recently, they were almost entirely written out of Hong Kong film history? A likely answer to this can be found in what Hector Rodriguez (2001) terms the era's 'film cultural field', 'an interlocking network of public spheres where critics and aspiring filmmakers came together as a community with a shared interest in film as art' (55). Rodriguez (2001, 54–6) argues that this community defined itself in opposition to Hong Kong cinema's commercialism, and especially against the work of major studios like Shaw Brothers, which, as we have seen, was behind many pioneering 1970s

---

[1] The first article predicting a New Wave in local cinema appeared in *Close-Up* as early as September 1976 (Zoeng 1976).

[2] Of all the films discussed in Chapters 3 and 4, only Leong Po-chi and Josephine Siao's *Jumping Ash* (1976) is occasionally touted as an early New Wave work, for example by Teo (1999, 17).

crime films. The film cultural field's agenda is reflected in the title of an influential *Close-Up* article of the time, which asked: 'The Hong Kong Cinematic New Wave: Revolutionaries who Challenge Tradition?' (Jik 1978). The article expressed a strong hope that the young directors about to make their cinematic debuts would establish a new local (art) cinema.

Aside from resistance against the commercial film industry, critics assigned another mission to the New Wave: establishing a Hong Kong cinema that took the 'Hong Kong experience' as its foundation. Most clearly formulated in a 1979 article by Law Wai-ming in *Film Biweekly* (影 刊 *Dianying shuangzhoukan*; *Close-Up*'s successor), this objective hints at another reason for the film cultural field's opposition to commercial cinema: the big studios' (perceived) focus on escapist period films (martial arts films and imperial dramas), which, in the case of Shaw Brothers, were often still shot in Mandarin rather than Cantonese.[3] The young filmmakers' works would indeed push the cinematic localisation trend that started in the 1970s to a new height, predominantly using contemporary Hong Kong as a setting and Cantonese for dialogues. That merely two years later critics nevertheless expressed disappointment with the New Wave (for example, Li 1981) was mainly due to the directors' tendency to work within the existing genres and commercial imperatives of Hong Kong cinema. Some critics, perhaps, had expected a Godard, but instead they 'merely' got a Spielberg. For others, the disappointment stemmed from the perceived failure of most New Wave filmmakers to translate the realist aesthetic of their television days into cinema (Li 1981). Regardless of the varied evaluations of filmmakers' artistic accomplishments, there can be little doubt that the discourse of a New Wave successfully brought the idea of film as art to a more prominent position in the Hong Kong film cultural field. This film cultural field and its aspirations endure to the present, which explains why every few years the arrival of a new 'New Wave' is proclaimed, from the so-called Second Wave in the late 1980s (Teo 1997), to the post-1997 'HKSAR New Wave' (Szeto and Chen 2012).

Another enduring legacy of the 1970s film cultural field that produced the New Wave is what Rodriguez (2001, 60–1) has called local critics' 'normative realism' – 'the conviction that filmmakers ought to depict their social and historical reality'. Many of these critics had in mind the kind of realist (melo)dramas found

[3] It is worth adding that Law (1979, 4) saw the critical community's goal as more ambitious than just stimulating the creation of artistic films based on the Hong Kong experience: he argued that to achieve this kind of cinema, the whole of Hong Kong society needed to be changed, something which could only be done if different actors in the 'film cultural field' collectively strived for it (he names the newly established Hong Kong International Film Festival, a recurring local competition of experimental short films and several prominent cultural magazines as potential partners in this struggle).

among New Wave filmmakers' TV output as well as the vaunted tradition of 1950s Cantonese *lunlipian*. Instead of pursuing this normative realism, however, most New Wave filmmakers opted to work within what I have been calling criminal realism. Rodriguez insightfully argues that normative realism was in fact the flipside of the reflectionist framework employed by the critics – this is a framework that explains 'the presence of stylistic, narrative, and thematic devices [in films] by reference to societal processes, structures, and events' (61–2). This reflectionism could take different forms. Sek Kei (1988, 19), for instance, claimed that Hong Kong films' long-standing detachment from local social reality was due to the city's colonial nature, and in particular the government's film censorship – a claim at least in part supported by this book. The most pervasive application of a reflectionist approach in the 1980s and 1990s, however, was the (sometimes forced) interpretation of nearly all Hong Kong films through the lens of the 1997 Handover. The sociopolitical concern manifested in reflectionism explains why, in a continuation of the censorship struggles of the late 1960s and early 1970s, New Wave filmmakers and critics would clash on several occasions with the censors. A prominent voice in the film cultural field, *Film Biweekly* for example frequently criticised government censorship on its pages and proactively pushed for reform (especially the introduction of film classification) throughout the 1980s.

Finally, the relationship between the overlapping terms 'Hong Kong New Wave' and 'New Hong Kong Cinema' should be considered, as it helps to clarify the scope of this chapter. As we have seen, the Hong Kong New Wave was to an important extent the product of local critical discourse. It therefore has a strong evaluative and auteurist dimension. Cheuk Pak-tong's approach in his book *Hong Kong New Wave Cinema (1978–2000)* is representative: he divides the Hong Kong New Wave into 'core' and 'non-core' directors, with the core group comprising those who, in his opinion, made a sizeable number of more experimental, influential and consistent works (Ann Hui, Tsui Hark, Patrick Tam 家明, Yim Ho 嚴 , Allen Fong 方 平 and Alex Cheung). The non-core directors (Kirk Wong, Clifford Choi 光, Lau Shing-hon 劉成 , Terry Tong 唐基明, Peter Yung and Dennis Yu 余允抗) either made very few films (Peter Yung, Lau Shing-hon), or mainly critically less-acclaimed commercial works (Kirk Wong, Dennis Yu) (Cheuk 2008, 8). As is usually the case with such evaluative criteria, other critics might disagree with Cheuk's selection and classification of directors. Other critical disputes on the New Wave have involved its duration and, as we have seen, even its very existence (Li 1981). Some, like Teo (1997, 1999) have preferred to limit the New Wave moment to the years between 1978 and 1982, with the New Wave directors absorbed into the mainstream since. Cheuk (2008), however, also considers the works of New Wave directors made in later decades.

'New Hong Kong Cinema' or *xin dianying* 新 影 (*san dinjing*) was sometimes used as an alternative term for the Hong Kong New Wave in the late 1970s and 1980s. In English, it has been popularised mainly through its use as a book series title published by the Hong Kong University Press (2003–16). Series editors Ackbar Abbas and Wimal Dissanayake used the term to refer to Hong Kong cinema since the 1980s in general (including but not limited to the New Wave directors), while also linking it to the city's 1997 change of sovereignty, specifically evoking Abbas's influential theorisation of Hong Kong culture as a culture of disappearance (Abbas 1997). Privileging the Handover in our understanding of all Hong Kong cinema since the 1980s is in my view an overly reductive approach, but the term 'New Hong Kong Cinema' can still be useful as a more inclusive way of describing 1980s and 1990s Hong Kong cinema. In this more descriptive sense, the term also covers directors of roughly the same generation as the New Wave filmmakers who came up through the traditional studio system, such as John Woo, Ringo Lam, Johnnie To, Jackie Chan and Danny Lee 李修 , as well as what Teo (1997) describes as the 'Second Wave' of directors who made their debut in the late 1980s and early 1990s, such as Lawrence Lau 劉國昌, Mabel Cheung 張婉婷, Clara Law 卓 , Wong Kar-wai 家 and Stanley Kwan . Avoiding the evaluative dimension of the term New Wave, 'New Hong Kong Cinema' captures the profound generational shift that reshaped the Hong Kong film industry. While in this chapter I mainly focus on films associated with the New Wave, I will occasionally also consider films made by young directors not usually discussed under that label. My goal, after all, is to give an overview of the changes taking place in the Hong Kong crime film during this period – changes which the auteurist category of the New Wave has tended to obscure.

Problem Youth Revisited

Mapping out the landscape of 1980s Hong Kong crime cinema is no simple task, as – unlike in earlier decades – the crime film became one of Hong Kong cinema's dominant genres, sparking several intersecting trends and cycles. Nevertheless, it is possible to delineate a broad shift that took place in local crime cinema over the decade, from the pursuit of criminal realism carried over from the 1970s to the dominance of melodramatic action-crime following the release of *A Better Tomorrow* in 1986. In the first half of the decade, filmmakers built on the precedents set in the late 1960s and 1970s, not only by pursuing realism and returning to the topic of youth crime, but also by exploring other dimensions of the local in depictions of the Royal Hong Kong Police Force and triad gangsters. In the account that follows, my focus remains on the developments in criminal realism and on the three figures that I posit dominated the Hong Kong crime film from the late 1960s onwards: the youthful delinquent, the (triad) gangster and the cop. It will conclude with a discussion of several films that in various ways prefigured *A Better Tomorrow*'s decisive shift away from criminal realism. My account here mostly skips over the many action-crime comedies that dominated the first half of the 1980s: these perhaps deserve their own dedicated study.[4] Other genres will be left out because they were minor in the 1980s. This includes detective films and suspense/mystery thrillers, the dominant crime genres of the 1950s and 1960s. Aside from a few notable exceptions such as Ann Hui's debut *The Secret* (1979) – an accomplished, highly localised and personal riff on Hitchcock's *Vertigo* (1958) – these genres have remained largely dormant until they staged a very modest return around the turn of the millennium. Examples of efforts in other minor crime genres can be found in the oeuvre of other New Wave filmmakers, such as Dennis Yu's rape-revenge movie *The Beasts* (山 *Saan gau*, 1980) and Patrick Tam's serial killer film *Love Massacre* (愛殺 *Ngoi saat*, 1981). While a serial killer film cycle would eventually take shape in the 1990s, rape-revenge films have remained few and far between. Finally, the courtroom drama and the prison film were explored by some filmmakers: in the case of the former, Ng See-yuen's *The Unwritten Law* (外情 *Faatngoi cing*, 1985) and its two sequels are best-known,[5] while the latter saw occasional new entries, especially following the success of Ringo Lam's *Prison on Fire* (*Gaamjuk fungwan*, 1987).

As already mentioned, youth crime remained an important preoccupation for the government and police force throughout the 1980s, with the alarm raised once again by Governor MacLehose in his 1980 policy address. Given the moral panics surrounding youth and crime, it is unsurprising that young directors dealt with these topics in their films. Sometimes this led to efforts in the mould set by Patrick Lung's *Teddy Girls* (1969) and *The Call Girls* (1973, both discussed in Chapter 3). The most prominent example of this is David Lai 大 's debut film, *Lonely Fifteen* (妹仔 *Lengmuizai*, 1982). One of the year's top-earning local productions, it follows a group of adolescent schoolgirls as they get caught shoplifting, are expelled from school, and sink deeper and deeper into the sex industry and the violent underworld. Like Lung's films, *Lonely Fifteen* combines sensationalism and melodrama with a sociological impulse: the film credits a team of four for 'collecting data' and contains a great deal of realistic detail. This sociological impulse was a

---

[4] This includes immensely popular films such as *Aces Go Places* (最佳拍檔 *Zeoigaai paakdong*, 1982), *Winners and Sinners* (奇 妙 五 星 *Keimau miugai ng fuksing*, 1983) and *Pom Pom* (勇   *Sanjung soenghoengpaau*, 1984), each of which was followed by several sequels.

[5] For a recent discussion of these films, see Wan (2021, 26–45).

natural correlative of young filmmakers' pursuit of Hong Kong-focused realism and paralleled the rapid growth in local social science research since the 1970s – an important aspect of Hong Kong's governmentality. In perhaps the clearest New Wave example of this impulse – Rachel Zen 單慧 's *Cream Soda and Milk* (忌廉奶 *Geilim kau sinnaai*, 1981) – a social worker protagonist links together various characters that present a broad spectrum of social problems in Hong Kong (such as teenage prostitution and crime, racial discrimination, poverty, the plight of the disabled and so on). In *Lonely Fifteen*, the final diagnosis of the causes for female youth crime echoes the patriarchal paternalism of *Teddy Girls*: while the film acknowledges a range of factors, the main female protagonist's delinquent behaviour is primarily attributed to her parents' divorce and subsequent neglect. It is only when the mother breaks up with her boyfriend that she and her daughter can try to have a fresh start. In this way, the film, like *Teddy Girls*, reproduces a form of gender discrimination, placing the blame for the daughter's criminality primarily with the mother. In the end, it is the mother, not the father, who must sacrifice to 'save' the daughter.

A similar debut film that enjoyed more critical acclaim but less commercial success was Lawrence Lau's *Gangs* (*Tungdong*, 1988). Considered one of the 'Second Wave' directors, Lau also takes a sociological approach to the subject of youth gangs but does so in a grittier register. *Gangs* deals primarily with the recruitment of adolescents into the triads and closely paralleled the official/police discourse of the time: the 1988–9 Fight Crime campaign was dedicated to this very same problem (Jones and Vagg 2007, 515–6). In the film, a small group of adolescent boys are recruited into a triad society. Following a deadly turf battle, they must hide from the police, find themselves betrayed by their triad boss, and are sucked deeper and deeper into a cycle of violence. Aside from its parallels with official discourse, *Gangs* can also be considered an attack against the glorification of triad heroes and the romanticisation of traditional triad values that were then running rampant in Hong Kong cinema. Rather than being righteous and loyal, the triad leaders that direct these youth gangs are depicted as motivated by cynical self-interest: they sell out their young followers to the police when convenient, and disregard the rules that once, supposedly, governed the relations within and between triad groups. Lau's film is more sophisticated than most earlier problem youth films in its analysis of the causes of youth crime: poverty, inequality and the pervasive presence of the triads in poor neighbourhoods are implicitly presented as important factors. Family matters too, but *Gangs* offers an interesting twist on this theme by focusing on the main protagonist's father, who was a triad member himself in the past. Early in the film, in a brief run-in with the police, the father vents his anger against law enforcement and shows off the battle scars from his shady past. At the same time, he desperately does not want his sons to follow in his footsteps, going as far as asking a few former triad friends to teach his eldest boy a lesson. It is the father's inability to communicate with his two sons except through violence and his ambivalent attitude towards his own chequered past that ultimately pushes the youngsters down the wrong path. In the end, the father sacrifices his own life to save that of his son. Intentionally or not, *Gangs* in this way provides a corrective for the misogyny in *Lonely Fifteen* and earlier films.

Some New Wave works dealing with youth and crime were less interested in exploring social problems per se and instead used the subject to express a more general social and/or political discontent. The appearance of films showing 'the symptoms of a disease-ridden society' was recognised with some concern by the Hong Kong government's censors as a significant trend in local film production in 1980. They took special note of two films dealing with problem youth: Yim Ho's *The Happenings* (夜　*Jece*, 1980) and Tsui Hark's *Dangerous Encounter of the First Kind* (1980) (Report on the Trend of Films in HK between January 1976 and January 1981, January 1981, HKRS313-7-3, HKPRO). The censors' concern was understandable, as critics at the time likened *The Happenings* to Walter Hill's *The Warriors* (1979), a film about violent youth gangs that in the United States had been linked to vandalism and even murders when it was first screened (Robin Herman, 'Ads Resumed for a Gang Movie after Sporadic Violence at Theaters', *New York Times*, 23 February 1979). Writing in *Film Biweekly*, Soenggun Gwanbou (1980) acknowledged the similarities between the two films – both follow a group of young delinquents during a violent night on the run throughout the city – but also pointed out that unlike the American film, Yim Ho didn't romanticise or heroise the youngsters. Although *The Happenings* didn't push its anti-establishment sentiment as far as *The Warriors*, it certainly contains strong hints of social/political discontent. This becomes clear when one considers how the film treats the sociological impulse found in other problem youth films at the time. Although a promotional trailer for the film boasted of the research that went into its making ('5,000 questionnaires, 300 interviews!'), *The Happenings* is not interested in rehashing once more the various presumed causes of youthful delinquency. Instead, it highlights the disconnect between working-class youngsters and the young intellectuals who befriended them, with the latter standing in for 'respectable' middle-class society (including the filmmakers themselves). In an argument between the two groups towards the end of the film, one of the 'delinquents' pointedly says: 'You guys act as if you're social workers. I hate social workers the most! They're government, and government harms people!' Resisting the paternalism inherent in the sociological approach and instead hinting the problem lies with the government, *The Happenings* also suggests the fragility of 'normal life' and social stability in Hong Kong, with extreme and irrational violence lurking just below the surface. This theme is signalled in the film's opening sequence, which combines shots of the city with images of the youthful protagonists having fun, until, without any warning, one of them throws a bicycle through the window of a luxury fashion store – a moment accentuated through the use of slow motion. Crucially, the film indicates that this barely contained violence is not just a part of the 'youth problem' but is a feature of society in general: the youngsters' fatal journey starts only after two middle-aged gas station attendants violently beat one of them for failing to pay the bill.

Although *The Happenings* also portrays the Hong Kong Police Force as incompetent buffoons (at the end tellingly shown to be commanded by a Caucasian officer), it only vaguely suggests that Hong Kong's colonial status is to be blamed for the profound social malaise it depicts.[6] That the oppressiveness of British rule was on some New Wave filmmakers' minds is confirmed by the other problem youth film noted by the censors, Tsui Hark's *Dangerous Encounter of the First Kind* (hereafter *Dangerous Encounter*). Law Kar has described the film as 'an extremely rare film in the history of Hong Kong cinema that brims with accusation and subversive ideas' (Law, Ng and Cheuk 1997, 47). Indeed, the film was initially banned by the censors and was only released in a significantly revised cut in late 1980.[7] While the original version – screened at the Berlin International Film Festival prior to the ban – was long thought to be lost, a 'director's cut' has been circulating for over a decade now, reconstructing the original film with footage recovered from a VHS tape. This version starts with an insert explaining the film's title: 'In the third section of the 1956 law dealing with dangerous objects, explosives are classified as "dangerous objects of the first kind". People possessing such objects are called . . .' This is followed by the film's Chinese title, which translates as 'dangers of the first kind'. Cut from the censored version, this introductory text hints that the film will deal with the Hong Kong government's greatest fear – violent resistance against colonial rule. This message is reinforced by the film's allusions to past periods of social unrest in Hong Kong. The year 1956 mentioned in the opening text recalls that year's deadly Double Ten riots, which were sparked by tensions between local Communists and Kuomintang supporters, but which also involved violence against foreigners. The film's ending echoes this by inserting a rapid montage of black-and-white pictures from the 1967 Leftist riots, an explicit reminder of the greatest challenge to colonial rule in the post-war period.

---

[6] The English synopsis of the film on a handbill created for its Southeast Asian release concludes: 'Then the lost young men hear the laughter. Yes, they are laughing. The police, the police are laughing' (Hong Kong Film Archive HB1580X). Interestingly, these lines, which make the anti-establishment/anti-colonial subtext much more obvious, are missing from the Chinese version of the synopsis on the same handbill.

[7] For an account of the censorship controversy, including the various debates about censorship and cinematic violence it inspired in the public sphere, see Tan (1996, 83–91).

Figure 5.1 Youngsters preparing Molotov cocktails in *Dangerous Encounter of the First Kind* (1980).

Dangerous Encounter's plot further elaborates on this theme. Cut from the censored version, the film starts with three high school students manufacturing a bomb and detonating it in a movie theatre just for kicks. Wan-chu (Lin Chen-chi 林 奇), a rebellious girl shown to enjoy torturing animals, recognises the boys and blackmails them into making another bomb which she herself places in a public toilet. She next forces them to join her in hijacking a bus of Japanese tourists. Aside from the placing of bombs in public spaces recalling similar activities during the 1967 riots, Tsui also pits the youngsters against a gang of Caucasian criminals, which further reinforces the film's anti-colonial message. Although the boys abandon Wan-chu halfway the hijacking of the bus, they later support her when she gets into an altercation with an obnoxious American. Making off with a box in the foreigner's car, Wan-chu and the boys find themselves in possession of a large amount of money orders in Japanese yen. The American turns out to be part of a group of Vietnam veterans engaged in weapons smuggling, and the youngsters end up being chased by the police, the triads and the smugglers. This finally culminates in a gruelling shootout at an enormous cemetery, involving Wan-chu's policeman brother Ah Tan (Lo Lieh   ), the smugglers and the three boys – with Wan-chu herself earlier already killed by the foreigners.

Like Yim Ho, Tsui does not heroise or romanticise his protagonists, often showing them to be as vicious as their enemies. Tan (1996, 84) aptly calls the film a 'militant and cautionary anti-colonialist tract; militant because Tsui appears to espouse a struggle for freedom through violence, and cautionary because while seeing violent struggles as inevitable, he refuses to romanticise them'. But while Tan focuses his argument on the film's anti-colonialism, Tsui's critique in fact extends beyond the colonial situation in Hong Kong. The director himself has claimed his dominant feeling during the making of *Dangerous Encounter* was anger (Morton 2001, 41), and this anger is also directed against American imperialism in Asia (the presence of crazed Vietnam vets), the Japanese economic 'invasion' (the bus of tourists and the money orders), and the logic of global capitalism (international arms smuggling and universal greed). One could go even further and argue that Tsui presents human nature as essentially violent and self-interested. In the diegetic world of the film, not only is violence continuously broadcast and normalised via the media (in the bombed movie theatre and on various TV sets seen in the first half of the film), it also characterises nearly all social interactions. Society is shown to operate according to the law of the jungle. For instance, aside from torturing mice, Wan-chu at one point casually throws a cat out of the window, impaling the poor animal. Later, she receives the same treatment at the hands of the Vietnam vets, ending up impaled next to the cat. Even though people are shown to work in groups (the triads, the four youngsters, the smugglers, the police), they also distrust and easily turn against fellow group members. Repeated images of cages, window bars and barbed wire further stress that society is a prison where the strong suppress the weak – a message that resonates with Hong Kong's colonial status and cramped living conditions. In this sense, *Dangerous Encounter* echoes the theme of Tsui's previous film, *We're Going to Eat You* (地　　 *Deijuk mou mun*, 1980), which focuses on a village of cannibals and is sometimes read as a Lu Xun-inspired satire of Cultural Revolution-era China (Lee Y. 1999, 77–8).

What I want to stress here is how *Dangerous Encounter* and its collision with the colonial censors exposed the role of the youth problem in Hong Kong's governmentality. This becomes clear when one puts the original version of the film next to the censored one. Aside from removing the most sensitive references to anti-colonial resistance (the bombing activities of the three boys), Tsui also had to add in scenes showing how the Hong Kong authorities were all along on the trail of the smugglers.[8] Another difference between the two cuts is even more interesting: instead of being spotted planting a bomb in a theatre, in the revised version the three boys are seen by Wan-chu when they kill a pedestrian in a car accident. In this way, the boys simply become naughty kids with some bad luck. The anarchism of Wan-chu's character is similarly contained in the censored version: we learn that she has previously spent time in a correctional facility and is receiving support from a social worker. In this way, her nihilistic tendencies are reduced to an individual problem that the

---

[8] While Tsui complied with the censor's demands, he did so in a mildly subversive way: the police unit depicted is the Special Branch, known for its history of political policing in Hong Kong. Not only does Tsui show these Special Branch officers as unable to prevent the massacre at the end of the film or capture any of the criminals, but he also cast several fellow New Wave directors as Special Branch officers, allowing for a show of solidarity in the face of government censorship.

government is trying to solve through social work. That the changes make *Dangerous Encounter* more like *The Happenings* shows that the problem youth film's potential for political critique was policed by the Hong Kong government censors, who made sure that any anti-government and anti-colonial sentiments were largely diverted to the 'youth problem' and other social problems, which, supposedly, were already being addressed through the government's social work programmes.

A final film worth mentioning in this context is Ringo Lam's *School on Fire* (學校 *Hokhaau fungwan*, 1988), which came out in the same year as *Gangs*. Like Lau's film, *School on Fire* deals with triad recruitment among teenagers and provides an antidote to the triad glorification then common in Hong Kong cinema. The third film in Lam's *On Fire* series, *School on Fire* has an over-the-top arch-villain, a triad boss who gets his comeuppance at the end. Given the film's relentless violence and pessimism, however, the villain's final perishing does not give the sense that social order is somehow restored. Like *The Happenings* and *Dangerous Encounter*, *School on Fire* contains a subtle critique of British rule in Hong Kong: on several occasions throughout the film a solo bagpipe theme can be heard, which, given its association with Britishness, the director has claimed was his way of holding the British accountable for the social problems depicted in the film (Odham Stokes and Hoover 1999, 73). The film's frantic despair and apocalyptic atmosphere also can be seen as a reaction to the approaching change of sovereignty to which the British agreed under the 1984 Joint Declaration. This is hinted at early in the film, when a teacher and a cop engage in a debate common in problem youth films since at least 1969, with the cop blaming teachers for not doing a good job and the teacher arguing youth crime is part of a broader social problem and cannot be solved by teachers alone. At this point, a senior officer intervenes in the increasingly heated argument, saying: 'Just stop it. Let's wait until after 1997 to further discuss this.'

Ambiguous Cop Thrillers

The ambiguous explorations of Self and Other in immigrant gangster films since the late 1970s was one way by which young filmmakers articulated local identity, while the sociological impulse found in problem youth films since the late 1960s was another. The police thriller subgenre provided a third way. As we have seen in Chapter 4, the local police thriller emerged as part of the 'true crime' trend in the mid-1970s, with Leong Po-chih and Josephine Siao's *Jumping Ash* (1976) often considered a landmark film and a precursor to the New Wave. Writing about the origins of the Hong Kong police thriller, Karen Fang (2017, 93–125) has argued that from the mid-1970s onwards a mutually beneficial collaboration developed between local law enforcement and the film industry, which supported the latter's commercial success while helping to improve the former's public image. Examples of such synergy can indeed be found – from Chang Cheh's pioneering *Police Force* (1973) being made with police assistance and released to coincide with the first Fight Crime campaign, to the theme song of Jackie Chan's *Police Story* (察故事 *Gingcaat gusi*, 1985) being adopted by the police's weekly public service broadcasts (Fang 2017, 112). By placing local police thrillers on a continuum with the police force's public relations efforts, however, Fang inadvertently plays down the great variety of police images and thematic concerns that can be found in such films. As discussed in Chapter 4, the police populism pioneered by *Jumping Ash* did encourage sympathy with grassroots cops, but, importantly, these same cops are also often shown to be in conflict with the very judicial and law enforcement systems they presumably serve. The films discussed in this section all stay true to this genre convention, which, as various scholars have noted, is one familiar from police thrillers around the world (Rafter 2000, 71-92; Leitch 2002a, 215–40). Each of these films nevertheless also offers novel variations and elaborations on this theme, which often can be related to the local realities of crime and policing. As will be discussed in the final section, the figure of the undercover cop in particular began to provide an evocative metaphor for the urgent questions surrounding Hong Kong identity.

One of *Jumping Ash*'s scriptwriters, Philip Chan was a key person in the late 1970s in bringing these local realities to the screen. Following the success of *Jumping Ash*, Chan quit the police force and embarked on a full-time career in the entertainment industry, specialising in playing cops on TV and in movies, and writing and occasionally directing crime films. As such, he was involved in several New Wave films, co-writing and co-directing *The Servants* (內 外 *Coengnoi coengngoi*, 1979), in which he also starred, and portraying a senior officer in *Cops and Robbers*. To be sure, his participation in films didn't guarantee the pushing of a pro-police message: Chan was also the sole scriptwriter for the first *Long Arm of the Law* film, which as we have seen in Chapter 4 was scathing in its depiction of the police. Instead, his presence either behind or in front of the camera above all signified 'authenticity' to an audience still craving for (criminal) realism in films. This is best illustrated by *The Servants*, originally conceived as a sequel to *Jumping Ash* but eventually promoted as a standalone film. Chan's co-director was Ronny Yu 于仁 , who in an interview prior to the film's release claimed to have done most of the directing himself, with Chan's name only added for promotional purposes (Maa 1979, 16). The film's plot is rather straightforward: from behind prison bars, a drug lord plans his revenge on Inspector Chow (Chu Kong 朱), the cop who caught him. In typical buddy cop fashion, Chow is a strictly by-the-book and idealistic officer, while his partner, Inspector Pang (Philip Chan), is savvier but also less morally upright. Pang, who likes to gamble, accepts a bribe from one of the men working for the drug lord and

Figure 5.2 In the midst of a vicious gunfight in *The Servants* (1979), Inspector Chow (Chu Kong) insists on doing things by the book.

his complicity contributes to the death of Chow's fiancé, sister and mother in a failed assassination attempt on Chow. Despite the gangsters' blackmail, Pang eventually helps Chow to bring the villains to justice in a violent climax. As Sek Kei (2005, 376–7) noted in a contemporary review, the plot of *The Servants* is rather shoddy, but the film is saved by its realistic details. This includes a joke referring to the bad relationship between the police and the ICAC, a scene of Pang doing a home screening of 'indecent' films confiscated by the police, and a humorous argument between Pang and a street cop after the latter gives Chow a parking ticket. Pang's corruption is also noteworthy: Fang (2017, 104), for instance, has argued that many 1970s police films 'encode generational change into their production or plot', acknowledging the corruption of the past while indicating the reform brought by a new generation. To some extent, this dynamic is observable in *The Servants*, with the righteous Chow the obvious counterweight to the corrupt Pang. As there is no observable age difference between the two characters, there is however no sense that the present and the future are all rosy: instead, the film indicates that even after the establishment of the ICAC, police corruption remains a real possibility with potentially tragic consequences.

Although *The Servants* replicated the commercial success of *Jumping Ash*, was director Ronny Yu's first film, and came out in 1979, the year that marked the arrival of the New Wave, local critics appeared reluctant to grant the film New Wave status. Perhaps, as Law Kar (1999, 49) suggests, *The Servants* was a bit too popular for the critics' taste. Sek Kei (2005, 240) – writing for the *Ming Pao* newspaper and thus less beholden to *Film Biweekly*'s mission of promoting the New Wave – compared *The Servants* to New Wave films such as *Jumping Ash*, *Cops and Robbers* and *The System* (*Hangkwai*, 1979), but also to Shaw Brothers' *Bank Busters* (1978, discussed in Chapter 4). He found that all these films by young directors contained a strong '*qiqing* flavor', thereby indicating the continuity with the sensationalist true crime films of the mid-1970s. The *Film Biweekly* critics were certainly aware of the affinity of the new police thrillers with these older local films and as a result often remained somewhat ambivalent even about works such as *Cops and Robbers* and *The System* to which they did grant New Wave status. Even though very few cop films had been made in Hong Kong before 1979, popular TV series in preceding years, such as 'C.I.D.' (1976), 'Operation Manhunt' (大丈夫 *Daaizoengfu*, 1977) and 'Interpol' (國 刑 *Gwokzai jingging*, 1978) – often made by filmmakers who would eventually join the New Wave – had already frequently focused on the work of local police. In addition, many foreign police thrillers and TV series, especially from the US, had been screened in Hong Kong throughout the 1970s. In a 1980 *Film Biweekly* essay on the police film that drew heavily on Stuart M. Kaminsky's pioneering book *American Film Genres* (1974), the author claimed that the genre had moved out of the Hollywood mainstream after 1977, after six years of intense production (Ziu 1980, 7). In the same issue, another critic even wondered whether after a few recent successes, the Hong Kong police film was also reaching generic exhaustion (Man 1980).

Like the critics, local filmmakers were certainly familiar with American cop films and in interviews frequently referred to ones that influenced their own work. In an interview about *The Servants*, Ronny Yu compared his film to *Dirty Harry*, describing Don Siegel's film as 'a commercial film with something to say' and saying he watched it with his cinematographer for inspiration (Maa 1979, 15–16). This American influence is more obvious in Yu's next film, *The Saviour* (救世 *Gausaize*, 1980), in which the protagonist's look and characterisation were based on Clint Eastwood's Dirty Harry. The film is further noteworthy for its use of Christian symbolism: the 'saviour' of the film's title refers both to the police protagonist, Inspector Tom (Bai Ying   ), who is at one point scolded by his British superior for trying to 'save humanity like Jesus', and to the serial killer of prostitutes he is trying to catch. The latter is a psychopath whose hatred of prostitutes stems from his Catholic mother's suicide due to his father's unfaithfulness. This doubling of a psycho-killer and the stereotypical cop who places himself above the law in his pursuit of 'justice' is a rather extreme expression of one of the genre's conventions as described by Kaminsky (1985, 230–1) and it places a big question mark over the cop's supposed heroism.

This 'saviour complex' also characterises the protagonist of Peter Yung's *The System*, where it however appears in a much subtler and understated fashion. This film, based on real events and real people, focuses on a cop's persistent efforts to bring to justice a powerful drug lord through use of a well-placed informer. After a failed sting, the cop (again played by Bai Ying) takes a brief vacation to go bird-watching on one of Hong Kong's outlying islands. On the way to the ferry, he passes by several posters on which the camera lingers, along with the beggars standing in front of them. The posters include both government messages to 'cherish one's health for a better future' as well as one promoting the Hollywood blockbuster *Superman* (1978). The contrast of the posters with the old and frail beggars captures the protagonist's state of mind: his desire to be a 'superman' who single-handedly takes on a corrupt system, and his belief in progress, which are both being challenged by a sobering social reality. As he later muses during his solitary stay on the island, he might very well die in his attempt to break the 'system' of police and criminal entanglement that ensures the survival of the local drug trade. In a departure from genre conventions, Yung has the cop and his informant abruptly stabbed to death by hired thugs at the end of the film: the drug lord and the 'system' remain untouched. It was however the film's style that evoked most discussion among contemporary critics. Yung made unprecedented use of location-shooting with handheld or hidden cameras in crowded urban areas, avoided canned music, and instead extensively used direct sound recording, then uncommon in Hong Kong cinema (Cheuk 2008, 222). Having previously participated in the making of 'Opium: The White Powder Opera' (1976–7), a British TV documentary on the Hong Kong drug trade, Yung also included plenty of real detail on the practices of local drug dealers, as well as those of the police anti-drug unit, with some of the film's finest sequences depicting police surveillance operations and technologies, as well as traffickers' elaborate tricks to avoid capture. Critics at *Film Biweekly* were enthusiastic about *The System*, with fellow New Wave filmmaker Lau Shing-hon even coining a novel genre term for it, the *jingcha wenti pian* 察問 (*gingcaat mantai pin*, 'police problem film'). In his review, Lau (1979) expressed some surprise that *The System* managed to get past the censors, as the film strongly hinted that the cop's repeated failures were due to his corrupt British supervisors' protection of the drug lord and because it touched upon the nefarious rivalry between the government's different departments fighting the drug trade.

Among the New Wave police thrillers, *The System* offers the sharpest rebuttal of Fang's characterisation of the genre as a kind of extension of police public relations efforts. Alex Cheung's debut *Cops and Robbers*, however, fits Fang's

Figure 5.3 Posters for an anti-drug campaign and the movie *Superman* (1978) are contrasted with the reality of the frail beggars in front of them in *The System* (1979).

description almost perfectly, at least at first sight. Unlike most of his fellow New Wave filmmakers, Cheung had not received overseas training. Instead, he gained a reputation as a self-taught wunderkind, making award-winning experimental shorts and then moving into television. His first two feature films, *Cops and Robbers* and *Man on the Brink*, managed a rare balancing act by achieving both commercial success and critical acclaim. *Cops and Robbers* centres on a closely knit team of police officers, among which three characters are more developed: there is the hot-headed Dirty Harry-style cop Chan Lap-kei (Wong Chung), his more restrained but sympathetic boss Deputy Chow (Kam Hing-yin   ) and rookie Ah Wing (Cheung Kwok-keung 張國強). The team investigates a small gang that has robbed some beat cops of their guns and has used these weapons for a bank robbery. Soon enough, the gang is located, with a large-scale police raid resulting in the capture of one of the criminals and the death of another. The remaining gangster, Biu (Hui Bing-sam   森), manages to get away. The cops celebrate, and Chan and Chow meet the press to talk about the operation's success. However, Biu sets out to avenge his brother's death, kidnaps Chan's son and, in a surprising twist, kills Chan when he comes to meet him without backup. The rules have clearly changed: Biu also ambushes Chow, nearly killing him, and then corners Ah Wing in a corridor with no way out. In a scene now considered a classic of Hong Kong crime cinema, the unarmed Ah Wing makes a desperate attack but slips on a baseball, inadvertently saving him from Biu's bullets. As just then Biu runs out of ammunition, Ah Wing crazily beats him to a pulp with a baseball bat he earlier picked up in the corridor.

Cops and Robbers largely plays as an extended paean to the Hong Kong Police Force. The friendship between the team of cops is highlighted in a way not seen before in Hong Kong movies. Even the superior officers (played by Philip Chan and a Caucasian actor) escape the conventional negative portrayal and are shown to be on cordial terms with the main characters. Important in this regard is an early sequence in which the team plays baseball together – the appearance of a baseball and a baseball bat during Ah Wing's vanquishing of Biu at the end of the film is therefore highly symbolic. In another scene, the colleagues after work go to a bar where a musician friend performs. Played by pop star Teddy Robin (who also wrote the film's theme song), this musician sings a song for them with lyrics celebrating police brotherhood and the force's desire to fearlessly fight against evil. Aside from highlighting police camaraderie, courage and service to society, Cheung's film also elicits sympathy for the force by emphasising the various difficulties, prejudices and dangers officers face every day. In one vignette, a street hawker who witnessed a bank heist refuses to step forward and cooperate, so that the cops must resort to trickery to get the information they need. This episode reinforces the message that citizens should collaborate with the police – a frequent appeal in the police public relations efforts of the 1970s. Other scenes show common people's ridiculing of the police and their abilities, while in a subplot Deputy Chow's relationship with his girlfriend comes under pressure when she gets increasingly worried about the deadly dangers he faces in his work. Taken together, the image presented of the police is one of courageous, self-sacrificing public servants doing a dangerous and often thankless job. This image, however, is simultaneously undermined by *Cops and Robbers*' much-noted theme of fatalism. Establishing this theme early, the film starts with a group of children playing 'cops and robbers', in which the roles of 'cops' and 'robbers' are decided by chance. Likewise, we learn that the film's main villain, Biu, originally wanted to be a cop but was rejected for being cross-eyed, so instead he became a robber with an intense hatred of the police. The film's ending, where the roles of cop and robber are reversed (with the robber chasing the cops), and where Ah Wing only overcomes Biu by sheer luck, returns the film to the theme of fatalism. As several critics at the time noted, however, this theme feels somewhat tagged on, with Sek Kei (2005, 359) arguing that in the final analysis *Cops and Robbers*' focus is still on praising the police.

While *Man on the Brink* in some ways plays as a variation on *Cops and Robbers*, it also significantly departs from Cheung's debut. The film in fact can be placed in a distinct subgenre of the crime genre, the undercover cop film. Although undercover cops had appeared in Hong Kong cinema since at least the 1960s (as in the Jane Bond cycle discussed in Chapter 1), *Man on the Brink* is often considered the real starting point of the subgenre locally, informing several major undercover cop films that followed, such as *City on Fire* and *Infernal Affairs* (Mougaandou, 2002). The film follows a rookie cop, Chiu (Eddy Chen), who gets recruited to work as an undercover. As his job (and survival) depends on him acting like a criminal, Chiu increasingly gets estranged from his girlfriend and his sister, to whom he is not supposed to reveal his job. More and more confused about his own identity, he finally snaps when his girlfriend breaks up with him, taking revenge on her new lover by robbing and vandalising the latter's jewellery shop. After his dismissal from the force, Chiu participates in the robbery of a family in a housing estate, but secretly tips off the police, resulting in the arrest of the gang. With the estate's residents alerted to the robbery, however, a riot breaks out as they want to take justice into their own hands. Although the cops manage to bring the arrested gangsters to safety, Chiu remains stranded in the building and eventually is beaten to death by the angry mob. Having spoken of his desire for a heroic death at earlier points in the film, Chiu dies asking his former boss and an ex-undercover friend whether this is a heroic death or not.

Characterising Hong Kong's distinct sociocultural formation as 'collaborative colonialism', Law Wing-sang (2008, 528) has argued that the undercover cop subgenre is 'a key enabling us to grasp the structures of feeling embedded in Hong Kong's cultural and ideological landscape'. The subgenre is indeed focused on how the collaborator's double identity results in a split subjectivity, 'always torn apart by endless interrogations (or self-interrogations) of loyalty' (Law W. 2008, 527). Starting his brief account of the subgenre's landmark works with *Man on the Brink*, Law places Cheung's film in the 1970s context of the establishment of the ICAC and 'people's perception of the colonial establishment's incompetence', as well as the start of negotiations over the future of Hong Kong (529). Given Cheung's strong pro-police message in *Cops and Robbers*, Law's generalisation of late 1970s attitudes towards the colonial establishment can be questioned, but it is true that *Man on the Brink*'s picture of the police is much less flattering than the earlier film's. This is signalled by its opening scene, which shows the police staging a raid against illegal street hawkers. These raids were part of a highly unpopular government policy that tried to regulate and limit street hawking.[9]

---

[9] For two illuminating studies on Hong Kong's hawkers and the government's attempts to control them roughly contemporary to *Man on the Brink*, see Smart 1983, 1986. It should be noted that the main government department responsible for managing hawkers was the Urban Services Department. While the police's nuisance squad also took enforcement action, they were not the main department responsible. Films, however, almost uniformly show police officers acting against hawkers. To this day, these attempts to limit unlicensed hawking remain highly unpopular in Hong Kong: the so-called 'Fishball Revolution' in 2016 was sparked by a crackdown on street hawkers during the Chinese New Year holidays.

In the film, Chiu's character is established when he decides to let an old lady go in response to a bystander's loud condemnation of the police raid, which then promptly leads to a scolding by his superior. This basic scenario replays itself throughout the film: Chiu is essentially a good person trapped in the middle and misunderstood by others. His worsening identity crisis and wrongful death at the hands of the people he is trying to protect show this in-between identity to be a kind of living hell. In this sense, the undercover cop film is a concentrated and highly pessimistic expression of the kinds of ambiguities surrounding cops and gangsters in Hong Kong cinema that we have encountered throughout this book. Rather than limiting this reading to the undercover cop subgenre as Law Wing-sang does, I argue that local politics have been a persistent theme in Hong Kong crime cinema throughout its history.

Towards *A Better Tomorrow*: Ending Criminal Realism's Dominance

It is important to note that contemporary critics did not read *Man on the Brink* in terms of Hong Kong identity, nor did Alex Cheung himself hint at such an allegorical reading. While this does not invalidate Law Wing-sang's interpretation, contemporary critics' discussions do shed light on another reason for *Man on the Brink*'s importance in the history of the Hong Kong crime film. Although Cheung himself in an interview positioned *Man on the Brink* as a further elaboration on the theme of fatalism (Cheung 1981), several critics instead explored the film's affinity with tragedy. One critic for instance pointed out that throughout *Man on the Brink* Chiu makes his own choices, so that his death is caused not by fate, but by his own tragic personality, as evidenced in his repeatedly stated desire to die gloriously (Cang 1981). Another critic compared the death of the film's hero with similar deaths in the works of Chang Cheh and Patrick Lung, as well as with ones found in several other New Wave films, placing *Man on the Brink* somewhere in the middle: while the film doesn't elicit the detached sentiment of other New Wave works, it also does not unreservedly go for the powerful emotions in the films of Chang and Lung. The semi-romanticisation of Chiu's tragic 'non-hero', Liu argues, makes the film a 'point of departure for current action films', as does its focus on an individual's story and its avoidance of broader political and/or social messages of films like *Dangerous Encounter of the First Kind* and *The System* (Liu 1981).

From our current vantage point, *Man on the Brink* can be seen as a transitional crime film between the New Wave moment and John Woo's *A Better Tomorrow*. Indeed, brotherhood, tragic heroism and spectacular violence connect these two films, but the links go even deeper, as they both draw on Christian imagery to

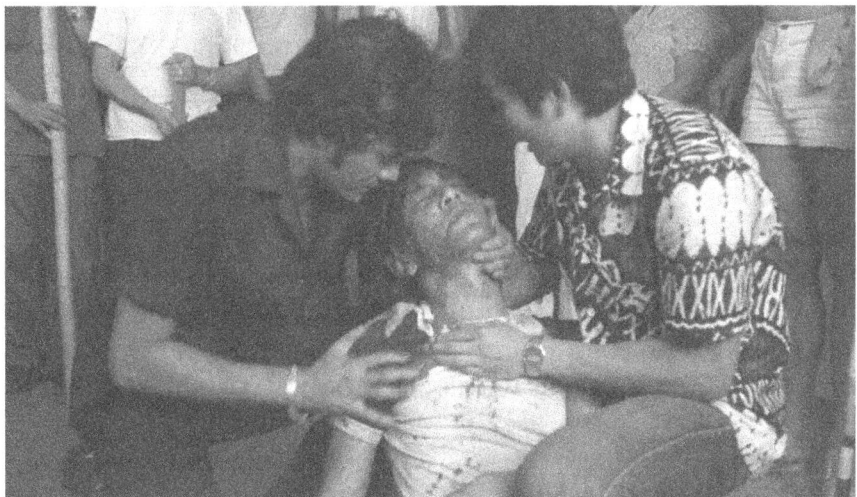

Figure 5.4 Death of an undercover: the pietà scene concluding *Man on the Brink* (1981).

heighten the viewer's affective response.¹⁰ This return to the melodrama and emotionalism that characterised the late 1960s and early 1970s works of Chang Cheh and Patrick Lung indicated that the criminal realism of the late 1970s was losing some of its appeal. Three films released in 1981 and 1982 embodied the transition that was taking place. While Kirk Wong's *The Club* and Terry Tong's *Coolie Killer* (殺出　　Saatceot Saijingpun*, 1982) are sometimes considered part of the New Wave and are frequently cited as precursors to Woo's *A Better Tomorrow*, Stanley Siu's nearly forgotten *Outlaw Genes* (1982) is, just like Woo's film, a remake of Patrick Lung's *Story of a Discharged Prisoner* (1967, discussed in Chapter 1). Siu's version offers a most telling contrast to both Lung and Woo's films.

The Club, knowingly or unknowingly, picked up the model first explored in the 1976 Shaw Brothers film, *Brotherhood* (discussed in Chapter 4), spinning an action-oriented tale around the brotherhood and loyalty of fictional rank-and-file triad heroes. Seemingly shot entirely on location and containing lots of convincing real-life detail about the film's main setting, a nightclub, Wong's film is more realistic than its predecessor – not in the least because it starred Michael Chan, whose impressively tattooed body was prominently displayed in many gangster films of the period to remind the audience of his past life as a triad gangster. Filled with stylishly shot chases and fight scenes, *The Club* set a new standard for the action-crime

---

[10] In an interview, Alex Cheung compared Chiu's death at the hands of the crowd to Christ's crucifixion (Cheung 1981). As Woo would also repeatedly do, *Man on the Brink* stages a pietà-like death scene, with the protagonist cradled and mourned by his (male) friends.

film in the criminal realist tradition. Its criminal realist credentials are confirmed at the end of the film, when after the two triad brothers have single-handedly vanquished the rival gang, we get a series of stills of contemporary newspapers with headlines about gang violence and photographs of people being arrested. While the film's action scenes frequently stretch the realm of the possible – one character is murdered with motorboat propellers – Kirk Wong overall stayed close to reality in having his triad gangsters fight with blades rather than guns. Terry Tong's *Coolie Killer*, in contrast, moves decidedly beyond the criminal realist mainstream and is the most direct predecessor of Woo's heroic bloodshed films. The film focuses on the leader of a gang of assassins who sets out to avenge his 'brothers' after they have been killed as part of a convoluted underworld plot. The film's action is more outlandish than *The Club*'s, featuring killers on rollerblades and motorcycles, as well as plenty of stylish gunfights. With the theme of brotherhood and the motif of a cop bonding with the righteous assassin he is investigating, *Coolie Killer* clearly operates in a romantic universe similar to Woo's, especially the latter's *The Killer* (1989).

The most fitting film to conclude this account of criminal realism is however *Outlaw Genes*. Nearly forgotten today, the film was in fact co-scripted by the renowned film critic and scholar Law Kar 卡, who claimed he consulted both *Story of a Discharged Prisoner* and *Once a Thief* when writing the script. While it is unclear whether John Woo saw *Outlaw Genes*, this 1982 film made some changes to the original story that also appear in *A Better Tomorrow*. The most significant of these is the addition of a righteous and loyal triad 'brother' for the ex-con character, who joins him in a suicide mission to rescue his brother by birth and to avenge his father. Again starring Michael Chan, this final battle is very similar to *The Club*'s, but this time the triad heroes chase their enemy over the streets of Kowloon, hacking at him with their knives until they are shot in the back by the police. At this point, the two men stop their attack, clasp each other's hand, and exclaim 'Good brother!' The end credits appear over a still shot of this image. While this ending is certainly over the top, the film still comes across as the most realistic of the many versions of this reformed gangster story. In a recent YouTube discussion of the film between local film critics Honkaz Fung and Shu Kei, a similar opinion is expressed. Shu Kei, an active participant in New Wave discourse and filmmaking in the late 1970s and 1980s, is clearly surprised by the type of realism evident in *Outlaw Genes*, a film which almost entirely slipped under critics' radar in the early 1980s, including his own. He even describes the film as a kind of 'direct cinema': with this he does not mean the specific approach to documentary filmmaking the term typically is used for, but instead the direct, visceral impact of *Outlaw Genes* and other crime films of that time. They are based on reality, albeit a reality most people back then only encountered in newspaper headlines. At the same time, these films powerfully reflect the era's mentality – the cynicism, pragmatism and materialism of a society experiencing a prolonged economic boom. Agreeing with this characterisation, Honkaz Fung muses that this type of crime film is in fact a kind of history of Hong Kong at the time (Fung and Shu 2020).

With the benefit of hindsight, it thus appears that also local critics can now appreciate the unique form of realism of this period. This is what this book has called 'criminal realism', a type of realism one finds in Hong Kong crime films since at least the 1930s, but which really flourished from the late 1960s to the early 1980s as a result of the gradual relaxation of censorship, a growing awareness of a distinct Hong Kong identity, public concern with crime, and international cinematic trends. Obviously, the criminal realism in crime films only captured a particular slice of reality, and this slice through repetition quickly lost its novelty and ability to entertain. With most censorship restrictions on the depiction of crime lifted, the stage was now set for a new era of Hong Kong crime films, one in which criminal realism was only one of the approaches that filmmakers could adopt.

Afterword: The Uncertain Present and Future of Criminal Realism in Hong Kong

CRIMINAL REALISM, SIMPLY speaking, is the kind of realism one finds in many crime films. Tending towards sensationalism, it finds inspiration in real-life crimes, often events of a particularly violent and/or sexual nature. While action sequences can be found in criminal realist films, these sequences are not the primary objective and tend towards the gritty and (relatively) plausible. These films instead edge closer to social problem films and address, often in a populist voice, issues that are of broader social concern at the time (such as worries about violent crime or juvenile delinquency). Limited neither in time, nor even in space, incarnations of criminal realism can be found in cinemas around the world since the medium's early years. As in Hong Kong, criminal realism elsewhere often encountered problems with censorship organs as well as disparagement by film critics and other commentators.

This book has argued that criminal realism was particularly pertinent to Hong Kong cinema from the late 1960s to the early 1980s, when it was the dominant mode of the local crime film. Its pursuit by filmmakers at this time was driven by a broader societal desire to engage with local issues and politics, as well as the unique texture of life in a city that was and still is a colonial and postcolonial paradox. While overt politics remained largely taboo in local cinema until well into the 1980s, films about crime were a politically and commercially safer way to comment on the sociopolitical issues of the day. The growing presence of criminal realism in Hong Kong cinema was therefore not only part of an international fad for realist crime films, but also a response to local circumstances. As we have seen, this pursuit of a realist aesthetic ran parallel to the programmatic calls by local film critics for a greater realism in Hong Kong cinema, even if these critics mostly overlooked or dismissed the criminal realism one could then find in commercial crime films. The increasing prominence of criminal realism meanwhile was also a side effect of the sensitivity of the local censors towards the depiction of contemporary crime in Hong Kong – filmmakers were eager to give audiences what the censors for a long time had turned into a forbidden fruit, and therefore continuously pushed the boundaries of the permissible.

The question of agency is a crucial one here. In a recent book on the history of political censorship in Hong Kong media, Michael Ng (2022, 6) argues:

> What has defined and confined the Hong Kong people's right to speak has not, unfortunately, been how dearly held the values of common law are or how hard the Hong Kong people have fought to secure that right. What has mattered more . . . has been the bigger picture of global and regional politics: the political-economic situation of China, China's relations with the major world powers and those powers' China strategies over time.

While there is much truth to this, Ng's argument may be slightly skewed due to his book's focus on changes in Hong Kong laws related to freedom of expression, with less attention to how censorship was practised on a day-to-day basis and how people responded to it. What I hope my more fine-grained account of the censorship of crime and violence in films has highlighted is that filmmakers, audiences and critics did play an important role in pushing and expanding the boundaries of the permissible, for instance by talking about politics indirectly (often using crime films for that purpose) or by directly challenging the censors. The latter they did, amongst others, by daringly broaching previously taboo subject matter in films, appealing the decisions of the censors, speaking out against censorship in the press, and so forth. Importantly, this pushing of boundaries was not only the work of outspoken individual artists, such as Patrick Lung, Kuei Chih-hung, Mou Tun-fei or Tsui Hark, but also of film companies, which had a commercial interest in expanding these boundaries.

This history of 'everyday resistance' (Scott 1985) is sadly very relevant again in Hong Kong today, with the introduction of the National Security Law in 2020 leading to a degree of political censorship not seen in the territory since at least the 1970s. The National Security Law was passed by the Standing Committee of the National People's Congress of the People's Republic of China (PRC) on 30 June 2020, in a process that bypassed Hong Kong's own legislative system protected under the 'One Country, Two Systems' arrangement since 1997. The law was introduced after the massive and sometimes violent protests of 2019 and 2020, which started as a campaign against legislation planned by the Hong Kong government that would make the extradition of fugitives to mainland China possible. As the government ignored some of the largest peaceful protest marches in Hong Kong history and as heavy-handed police action against protesters incurred widespread condemnation, the movement from June 2019 onwards quickly escalated to include calls for democratisation and later even independence. The outbreak of COVID-19 and the imposition of the National Security Law brought an end to these protests but has also caused an ongoing emigration wave as Hongkongers seek to escape an environment of political persecution, censorship, forced national education and harsh COVID-19-related restrictions.[1]

The National Security Law focuses on the four crimes of secession, subversion, terrorism and collusion with foreign organisations, but also criminalises 'incitement' to those acts, which has raised fears for the freedom of speech supposedly guaranteed by Hong Kong's Bill of Rights. In the realm of cinema, these fears have become more concrete after, for the first time in decades, the government decided to make substantial amendments to the Film Censorship Ordinance to bring it in line with the National Security Law. The amended law, passed by Hong Kong's Legislative Council in October 2021, has a new clause asking the censor to consider 'whether the exhibition of the film would be contrary to the interests of national security'. This in effect brought back a form of political film censorship that had been removed from the law in 1994, shortly before the Handover. The phrasing 'contrary to the interests of national security' is intentionally broad and vague and marked an expansion from the one used in the 'Film Censorship Guidelines for Censors' which were revised just a few months before the Ordinance was amended. This earlier document targeted only films '(likely to) endanger national security' (see also K. Ng 2022, 76–7).[2] The amended Ordinance introduced many significant changes, such as making it impossible to appeal the decision of the censors if that decision was made on national security grounds and granting the Chief Secretary the power to withdraw permission to screen a film that had earlier passed the censors. Most relevant to the topic of criminal realism, however, is a new clause in the Film Censorship Guidelines for Censors that aims directly at films that 'may be perceived as a documentary of or appear to be based on or re-enacting real events with immediate connection to the circumstances in Hong Kong' (par. 50). Censors are told specifically to carefully consider whether 'such contents' may 'lead viewers to commit or imitate any act or activity endangering national security' (par. 50). In the version of the Guidelines

---

[1] In August 2022, the population outflow was estimated at over 200,000 people since mid-2020 (William Yiu, '113,200 Residents Leave Hong Kong in 12 Months, Contributing to 1.6 Per Cent Drop in Population, Census Figures Show', *South China Morning Post*, 11 August 2022).

[2] The current Film Censorship Guidelines can be found at https://www.ofnaa.gov.hk/filemanager/ofnaa/en/content_1398/filmcensorship.pdf.

published in June 2021, this sentence reads somewhat differently, as it highlights contents that may 'lead viewers to imitate the criminal or violent acts depicted' (par. 17). This uncannily echoes the distinction made in the 1965 General Principles between violence 'in conditions entirely alien to Hong Kong's' and the more dangerous violence 'in familiar surroundings', as discussed in the Intermezzo.

This paragraph was undoubtedly written with the many documentaries about the 2019 protests in mind that were then coming out: even prior to the changes in censorship legislation, one such documentary – *Inside the Red Brick Wall* (大圍城 *Leidaai waising*, 2020) – had already become the target of the Communist-affiliated press in Hong Kong, with a screening of the film in March 2021 cancelled at the last minute, likely due to this pressure (Candice Chau, 'Hong Kong Campus Protest Documentary Screening Cancelled Hours Before Showing Following Attack by Pro-Beijing Paper', *Hong Kong Free Press*, 15 March 2021). Other filmmakers subsequently decided to forego a Hong Kong release altogether for their protest documentaries, instead opting for screenings overseas.³ When films that only indirectly touch upon the 2019 protests – such as *Far From Home* (執屋 *Zapnguk*, 2021) and *The Dancing Voice of Youth* (亂世共 *Jyu lyunsai gungmou*, 2021) – have been submitted to the censors, they have since June 2021 almost invariably run into trouble.⁴ Unlike the 1965 General Principles, the current censorship (so far) has not expanded to cover crime films in the conventional sense, focusing instead on films that are deemed to constitute 'national security crimes'. Given the abysmal public image of the police due to their role in suppressing recent social movements, it remains to be seen whether at some point the depiction of police corruption or police abuse of power are also considered 'contrary to the interests of national security'. In view of the current harsh censorship of crime films in mainland China, this certainly belongs to the realm of possibilities.⁵

---

³ The most prominent example of this was Kiwi Chow 周冠威's *Revolution of Our Times* (時代 命 *Sidoi gaakming*), which was launched at the Cannes Film Festival in July 2021.

⁴ In a replay of political censorship during the Cold War, films from Taiwan have also already repeatedly encountered problems with the Hong Kong censors, especially those that touch upon social movements on the island – such as *The Lucky Woman* (人 *Toupaau dik jan*, 2020) – or touch upon Taiwan-mainland China politics – such as the dystopian short film *Islander* (島 *Cekdou*, 2021).

⁵ Most recently, a planned screening of the Batman movie *The Dark Knight* (2008) was cancelled, which led to widespread speculation that the censors had objected to a part of the film where Batman comes to Hong Kong to capture a corrupt Chinese businessman who has bribed local police for protection. The government later argued that it had raised its concerns about the screening to the organisers as it considered the film 'too violent' for an outdoor event (Hillary Leung, 'Screening of Batman Film Scrapped after Hong Kong Censors Say It Is "Not Appropriate" for Outdoor Showing', *Hong Kong Free Press*, 21 October 2022).

Notwithstanding these clouds now on the horizon, filmmakers in recent years have occasionally drawn on the tradition of criminal realism to significant acclaim. Philip Yung's *Port of Call* (尋梅 *Daap hyut cam mui*, 2015), based on a 2008 murder of a teenage prostitute, is perhaps the most prominent example, winning multiple awards in Hong Kong and Taiwan. At the time of writing, Ho Cheuk-tin 何　天's *The Sparring Partner* (正　廊 *Zingji wuilong*, 2022), based on a grisly 2013 murder, is proving a local hit. In a review of Ho's film, veteran critic Sek Kei (2022) links it explicitly to the 1970s trend for true crime films. Noting how in the past decade or so only a few films have come out in this subgenre, he rightfully points out that Hong Kong films based on real people and real events have nevertheless been proliferating in recent years. Indeed, it can be argued that over the past decade a new form of criminal realism has been developing, with a steady trickle of films coming out that tackle social issues and show a deep commitment to the local.[6] Crime is sometimes the focus of these works (as in the above-mentioned examples), but their range is broader than this. To name just two recent films in this vein, Jun Li 李　's *Drifting* (　*Zukseoi piulau*, 2021) and Adam Wong 修平's *The Way We Keep Dancing* (　3 *Kongmoupaai 3*, 2020) are, respectively, a drama about street sleepers who sue the government over the removal of their possessions, and a dance film that tackles the problem of 'real estate hegemony' and gentrification. Given their self-consciously local focus and sometimes political subtexts, it remains to be seen whether this trend can continue under the revised censorship rules, especially now that the insistence on a distinct Hong Kong identity and culture has become politically suspect.

One film that points to a possible direction for criminal realism under the new censorship regime is Rex Ren 任俠 and Lam Sum 林森's *May You Stay Forever Young* (2021). Set during the 2019 protests, the film follows a group that tries to prevent the suicide of a female high school student recently arrested during a protest. Such volunteer 'suicide prevention teams' coordinated via social media really did operate during the protests, and while the film's story is fictional, the filmmakers clearly aimed to make it a truthful record of the times (Wong Yui-hin 　, 'Dinjing "Siunin" congzokze: cozung seonseoi, soengseon gusi zikdak jinsyut' 　影'少年'創作　：初　，　信故事值得　[Creators of *May You Stay Forever Young*: The Original Intention Was Pure, We Believe This Is a Story Worth Telling], *InMedia*, 15 October 2021). Not only is documentary footage of the protests seamlessly weaved into the film, but the film's story is also structured to include several 'typical' protest characters, such as a *yongwu* 勇武 (*jungmou*,

---

[6] The unprecedented flourishing of documentary filmmaking in Hong Kong over the past ten years is just one dimension of this broader change.

Figure AW.1 Cops intimidate and harass protesters in *May You Stay Forever Young* (2021).

'valiant') protester (that is, a protester who does not disavow the use of more violent methods), an older social worker, a brother and sister who serve as getaway drivers, and so on. The police meanwhile are depicted as rather one-dimensional villains, sexually harassing female arrestees and abusing their power in often violent ways. As with the different 'types' of protesters, this depiction matches common perceptions of the police among supporters of the movement in 2019 and 2020. Opting not to release the film in Hong Kong where – as highlighted in the overseas marketing for the film – it would certainly have been banned, *May You Stay Forever Young* had a successful run in Taiwan, at international film festivals, and at numerous events organised by Hongkongers abroad.[7]

May You Stay Forever Young is an interesting case to consider the possible directions of local criminal realism, not only because of the new censorship context, but also because the filmmakers behind it are motivated in part by a desire to inherit the tradition(s) of Hong Kong cinema. Director Rex Ren and producer Daniel Chan 力 were amongst the initiators of a 2022 'Manifesto for a Free Hong Kong Cinema' which, alongside a commitment to free expression and to Hong Kong itself, called on filmmakers to draw on Hong Kong cinema's traditions in their

---

[7] When the film was nominated for awards at the Golden Horse Awards in Taiwan, the pro-communist Hong Kong newspaper *Wen Wei Po* launched an attack against it, quoting a legal scholar who argued that the filmmakers should be considered guilty of inciting subversion under the National Security Law (Gong Xueming 學 , '"Siunin" sinbou sinsau, sip wai gwokngonfaat' '少年 暴 仇 國安 [*May You Stay Forever Young* Incites Violence and Hatred, Violates the National Security Law], *Wen Wei Po*, 15 October 2021). No legal action has so far been taken against the filmmakers.

creative work.[8] Hence, although *May You Stay Forever Young* is without a doubt quite different from the Hong Kong crime films discussed in this book, it can still be productively placed next to some of the problem youth films earlier highlighted, in particular Patrick Lung's *Teddy Girls* (1969) and Tsui Hark's *Dangerous Encounter of the First Kind* (1980). As argued in earlier chapters, *Teddy Girls* combined sensationalism with a serious commitment to social analysis to promote a vision that was paternalistic but also reformist. In this way, Lung's film can be said to have prefigured the governmental mindset of Hong Kong in the 1970s. Before it was censored, Tsui's film about ten years later deconstructed the official narrative that turned youthful discontent into a social – not a political – problem and gave expression to an anti-colonial anger never seen before in the history of Hong Kong cinema. It could be said that where Patrick Lung treated youth as a problem, Tsui Hark indicated that society, or perhaps human nature in general, was the problem. Tsui's vision in the film is utterly nihilistic and amoral: his tale has no heroes and depicts a reality that is essentially lawless.

Ren and Lam take yet another unprecedented step. Like Tsui, they show the law and its enforcers to be corrupt and unjust, but unlike Tsui, they simultaneously express a belief in a civic morality beyond the law. Indeed, we see the film's protagonists commit various crimes – assaulting a police officer, resisting arrest, breaking and entering – but tend to condone their actions because they do all this to save a schoolgirl's life and because the police are unambiguously evil. Indeed, the film depicts its protester protagonists in a heroic manner. This very well captures the essence of the revolutionary atmosphere of 2019, when a large – perhaps a dominant – section of the public came to accept 'illegal' acts of resistance (including vandalism, arson and attacks on the police) as justified vis-à-vis the greater evil of state violence. A term often used at this time was *liangzhi* (*loengzi*, 'conscience'), in essence an appeal to an individual morality considered more just than the statements coming from the authorities and the courts, which simply condemned protesters' actions for breaking the law. These events and the crackdown that followed have, in the eyes of many, increasingly been turning the law and its enforcers into tools of oppression, rather than protectors of citizens' rights. More than most documentaries about the 2019–20 protests, *May You Stay Forever Young* – perhaps due to the process of simplification that often accompanies commercial filmmaking – captures this attitude towards the law very well, turning it in the final analysis into a highly original crime film.

---

[8] The manifesto was initially published on social media but has since been published in print in *Film Appreciation Journal* (影欣 *Dianying xinshang*), a Taiwanese publication. See Ren, Ngon, Chow and Chan 2022. The other director of *May You Stay Forever Young*, Lam Sum, was one of the manifesto's signatories.

Certainly, the current censorship environment and the financial pressures on filmmakers make it unlikely that many films will follow the example set by *May You Stay Forever Young*. As their predecessors did in the past, most current Hong Kong filmmakers will likely work within the boundaries set by the censors to survive. But perhaps more than at any time in the past, some will also try hard to find ways to push against these boundaries or to slip around them. As the earlier-mentioned 'Manifesto for a Free Hong Kong Cinema' puts it: 'We have to believe that we can bring about change; we have to believe that our films can create a future for Hong Kong.'

Glossary

Chinese-Language Persons

Ba Jin	巴
Bai Guang	光
Bai Ying	
But Fu	
Chan, Connie	寶
Chan, Daniel	力
Chan, Jackie	成
Chan King-sam	景森
Chan Koon-tai	
Chan Lit-bun	品
Chan Man	文
Chan, Michael	惠敏
Chan Pei	
Chan, Philip	欣健
Chan Wan	
Chang Cheh	張徹
Chang Kung	張弓
Chang, Paul	張
Chen, Eddie	
Cheng Kang	剛
Cheng Xiaoqing	小
Cheng Yuet-ying	月
Cheung, Alex	國明

Cheung, Irene	張　　夫人
Cheung Kwok-keung	張國強
Cheung, Mabel	張婉婷
Cheung Man-ping	張文
Cheung Sum	張森
Cheung Ying	張
Cheung Ying-choi	張　才
Chiang Wai-kwong	偉光
Chin, Charlie	林
Choi Cheung	昌
Choi, Clifford	光
Chor Yuen	楚原
Chow, Doven	周杜文
Chow, Kiwi	周冠威
Chow Kwun-ling	周坤
Chow Pak-ping	周
Chow Sze-luk	周
Chow Yun-fat	周
Chu Kea	
Chu Kong	朱
Chui San-yuen	徐　園
Chun Kim	劍
Chung Chang-hwa	昌和
Chung, Cherie	楚
Chung Kwok-yan	國仁
Deng Xiaoping	小平
Du Yuesheng	杜月
Fei Meng	
Fong, Allen	方　平
Fung Fung	峰
Furukawa Takumi	古川卓己
Ga Lun	嘉倫
Gou Dakhung	德
Gu Long	古
Guan Shan	山
Ha Ping	夏
Ho Cheuk-tin	何　天
Ho, Lily	何
Ho Meng-hua	何夢

Hua Shan	山
Hui, Ann	
Hui Bing-sam	森
Hui, Sam	冠傑
Hui Tak	德
Hung, Sammo	寶
Hung Sin-nui	女
Hung, William	士
Inoue Umetsugu	井上梅次
Kam Hing-yin	
Kam Ping-hing	
Kar, Patsy	嘉
Kong Chi-nam	之南
Kong Suet	
Kuei Chih-hung	桂
Kurosawa Akira	明
Kwan, Jason	智
Kwan Man-ching	文
Kwan, Stanley	
Kwan Tak-hing	德
Lai, David	大
Lam Chung	林
Lam Kwok-cheung	林國
Lam Nin-tung	林年同
Lam, Ringo	林嶺東
Lam Sum	林森
Lau, Andy	劉德
Lau Kar-leung	劉家
Lau Kei	劉
Lau, Lawrence	劉國昌
Lau Shing-hon	劉成
Lau, Stephen	劉文
Law Bun	斌
Law, Clara	卓
Law, John	
Law Kar	卡
Lee, Bruce	李小
Lee Choi-fat	李
Lee, Danny	李修

Lee Man	李敏
Lee Pang-fei	李
Lee Tit	李
Leong Po-chih	梁普智
Leung, Norman	梁乃
Leung Sing-po	梁
Li Han-hsiang	李
Li Jingguang	李敬光
Li, Jun	李
Li Li-hua	李
Li Pingqian	李　倩
Lin Chen-chi	林　奇
Lin Wen-wei	林文偉
Ling, Ivy	凌
Ling, Laurence	凌斯
Liu Wei-bin	劉　斌
Lo Lieh	
Lo Wei	
Lu Xun	
Lung, Patrick	剛
Ma Sik-chun	惜
Ma Sik-yu	惜如
Mak, Johnny	
Mak, Michael	傑
Maka, Karl	嘉
Matsuo Akinori	松尾昭典
Miao, Cora	人
Mo, Lily	愁
Mok Hong-si	康時
Mong Wan	望
Murayama Mitsuo	村山三
Nakahira Koh	中平康
Nam Hung	南
Ng Cho-fan	吳楚帆
Ng See-yuen	吳思
Ng Sik-ho	吳
Ng Wui	吳回
Ni Kuang	倪匡
Niu Ge	哥

Pak Yin
Pao Hsueh-li 學
Ren, Rex 任俠
Saam Sou 三
Shaw, Run Run 夫
Shek, Dean 天
Shek Kin 堅
Shiu, Stephen 元
Shum Wai 威
Siao, Josephine
Siu, Stanley 榮
Suet Nei 妮
Sun Chung 孫仲
Sun Liaohong 孫了
Sun, Robert 孫元
Szeto Wah 司徒
Tam, Patrick 家明
Tang, Alan 光榮
Tang Ching 唐
Tang Huang 唐
Tang Shu-shuen 唐書
Ting Ying 丁
To, Johnnie 杜　峯
Tong Kai 唐佳
Tong, Terry 唐基明
Tsai Yang-ming 揚名
Tsang, Kenneth 曾
Tsang Nam-sze 曾　施
Tse, Patrick
Tso Kea 左几
Tso Tat-wah 曹
Tsui, Elvis 徐
Tsui Hark 徐克
Wang, Jimmy
Wang Yin 引
Wang Yuan-long 元
Wong, Adam 修平
Wong Chung
Wong Hang

Wong Ho
Wong Jing 晶
Wong Kar-wai 家
Wong, Kirk 志強
Wong, Raymond
Wong Yiu 堯
Woo, John 吳宇森
Wu Lai-chu
Xiao Ping 小平
Xu Xu 徐
Yam Kim-fai 任劍
Yam Pang-nin 任彭年
Yam Wu-fa 任
Yang, Evan 易文
Yee Chau-shui 伊
Yee Tat (John Yip) 伊
Yeung Kuen 楊權
Yim Ho 嚴
Yu, Dennis 余允抗
Yu, Ronny 于仁
Yu So-chau 于
Yu Tsong 于
Yuan Qiufeng 楓
Yueh Hua 岳
Yuen Po-wan 步
Yuen Qiu 元
Yung, Peter
Yung, Philip 子光
Zen, Rachel 單慧
Zheng Dike 克

Chinese-Language Terms

Ah Fei
bangpian
caizi jiaren 才子佳人
ciji 刺
fanzuipian
feizei

haohan	好
heibangpian	幫
heishehuipian	會
Hongmen	
jiafa	家
jianghu	
jiating lunlipian	家庭倫
jingchapian	察
jingcha wenti pian	察問
jingfeipian	匪
jingqi	奇
jinzhang	張
jinzhang dashi	張大師
kongbu	恐怖
liangzhi	
lunlipian	倫
maopian	毛
nanyin	南
qi	奇
qiguai	奇怪
qiji	奇
qing	情
qingjie	情
qiqing	奇情
qiqingpian	奇情
qite	奇
qiyi	奇
quzhe	曲折
shehui	會
shehui lunlipian	會倫
shehui qiqingpian	會奇情
shehui xieshi	會寫實
wen	文
wenyi	文
wu	武
wuxia	武俠
xiangyan	
xieshi	寫實
xieshipian	寫實

xin dianying 新電影
yi 義
yingtan tiehan 影壇鐵漢
yingxiong 英雄
yiqi 義氣
zhenshi 真實
zhentan 偵探
zhuangguan 壯觀

Chinese-Language Magazines and Newspapers

Blue Cover Detective Magazine 藍皮書
Chinese Student Weekly 中國學生周報
Close-Up 大特寫
Film Appreciation Journal 電影欣賞
Film Biweekly 電影雙周刊
Hong Kong Movie News 香港影畫
Kung Sheung Daily News 工商日報
Ming Pao 明報
Oriental Daily 東方日報
Ta Kung Pao 大公報
Wah Kiu Yat Po 華僑日報
Wen Wei Po 文匯報

Filmography

48 Hours in Escape (亡 48 小時 *Toumong 48 siusi*). 1959. Dir. Evan Yang. Motion Picture & General Investment Co. Ltd.

999 Grotesque Corpse (九九九怪屍案 *Gau gau gau gwaai si ngon*). 1962. Dir. Ng Wui. Kong Ngee Co.

Absolute Monarch (手 天 *Zeksau ze tin*). 1980. Dir. Stanley Siu. The Wing-Scope Film Production Ltd.

Aces Go Places (最佳拍檔 *Zeoigaai paakdong*). 1982. Dir. Eric Tsang. Cinema City Co. Ltd.

Adventure in Fishing Harbor (恩仇 *Jyugong jansau*). 1967. Dir. Chan Lit-bun. Sin Hok Gong Luen.

All in the Family (城春 *Faa fei mun sing ceon*). 1975. Dir. Chu Mu. Golden Harvest Productions and New World Film Production Co.

Angel with the Iron Fists (*Tit gunjam*). 1967. Dir. Lo Wei. Shaw Brothers.

Anti-Corruption (廉政 暴 *Limzing fungbou*). 1975. Dir. Ng See-yuen. The Eternal Film (HK) Co. and Seasonal Film Corporation.

Arch, The (夫人 *Dung fujan*). 1970. Dir. Tang Shu-shuen. Film Dynasty Productions.

Asia-Pol (亞 密 察 *Ngaazau beimat gingcaat*). 1967. Dir. Matsuo Akinori. Shaw Brothers and Nikkatsu Corporation.

Assassin, The (大刺客 *Daai cihaak*). 1967. Dir. Chang Cheh. Shaw Brothers.

Back Street (後 *Hyutsaa haugaai*) (a.k.a. *The Bodyguards* 女保 *Sanneoi boubiu*). 1973. Dir. John Law. You Li Film Co.

Backyard Adventures (後 *Haucoeng*). 1955. Dir. Ng Wui, Chan Pei and Chu Kei. Liangyou Film Company.

Banana Cop (倫 *Jing Leon peipaa*). 1984. Dir. Leong Po-chi. Cinema City Co. Ltd.

Bank Busters (撈 *Lou gwo gaai*). 1978. Dir. Mou Tun-fei. Shaw Brothers.

Bat Girl (aka *The Lady Killer*) (女殺星 *Jukmin neoi saatsing*). 1967. Dir. Wong Fung. Tai Chee Film Co.

Battle of Hong Kong, The (攻 戰 *Hoenggong gungloekzin*). 1942. Dir. Tanaka Shigeo. Dai Nippon Film Company.

Beasts, The (山 *Saan gau*). 1980. Dir. Dennis Yu. The Pearl City Films Ltd.

Bedside Horror (枕 *Zambin gingwan*). 1963. Dir. Chow Sze-luk. Long Feng Film Company.

Better Tomorrow, A (本 *Jinghung bunsik*). 1986. Dir. John Woo. Cinema City Co. Ltd.

Between Justice and Love (情 *Faatmong cingsi*). 1966. Dir. Lee Tit. Bian Sing Motion Picture Co. Ltd.

Big Bad Sis (*Saadaam Jing*). 1976. Dir. Sun Chung. Shaw Brothers.

Big Boss, The (唐山大兄 *Tongsaan daaihing*). 1971. Dir. Lo Wei. Golden Harvest Productions.

Big Brother Cheng (大哥成 *Daaigo Sing*). 1975. Dir. Kuei Chih-hung. Shaw Brothers.

Big Holdup, The (大劫案 *Daai gip ngon*). 1975. Dir. Chor Yuen. Shaw Brothers.

Black Cat, The Cat Burglar (*Feicaak hakmaau*). 1956. Dir. Wong Hang. Man Wah Film Company.

Black Dragon, The (*Haklung*). 1973. Dir. Law Chi. IFD Films & Arts Ltd (Global).

Black Hero and Lee Ching-mei, The (俠 李 *Hakhap jyu Lei Cingmei*). 1948. Dir. Mong Wan. Great China Film Company.

Black Rose (*Hak muigwai*). 1965. Dir. Chor Yuen. Rose Motion Picture Company.

Blood Will Tell (棠 *Hoitong hung*). 1955. Dir. Evan Yang. Hsin Hwa Motion Picture Company, Dong He Film Company and Towa Co. Ltd.

Bloodshed on Wedding Day (新婚大 案 *Sanfan daaihyut ngon*). 1965. Dir. Wang Yin. Tien Nan Motion Picture Company.

Blood-Stained Begonia (染 棠 *Hyutjim hoitong hung*). 1949. Dir. Griffin Yueh. Great Wall Pictures Corporation.

Bloody Paper Man, The (人 *Hyutzijan*). 1964. Dir. Lee Tit. Union Film Enterprises Ltd.

Bloody Sucker, The (吸 婦 *Kaphyutfu*). 1962. Dir. Lee Tit. Union Film Enterprises Ltd and Hong Kong Movie Studio.

Boat People (投奔怒 *Tauban nou hoi*). 1982. Dir. Ann Hui. Bluebird Film Co. Ltd.

Boxer from Shantung, The (　　　 *Maa Wingzing*). 1972. Dir. Chang Cheh and Pao Hsueh-li. Shaw Brothers.

Boys and Girls (七彩　　女 *Catcoi hungnaam lukneoi*). 1969. Dir. Chiang Wai-kwong. Chung Kwong Motion Picture Company.

Brotherhood (　　子弟 *Gongwu zidai*). 1976. Dir. Hua Shan. Shaw Brothers.

Buddha's Palm (如來　掌 *Jyuloi sanzoeng*). 1964. Dir. Ling Yun. Foo Wa Film Company.

Bullet in the Head (喋　　 *Diphyut gaaitau*). 1990. Dir. John Woo. Golden Princess Film Production Ltd. and John Woo Film Production Ltd.

Bullets or Ballots. 1936. Dir. William Keighley. First National Pictures.

Bullitt. 1968. Dir. Peter Yates. Solar Productions and Warner Bros.-Seven Arts.

Bus Money Wiped out the Evils (巴士　妙　　三害 *Baasi Ngan miugai ceoi saamhoi*). 1966. Dir. Mok Hong-si. Fei Lung.

Call Girls, The (應召女　 *Jingziu neoilong*). 1973. Dir. Patrick Lung. Eng Wah & Co. HK.

Cause to Kill, A (殺機 *Saatgei*). 1970. Dir. Murayama Mitsuo. Shaw Brothers.

Chase of the Murderer at the Canidrome, A (　　剛　場　兇 *Titgamgong gaucoeng zeoihung*). 1965. Dir. Chan Kwok-wah. Lok Kei.

Chasing the Dragon (　　 *Zeoilung*. 2017. Dir. Wong Jing and Jason Kwan. Sil-Metropole Organisation, Bona Film Group Co. Ltd and others.

China Behind (再　中國 *Zoigin Zunggwok*). 1974. Dir. Tang Shu-shuen. Film Dynasty Productions.

Chinese Boxer, The (　　 *Lungfudau*). 1970. Dir. Jimmy Wang. Shaw Brothers.

Chinese Godfather (大　　 *Daai gaaulung*). 1974. Dir. Lui Gin. Star Sea Motion Picture Co.

City on Fire (　　 *Lung fu fungwan*). 1987. Dir. Ringo Lam. Cinema City Co. Ltd.

Cleopatra Jones and the Casino of Gold. 1975. Dir. Charles Bail. Harbor Productions, Shaw Brothers and Warner Bros.

Club, The (　廳 *Mouteng*). 1981. Dir. Kirk Wong. Verdull Ltd. (Film Dept.).

Coming Back to Life in a Dead Body (借屍　 *Zesi waanwan*). 1947. Dir. Hung Suk-wan. Chi Hsing (HK) Film Co.

Coolie Killer (殺出　　 *Saatceot Saijingpun*). 1982. Dir. Terry Tong. Century Motion Picture & Dist. Co. Ltd.

Cops and Robbers (　指兵兵 *Dim zi bingbing*). 1979. Dir. Alex Cheung. The Pearl City Films Ltd. and Yigao Entertainment.

Country Bumpkin, The (大　　 *Daaihoengleoi*). 1974. Dir. Richard Yeung. Foon Lok.

Cream Soda and Milk (忌廉　奶 *Geilim kau sinnaai*). 1981. Dir. Rachel Zen. Golden Fountain Publications Ltd.

Criminals, The (奇案 *Hoenggong keingon*). 1976. Dir. Cheng Kang, Hua Shan and Ho Meng-hua. Shaw Brothers.

Dancing Voice of Youth, The (亂世共 *Jyu lyunsai gungmou*). 2021. Dir. Erica Kwok.

Dangerous Encounter of the First Kind (一 型危 *Dai jat leoijing ngaihim*). 1980. Dir. Tsui Hark. Fotocine Film Production Ltd.

Dark Knight, The. 2008. Dir. Christopher Nolan. Warner Bros. Pictures, Legendary Pictures and Syncopy.

Dead and the Deadly, The (人嚇人 *Jan haak jan*). 1982. Dir. Wu Ma. Bo Ho Films Co. Ltd.

Dead End (死 *Seigok*). 1969. Dir. Chang Cheh. Shaw Brothers.

Death Valley (斷 *Tyunwan guk*). 1968. Dir. Lo Wei. Shaw Brothers.

Death Wish. 1974. Dir. Michael Winner. Dino De Laurentiis Corporation.

Delinquent, The (憤怒 年 *Fannou cingnin*). 1973. Dir. Chang Cheh and Kuei Chih-hung. Shaw Brothers.

Dial 999 for 24-Hour Murder Case (九九九廿四小時奇案 *Gau gau gau jaasei xiusi kei ngon*). 1961. Dir. Cho Kei. Kong Ngee Co.

Dial 999 for the Three Murderers (九九九 奇三兇手 *Gau gau gau leikei saam hungsau*). 1965. Dir. Wong Hok-sing. Lux Film Company.

Dial M for Murder. 1954. Dir. Alfred Hitchcock. Warner Bros.

Dirty Harry. 1971. Dir. Don Siegel. The Malpaso Company.

Discharged, The (出冊 *Ceotcaak*). 1977. Dir. Alan Tang and Stanley Siu. The Wing-Scope Film Production Ltd.

Don't Kill Me, Brother! (毒不丈夫 *Mouduk bat zoengfu*). 1981. Dir. Stanley Siu. The Wing-Scope Film Production Ltd.

Dragnet (aka *Dial 999 for Murder*) (九九九命案 *Gau gau gau ming ngon*). 1956. Dir. Chun Kim. Kong Ngee Co.

Dreadnaught, The (Titdaam). 1966. Dir. Chan Man. Kong Ngee Co.

Drifting (Zukseoi piulau). 2021. Dir. Jun Li. With You Film Production & Investment Ltd, MM2 Studios Hong Kong Limited and Medialink Holdings Limited.

Drug Connection, The (毒后 史 *Dukhau beisi*). 1976. Dir. Sun Chung. Shaw Brothers.

Drug Queen, The (大毒后 *Daai dukhau*). 1976. Dir. Yeung Kuen. Goldig Films (HK) Ltd.

Drug War (毒戰 *Dukzin*). 2013. Dir. Johnnie To. Huaxia Film Distribution Co. Ltd and Beijing Hairun Pictures Co. Ltd.

Duel, The (大 *Daaikyutdau*). 1971. Dir. Chang Cheh. Shaw Brothers.

Duel in Black Dragon Street (Hyutsaa haklunggaai). 1961. Dir. Yuan Qiufeng. Shaw Brothers.

Duel of Fists (拳擊 *Kyungik*). 1971. Dir. Chang Cheh. Shaw Brothers.
Easy Rider. 1969. Dir. Dennis Hopper. Pando Company Inc. and Raybert Productions.
Election (　會 *Haksewui*). 2005. Dir. Johnnie To. Milkyway Image (HK) Ltd and One Hundred Years of Film Company Ltd.
Encounter of the Spooky Kind (　打　 *Gwai daa gwai*). 1980. Dir. Sammo Hung. Bo Ho Films Co. Ltd.
Family (家 *Gaa*). 1953. Dir. Ng Wui. Grandview Film Company Limited and Union Film Enterprises Ltd.
Far From Home (執屋 *Zapnguk*). 2021. Dir. Mok Kwan-ling.
Fascinating Messenger, The (勾　使　 *Ngauwan saize*). 1956. Dir. Ng Wui. Tak Ngai Film Company.
Father and Son (　子 *Fu jyu zi*). 1954. Dir. Ng Wui. Union Film Enterprises Ltd.
Father Is Back (　幽 *Fofat jaulaan*). 1961. Dir. Lee Tit. Hwa Lien.
Five Tiger Heroes, The (五　將 *Ng fu zoeng*). 1955. Dir. But Fu. Taai Ga.
Forbidden Tales of Two Cities (　傳奇 *Gong Ou cyunkei*). 1975. Dir. Li Han-hsiang. Shaw Brothers.
Four Ways Out (*La città si defende*). 1951. Dir. Pietro Germi. Società Italiana Cines.
French Connection, The. 1971. Dir. William Friedkin. Philip D'Antoni Productions.
Friends (朋友 *Pangjau*). 1974. Dir. Chang Cheh. Shaw Brothers.
'G' Men. 1935. Dir. William Keighley. Warner Bros. First National Pictures.
Games Gamblers Play (　星 *Gwaimaa soengsing*). 1974. Dir. Michael Hui. Golden Harvest Productions and Hui's Film Production Co. Ltd.
Gangs (　 *Tungdong*). 1988. Dir. Lawrence Lau. Sil-Metropole Organisation Ltd.
Generation Gap (叛　 *Bunjik*). 1973. Dir. Chang Cheh. Shaw Brothers.
Ghost Returns at Midnight, The (午夜招　 *Ngje ziuwan*). 1964. Dir. Cheung Ying. Overseas Chinese Films.
Ghost That Was Not (夜半幽　 *Jebun jauling*). 1961. Dir. Chor Yuen. Kong Ngee Co.
Ghost That Was Not in the Moon-Light, The (殘月　 *Caanjyut leiwan*). 1962. Dir. Cho Kei. Shuangxi Film Company.
Ghostly Murderer, The (　兇手 *Gwai hungsau*). 1964. Dir. Cheung Ying and Hsieh Hung. Overseas Chinese Films.
Girl Detective 001 (　一　女探員 *Dai jat hou neoi taamjyun*). 1966. Dir. Lung To. Golden Orchid Movie Enterprises Co.
Girl in the Bus, The (巴士　巧　　 *Baasi Ngan haaupo houmungai*). 1965. Dir. Mok Hong-si. Fei Lung.
Girl with Long Hair, The (　姑娘 *Coengfaat gunoeng*). 1967. Dir. Chan Wan. Wing Aau.

Ghost Chasers (夜半﹝﹞影 *Jebun dik gwaijing*). 1966. Dir. Ng Wui. San Aau Movie-Making Company.

Glorious Festival, A (光﹝﹞日 *Gwongfai dik zitjat*). 1964. Central Studio of News Reels Production.

Godfather, The. 1972. Dir. Francis Ford Coppola. Paramount Pictures, Albert S. Ruddy Production and Alfran Productions.

Golden Butterfly, The Lady Thief (女﹝﹞﹝﹞ *Neoicaak gamwudip*). 1965. Dir. Mok Hong-si. Lan Kwong Film Co.

Goldfinger. 1964. Dir. Guy Hamilton. Eon Productions.

Gossip Street (多咀﹝﹞ *Dozeoigaai*). 1974. Dir. Wong Fung. Shaw Brothers.

Green Swan Nightclub, The (﹝﹞天﹝﹞夜﹝﹞會 *Luk tinngo jezungwui*). 1958. Dir. Li Pingqian. Great Wall Movie Enterprise.

Guangzhou Adventure of the Fearless, The (﹝﹞﹝﹞廣州 *Zau Sandaam naau Gwongzau*). 1947. Dir. Chan Pei. Hoi Yin Film Co.

Happenings, The (夜﹝﹞ *Jece*). 1980. Dir. Yim Ho. Golden Harvest Productions.

Her Fatal Ways (﹝﹞姐，你好﹝﹞！ *Biuze, nei hou je!*). 1990. Dir. Alfred Cheung. Bo Ho Films Co. Ltd and Paragon Films Ltd.

Hero of Our Time (一代梟﹝﹞ *Jatdoi hiuhung*). 1948. Dir. But Fu. Ng Chow Film Company.

Hong Kong 73 (﹝﹞73 *Hoenggong 73*). 1974. Dir. Chor Yuen. Shaw Brothers.

Hot Blood (入冊 *Japcaak*). 1977. Dir. Yeung Kuen. Goldig Films (HK) Ltd.

Hot-Tempered Leung's Adventure in Hong Kong (﹝﹞大﹝﹞ *Ngauzing Loeng daainaau Hoenggong*). 1947. Dir. Lee Tit. Laam Ying Film Company.

Hound Murderer Case (﹝﹞兇 *Mohyun zeoihung*). 1961. Dir. Wong Fung. Naam Wa Film Company.

House No. 13 (十三﹝﹞兇殺案 *Sapsaam hou hungsaat ngon*). 1960. Dir. Wong Fung. Overseas Chinese Films.

House Number Sixty-Six (六十六﹝﹞屋 *Luksapluk hou nguk*). 1936. Dir. Lee Tit. Dashidai Film Company.

House of 72 Tenants, The (七十二家房客 *Catsapji gaa fonghak*). 1973. Dir. Chor Yuen. Shaw Brothers.

How Inspector Dai Sum Shattered the Strange Cloaks Gang (戴森奇案: 大﹝﹞怪﹝﹞ *Daai Sam kei ngon: Daaipo gwaaijidong*). 1950. Dir. Ng Wui. Choeng Shing.

How Wong Ang the Heroine Caught the Murderer (女俠﹝﹞擒兇﹝﹞ *Neoihap Wong Ang kamhung gei*). 1959. Dir. Yam Pang-nin. Lap Tat Film Co.

How Wong Ang the Heroine Solved the Case of the Three Dead Bodies (女俠﹝﹞夜﹝﹞三屍案 *Neoihap Wong Ang je po saam si ngon*). 1959. Dir. Yam Pang-nin. Lap Tat Film Co.

In the Face of Demolition (危樓春曉 *Ngailau ceonhiu*). 1953. Dir. Lee Tit. Union Film Enterprises Ltd.

Infernal Affairs (無間道 *Mougaandou*). 2002. Dir. Andrew Lau and Alan Mak. Media Asia Film Company Limited.
Inside the Red Brick Wall (大圍城 *Leidaai waising*). 2020. Dir. Hong Kong Documentary Filmmakers.
Inter-Pol (特警009 *Dakging ling ling gau*). 1967. Dir. Nakahira Koh. Shaw Brothers.
'Interpol' (國際刑警 *Gwokzai jingging*). 1978. Prod. Lau Fong-gong. Television Broadcast (TVB). 11 episodes.
Ironside 426 (四二六 *Sei ji luk*). 1977. Dir. Lam Kwok-cheung. Golden Harvest Productions.
Islander (濁島 *Cekdou*). 2021. Dir. Wu Zi-En.
It's a Wonderful Life. 1946. Dir. Frank Capra. Liberty Films.
Joys and Sorrows of Youth, The (冷暖青春 *Laangnyun cingceon*). 1969. Dir. Chor Yuen. New Art Motion Picture Production Co.
Jumping Ash (跳灰 *Tiufui*). 1976. Dir. Josephine Siao and Leong Po-chi. Bang! Bang! Films.
Kid, The (細路祥 *Sailou Coeng*). 1950. Dir. Fung Fung. Datong Film Company.
Kidnap (天網 *Tinmong*). 1974. Dir. Cheng Kang. Shaw Brothers.
Killer, The (喋血雙雄 *Diphyut soenghung*). 1989. Dir. John Woo. Film Workshop and Golden Princess Film Production Ltd.
Kiss of Death (毒女 *Dukneoi*). 1973. Dir. Ho Meng-hua. Shaw Brothers.
Lady Black Cat (女黑俠木蘭花 *Neoicaak hakjemaau*). 1966. Dir. Chiang Wai-kwong. Tai Chee Film Co.
Lady Detective, The (女偵探 *Noei zingtaam*). 1963. Dir. Ng Wui. Kong Ngee Co.
Law Don (家法 *Gaafaat*). 1979. Dir. Alan Tang and Stanley Siu. The Wing-Scope Film Production Ltd.
Lifeline (生命線 *Saangming sin*). 1935. Dir. Kwan Man-ching. Grandview Film Company Limited.
Lion-Hearted Warriors (鐵血男兒 *Tithyut naamji*). 1948. Dir. Wang Yuan-long. Seung Lung Film Company.
Lonely Fifteen 靚妹仔 (*Lengmuizai*). 1982. Dir. David Lai. The Pearl City Films Ltd and Johnny Mak Production Co. Ltd.
Long Arm of the Law (省港旗兵 *Saang Gong kei bing*). 1984. Dir. Johnny Mak. Bo Ho Films Co. Ltd, Johnny Mak Production Co. Ltd and Paragon Films Ltd.
Long Arm of the Law II (省港旗兵續集 *Saang Gong kei bing zuk zaap*). 1987. Dir. Michael Mak. Golden Harvest Productions.
Long Arm of the Law III (省港旗兵第三集 *Saang Gong kei bing dai saam zaap*). 1989. Dir. Michael Mak. Johnny Mak Production Co. Ltd.
Lost Souls (打蛇 *Daa se*). 1980. Dir. Mou Tun-fei. Shaw Brothers.

Love and Hate in Jianghu (恩仇 *Gongwu jansau*). 1958. Dir. Wan Fang and Tang Huang. Mandarin Film Company.

Love Massacre (愛殺 *Ngoi saat*). 1981. Dir. Patrick Tam. David & David Investment Co. (Film Dept.) Production.

Lucky Woman, The (人 *Toupaau dik jan*). 2020. Dir. Tseng Wen-Chen.

Man from Hong Kong, The (搗 *Zikdou wonglung*). 1975. Dir. Brian Trenchard-Smith. Golden Harvest Productions and Paragon Films Ltd.

Man Killer against the Tricky Man, The (殺人 大戰扭 *Saatjanwong daaizin Naugai Sam*). 1961. Dir. Wong Tin-lam. Motion Picture & General Investment Co. Ltd.

Man on the Brink (人 *Binjyunjan*). 1981. Dir. Alex Cheung. Century Motion Picture & Dist. Co. Ltd.

Mandarin, The (人 *Munzaujan*). 1973. Dir. Katy Chin. Shijie Film Company.

March of the Guerrillas (擊 曲 *Jaugik zeonhangkuk*). 1941. Dir. Szeto Wai-Man. San Chiu Gung Shut.

Marnie. 1964. Dir. Alfred Hitchcock. Alfred J. Hitchcock Productions.

May You Stay Forever Young (少年 *Siunin*). 2021. Dir. Rex Ren and Lam Sum.

Mildred Pierce. 1945. Dir. Michael Curtiz. Warner Bros.-First National.

Million Dollars Snatch (七 元大劫案 *Catbaakmaan jyun daai gip ngon*). 1976. Dir. Ng See-yuen. Dak Lee Moving Picture Co.

Mobfix Patrol (*Cungfungce*). 1981. Dir. Wong Chung. Shaw Brothers.

Money Money Money (仙杜拉偷搶 *Gwai maa Sindoulaai tau coeng pin*). 1975. Dir. Yu Tsong. Pacific Motion Picture Co.

Motor Car Murder, The (兇殺案 *Heice hungsaat ngon*). 1962. Dir. Mok Hong-si. Kwok Ngai Film Co.

Murder on the Beach (九九九 命案 *Gau gau gau hoitaan ming ngon*). 1957. Dir. Chan Man. Kong Ngee Co.

Murderer in Town (城兇影 *Hoengsing hungjing*). 1958. Dir. Lee Tit. Union Film Enterprises Ltd.

Mystery of the Human Head, The (人 奇案 *Jantau kei ngon*). 1955. Dir. Kwan Man-ching. San Daat Company.

Net of Divine Retribution, The (天 恢恢 *Tinmong fuifui*). 1947. Dir. Yeung Kung-leung. Great China Film Company and Lianyi Film Company.

Night the Spirit Returns, The (回 夜 *Wuiwanje*). 1962. Dir. Cheung Ying and Choi Cheong. Haohua Film Company.

Once a Thief. 1965. Dir. Ralph Nelson. CIPRA.

Once a Thief (橫四 *Zungwaang seihoi*). 1991. Dir. John Woo. Golden Princess Film Production Ltd.

One-Armed Swordsman (刀 *Dukbei dou*). 1967. Dir. Chang Cheh. Shaw Brothers.

One by One (死對 Seideoitau). 1973. Dir. Chien Lung. First Distributors (HK) Ltd.

Operation Lipstick (嬌娃 Dipmong giuwaa). 1967. Dir. Inoue Umetsugu. Shaw Brothers.

'Operation Manhunt' (大丈夫 Daaizoengfu). 1977. Prod. Chung King-fai. Rediffusion (RTV). 8 episodes.

Orphan, The (人 孤 Janhoi gu hung). 1960. Dir. Lee Sun-fung. Hwa Lien.

Outlaw Genes (性 Caaksing). 1982. Dir. Stanley Siu. The Wing-Scope Film Production Ltd.

Over My Dead Body (殺妻案 Saatcai ngon). 1958. Dir. Cho Kei. Motion Picture & General Investment Co. Ltd.

Payment in Blood (Hyutzing). 1973. Dir. Kuei Chih-hung. Shaw Brothers.

Police Force (察 Gingcaat). 1973. Dir. Chang Cheh and Tsai Yang-ming. Shaw Brothers.

Police Story (察故事 Gingcaat gusi). 1985. Dir. Jackie Chan. Golden Way Films Ltd and Paragon Films Ltd.

Police Woman (女 察 Neoi gingcaat). 1973. Dir. Chu Mu. Great Earth Film Company.

Pom Pom (勇 Sanjung soenghoengpaau). 1984. Dir. Joe Cheung. Bo Ho Films Co. Ltd and Paragon Films Ltd.

Port of Call (尋梅 Daap hyut cam mui). 2015. Dir. Philip Yung. Mei Ah Film Production Co. Ltd and Mei Ah Entertainment Development, Inc.

Prison on Fire (Gaamjuk fungwan). 1987. Dir. Ringo Lam. Cinema City Co. Ltd.

Prodigal, The (子 Longzi). 1969. Dir. Chor Yuen. Tse Brother Motion Picture Production Company.

Psycho. 1960. Dir. Alfred Hitchcock. Shamley Productions.

Rascal Billionaire, The (Baakfan soenghung). 1978. Dir. Stanley Siu. Hang Faat.

Rear Window. 1954. Dir. Alfred Hitchcock. Patron Inc.

Rebecca. 1940. Dir. Alfred Hitchcock. Selznick International Pictures.

Red Detachment of Women, The (娘子 Hungsik noengzigwan). 1961. Dir. Xie Jin. Shanghai Tianma Film Studio.

Return of the Black Hero (俠歸來 Hakhap gwailoi). 1948. Dir. Fung Chi-kong. Yue Chow Film Company.

Revolution of Our Times (時代 命 Sidoi gaakming). 2021. Dir. Kiwi Chow.

Righting a Wrong with Earthenware Dish (冤 Ngaapun sanjyun). 1914. Dir. Benjamin Brodsky. Waa Mei.

Rock N' Roll Cop (　一　　　 *Saang Gong jat hou tungcapfaan*). 1994. Dir. Kirk Wong. Sky Point Film Investment Co. Ltd.
Rope. 1948. Dir. Alfred Hitchcock. Transatlantic Pictures and Warner Bros.
Rouge Tigress, The (　　 *Jinzifu*). 1955. Dir. Chun Kim. Kong Ngee Co.
Saviour, The (救世　 *Gausaize*). 1980. Dir. Ronny Yu. The Pearl City Films Ltd.
School on Fire (學校　　 *Hokhaau fungwan*). 1988. Dir. Ringo Lam. Cinema City Co. Ltd.
Secret, The (　劫 *Funggip*). 1979. Dir. Ann Hui. Unique Films Ltd.
Servants, The (　內　外 *Coengnoi coengngoi*). 1979. Dir. Philip Chan and Ronny Yu. Bang! Bang! Films.
Shadow, The (　克探案之　影　 *Leoi Hak taam ngon zi hyutjing gingwan*). 1961. Dir. Fung Fung. Yulin Film Co. Ltd, HK.
Shadow of a Doubt. 1943. Dir. Alfred Hitchcock. Universal Pictures and Skirball Productions.
Sima Fu's Encounter with the Honey Gang (司　夫大　　 *Simaa Fu daaipo mattong dong*). 1949. Dir. Hung Suk-wan. Nanxing Film Company.
Singing Thief, The (大　歌　 *Daaidou gowong*). 1969. Dir. Chang Cheh. Shaw Brothers.
Sisters in Crime (橫刀奪愛 *Waangdou dyutngoi* / 999 姊妹情殺案 *999 zimui cingsaatngon*). 1958. Dir. Lee Tit. Kong Ngee Co.
Social Characters (　女 *Feinaam feineoi*). 1969. Dir. Chan Wan. Yue Lok Film Company.
Sparring Partner, The (正　　廊 *Zingji wuilong*). 2022. Dir. Ho Cheuk-tin. Mei Ah Film Production Co. Ltd, The Film Development Fund of Hong Kong and Word By Word Limited.
Spy with My Face (　　　　 *Hak muigwai jyu hak muigwai*). 1966. Dir. Chor Yuen. Rose Motion Picture Company.
Stealing a Roasted Duck (偷　 *Tau siungaap*). 1914. Dir. Benjamin Brodsky. Waa Mei.
Story of a Discharged Prisoner (　本　 *Jinghun bunsik*). 1967. Dir. Patrick Lung. San Aau Movie-Making Company.
Story of Woo Viet, The (　　故事 *Wu Jyut dik gusi*). 1981. Dir. Ann Hui. The Pearl City Films Ltd.
Stowaways, The (偷　來客 *Taudou loihaak*). 1979. Dir. Tony Lou. Tin Ma.
Strangers on a Train. 1951. Dir. Alfred Hitchcock. Warner Bros.
Suspicion. 1941. Dir. Alfred Hitchcock. RKO Radio Pictures.
System, The (　 *Hangkwai*). 1979. Dir. Peter Yung. Trinity Asia Ltd.
Taxi Driver. 1976. Dir. Martin Scorsese. Bill/Phillips Productions and Italo-Judeo.

Teahouse, The (成　　樓 *Singgei caalau*). 1974. Dir. Kuei Chih-hung. Shaw Brothers.
Teddy Girls (　女正傳 *Feineoi zingcyun*). 1969. Dir. Patrick Lung. Eng Wah & Co., HK.
'Ten Sensational Cases' (十大奇案 *Sap daai kei ngon*). 1975. Prod. Loeng Wai-man. Rediffusion (RTV). 13 episodes.
Tenants of Talkative Street, The (　巷　 *Gaaizi hongman*). 1974. Dir. Yeung Kuen. Goldig Films (HK) Ltd.
To Catch a Thief. 1955. Dir. Alfred Hitchcock. Paramount Pictures Corp.
Tradition (傳　 *Cyuntung*). 1954. Dir. Tang Huang. Asia Pictures Limited.
Treasure Hunt (　剛　　奪寶 *Titgamgong hoihung dyutbou*). 1965. Dir. Wong Yiu. Chi Luen Film Company Limited.
Trouble with Harry, The. 1955. Dir. Alfred Hitchcock. Alfred Hitchcock Productions, Inc. and Paramount Pictures Corp.
Twin Corpses Mystery (九九九　　屍案 *Gau gau gau sanbei soengsi ngon*). 1965. Dir. Wong Hok-sing. Lux Film Company.
Underground Express (　旗兵　四　地下　 *Saang Gong kei bing dai sei zaap: Deihaa tungdou*). 1990. Dir. Michael Mak. San Heung Gong Din Ying Shing Gung Shut.
Unwritten Law, The (　外情 *Faatngoi cing*). 1985. Dir. Ng See-yuen. Seasonal Film Corporation.
Valiant Brothers, The (　克探案之　手凶刀 *Leoi Hak taam ngon zi hyutsau hungdou*). 1961. Dir. Yeung Kung-leung and Fung Fung. Yulin Film Co. Ltd, HK.
Vertigo. 1958. Dir. Alfred Hitchcock. Alfred Hitchcock Productions, Inc. and Paramount Pictures Corp.
Warriors, The. 1979. Dir. Walter Hill. Paramount Pictures Corp.
Way of the Dragon, The (　　 *Maanglong gwogong*). 1972. Dir. Bruce Lee. Golden Harvest Productions and Concord Productions Inc.
Way We Keep Dancing, The (　　3 *Kongmoupaai 3*). 2020. Dir. Adam Wong. Golden Scene Company Limited.
We're Going to Eat You (地　　 *Deijuk mou mun*). 1980. Dir. Tsui Hark. Seasonal Film Corporation.
We Want to Live (我　下去 *Ngo jiu wuthaaheoi*). 1960. Dir. Lee Tit. Union Film Enterprises Ltd.
Where the Wind Blows (　再　時 *Fung zoi hei si*). 2022. Dir. Philip Yung. Mei Ah Film Production, Dadi Century Films and Global Group Films.
White-Dappled Snake (　　 *Baakfaase*). 1954. Dir. Chen Huan-wen and Ding Lik. Ma Gong.

Window, The (　Coeng). 1968. Dir. Patrick Lung. Tse Brother Motion Picture Production Company.

Winners and Sinners (奇　妙　五　星 *Keimau miugai ng fuksing*). 1983. Dir. Sammo Hung. Paragon Films.

Yan Ruisheng (　　*Jim Seoisaang*). 1921. Dir. Yam Pang-nin. Commercial Press Film Department.

Yellow Giant (　毛怪人 *Wongmou gwaaijan*). 1962. Dir. Wong Fung. Sin Hok Gong Luen.

Yojimbo (　心棒 *Yojinbo*). 1961. Dir. Kurosawa Akira. Kurosawa Production and Toho.

Young People (年　人 *Ninhingjan*). 1972. Dir. Chang Cheh. Shaw Brothers.

Bibliography

Abbas, Ackbar. 1997. *Hong Kong: Culture and the Politics of Disappearance*. Hong Kong: Hong Kong University Press.

Altman, Rick. 1998. 'Reusable Packaging: Generic Products and the Recycling Process.' In Browne 1998, 1–41.

———. 1999. *Film/Genre*. London: BFI Pub.

Armstrong, Richard. 2005. *Understanding Realism*. London: British Film Institute.

Belton, John, ed. 2000a. *Alfred Hitchcock's* Rear Window. Cambridge: Cambridge University Press.

———. 2000b. 'Introduction.' In Belton 2000a, 1–20.

Benyahia, Sarah Casey. 2012. *Crime*. New York: Routledge.

Berry, Chris, and Mary Farquhar. 2006. *China on Screen: Cinema and Nation*. Hong Kong: Hong Kong University Press.

Bickers, Robert, and Ray Yep, eds. 2009. *May Days in Hong Kong: Riot and Emergency in 1967*. Hong Kong: Hong Kong University Press.

Bordwell, David. 1985. *Narration in the Fiction Film*. Madison: University of Wisconsin Press.

———. 2010. *Planet Hong Kong: Popular Cinema and the Art of Entertainment*. 2nd ed. Madison: Irvington Way Institute Press.

Boretz, Avron. 2011. *Gods, Ghosts, and Gangsters: Ritual Violence, Martial Arts, and Masculinity on the Margins of Chinese Society*. Honolulu: University of Hawai'i Press.

Braudy, Leo. 1998. 'Afterword: Rethinking Remakes.' In *Play It Again, Sam: Retakes on Remakes*, edited by Stuart Y. McDougal and Andrew Horton, 327–34. Berkeley: University of California Press.

Brooks, Peter. 1995. *The Melodramatic Imagination: Balzac, Henry James, Melodrama, and the Mode of Excess*. New Haven: Yale University Press.

Browne, Nick, ed. 1998. *Refiguring American Film Genres: History and Theory*. Berkeley: University of California Press.

Browne, Nick, Paul G. Pickowicz, Vivian Sobchack and Esther Yau, eds. 1994. *New Chinese Cinemas: Forms, Identities, Politics*. Cambridge: Cambridge University Press.

Cang Zanbong 曾振 . 1981. '"Binjyunjan" dik beikek singgaak kap dinjing jyujin' ' 人' 悲劇性格及 影 (*Man on the Brink*'s Tragic Character and Film Language). *Film Biweekly*, no. 53 (January 8): 32–3.

Carroll, John M. 2007. *A Concise History of Hong Kong*. Hong Kong: Hong Kong University Press.

Carroll, Noël. 1990. *The Philosophy of Horror, or, Paradoxes of the Heart*. New York: Routledge.

———. 1996. *Theorizing the Moving Image*. Cambridge: Cambridge University Press, 1996.

Chan, Johannes. 1988. 'Freedom of Expression: Censorship and Obscenity.' In *Civil Liberties in Hong Kong Kong*, edited by Raymond Wacks, 208–42. Hong Kong: Oxford University Press.

Chan, Keith, and Alvin Tse. 2011. 'The Bitter Tea of Big Brother Cheng: An Interview with Chan Koon-tai.' In *Kuei Chih-hung, the Rebel in the System*, edited by Sam Ho and Cheuk-to Li, 38–41. Hong Kong: Hong Kong Film Archive.

Chang, Cheh. 2004. *Chang Cheh: A Memoir*. Edited by Ain-ling Wong, Ching-ling Kwok, May Ng and Agnes Lam. Hong Kong: Hong Kong Film Archive.

Chang, Jing Jing. 2019. *Screening Communities: Negotiating Narratives of Empire, Nation, and the Cold War in Hong Kong Cinema*. Hong Kong: Hong Kong University Press.

Chapman, James. 2000. *License to Thrill: A Cultural History of the James Bond Films*. New York: Columbia University Press.

Chen, Timmy Chih-ting. 2019. '"The Orchid in Flames": Consanguinity, Community, and Criminality in *Father Is Back* (1961).' Paper presented at the 11th International Convention of Asia Scholars, Leiden, July 2019.

Cheng, Yu. 1989. 'Under a Spell.' In *Phantoms of the Hong Kong Cinema*, 20–3. 13th Hong Kong International Film Festival. Hong Kong: Urban Council.

———. 1990. 'Uninvited Guests.' In *The China Factor in Hong Kong Cinema*, 98–101. 14th Hong Kong International Film Festival. Hong Kong: Urban Council.

Cheuk, Pak Tong. 1999. 'Television in the 70s: Its State of Being.' In *Hong Kong New Wave: Twenty Years After*, 29–31. 23rd Hong Kong International Film Festival. Hong Kong: Provisional Urban Council of Hong Kong.

———. 2008. *Hong Kong New Wave Cinema (1978–2000)*. Bristol: Intellect.

Cheung Ka Chun 張嘉俊. 2009. 'Saam Sou siusyut jingau' 三蘇小說研究 (Study of San Su's Fiction). MPhil thesis, Lingnan University.

Cheung Shing-sheung 張承勷. 1981. 'Janzoeng: Zoeng Gwokming "Binjyunjan"' 印象：張國明《邊緣人》 (Impression: Alex Cheung's *Man on the Brink*). *Film Biweekly*, no. 53 (January 8): 46–7.

Chu, Yingchi. 2003. *Hong Kong Cinema: Coloniser, Motherland and Self*. London: Routledge Curzon.

Chu, Yiu-kong. 2000. *The Triads as Business*. London: Routledge.

Chu, Yiu-wai. 2017. *Hong Kong Cantopop: A Concise History*. Hong Kong: Hong Kong University Press.

Coengzi 澄子. 1978. 'Kithoi Zung Gwokjan dik sanbei daipaai' 揭開鍾國仁的神秘底牌 (Revealing Chung Kwok-yan's Mystery Card). *Southern Screen*, no. 242 (May): 44–5.

Cunliffe, Tom. 2021. 'Implicating the Social Order: *The Story of a Discharged Prisoner*.' *Film History* 33, no. 3 (Fall): 94–125.

Curtis, Scott. 2000. 'The Making of *Rear Window*.' In Belton 2000a, 21–56.

Davis, Brian. 1973. *The Thriller: The Suspense Film from 1946*. London: Studio Vista.

Deflem, Mathieu, Richard Featherstone, Yunqing Li, and Suzanne Sutphin. 2008. 'Policing the Pearl: Historical Transformations of Law Enforcement in Hong Kong.' *International Journal of Police Science & Management* 10, no. 3 (Autumn): 349–56.

Deleyto, Celestino. 2012. 'Film Genres at the Crossroads: What Genres and Films Do to Each Other.' In Grant 2012, 218–36.

Derrida, Jacques. 1980. 'The Law of Genre.' Translated by Avital Ronell. *Critical Inquiry* 7, no. 1 (Autumn): 55–81.

Derry, Charles. 1988. *The Suspense Thriller: Films in the Shadow of Alfred Hitchcock*. Jefferson: McFarland.

Desser, David. 2009. 'Triads and Changing Times: The National Allegory of Hong Kong Cinema, 1996–2000.' *Quarterly Review of Film and Video* 26 (3): 179–93.

Du, Ying. 2017. 'Censorship, Regulations, and the Cinematic Cold War in Hong Kong (1947–1971).' *China Review* 17, no. 1 (February): 117–51.

———. 2019. 'Hong Kong Leftist Cinema in the Cold War Era: In-Betweenness, Sensational Success and Censorship.' *Journal of Chinese Cinemas* 13 (1): 93–108.

Dungzi 冬子. 1973. '*Gingcaat* zotaamwui' 警察座談会 (Forum on *Police Force*). *Hong Kong Movie News*, no. 90 (June): 42–3.

Elliott, Paul. 2014. *Studying the British Crime Film*. New York: Columbia University Press.

Ellis, John. 1982. *Visible Fictions: Cinema, Television, Video*. London: Routledge & Kegan.

Fang, Karen. 2001. 'Arresting Cinema: Surveillance and the City-State in the Representation of Hong Kong.' *New Formations*, no. 44 (Autumn): 128–50.

———. 2017. *Arresting Cinema: Surveillance in Hong Kong Film*. Stanford: Stanford University Press.

Fonoroff, Paul. 1997. *Silver Light: A Pictorial History of Hong Kong Cinema, 1920–1970*. Hong Kong: Joint Publishing Co.

Forrest, Jennifer, and Leonard R. Koos, eds. 2002a. *Dead Ringers: The Remake in Theory and Practice*. Albany: State University of New York Press.

———. 2002b. 'Reviewing Remakes: An Introduction.' In Forrest and Koos 2002a, 1–36.

Foucault, Michel. 1992. 'What Is an Author?' In *Modernity and Its Discontents*, edited by James L. Marsh, John D. Caputo and Merold Westphal, 299–314. New York: Fordham University Press.

Frye, Northrop. 1957. *Anatomy of Criticism: Four Essays*. Princeton: Princeton University Press.

Fu, Poshek. 2000. 'The 1960s: Modernity, Youth Culture, and Hong Kong Cantonese Cinema.' In *The Cinema of Hong Kong: History, Arts, Identity*, edited by Poshek Fu and David Desser, 71–89. Cambridge: Cambridge University Press.

———. 2003. *Between Shanghai and Hong Kong: The Politics of Chinese Cinemas*. Stanford: Stanford University Press.

———. 2008. 'Introduction: The Shaw Brothers Diasporic Cinema.' In *China Forever: The Shaw Brothers and Diasporic Cinema*, edited by Poshek Fu, 1–25. Urbana: University of Illinois Press.

———. 2018. 'More than Just Entertaining: Cinematic Containment and Asia's Cold War in Hong Kong, 1949–1959.' *Modern Chinese Literature and Culture* 30, no. 2 (Fall): 1–55.

Fu, Winnie. 2014. 'Undercover Cops, Informants and Snitches.' Translated by Diane To. In Po 2014a, 114–24.

Fung, Honkaz 慶強, and Kei Shu. 2020. 'Sekpotinging waa Lung Gong! (Luk)' 天 剛! (六) (Discussing Patrick Lung with Insight and Originality! Part 6). The Glorious Record of Cantonese-Language Films, Episode 17. December 24. https://www.youtube.com/watch?v=C6ylmNcvrEA and https://www.youtube.com/watch?v=_35QWAM7kMg.

García-Mainar, Luis M. 2016. *The Introspective Realist Crime Film*. London: Palgrave Macmillan.

Gates, Philippa. 2011. *Detecting Women: Gender and the Hollywood Detective Film*. Albany: State University of New York Press.

Gaylord, Mark S., and Harold Traver. 1995. 'Colonial Policing and the Demise of British Rule in Hong Kong.' *International Journal of the Sociology of Law* 23, no. 1 (March): 23–43.

Gledhill, Christine. 1987. 'The Melodramatic Field: An Investigation.' In *Home Is Where the Heart Is: Studies in Melodrama and the Woman's Film*, edited by Christine Gledhill, 5–37. London: BFI Pub.

———. 2000. 'Rethinking Genre.' In *Reinventing Film Studies*, edited by Christine Gledhill and Linda Williams, 221–43. New York: Oxford University Press.

Grant, Barry Keith. 2007. *Film Genre: From Iconography to Ideology*. London: Wallflower.

———, ed. 2012. *Film Genre Reader IV*. Austin: University of Texas Press.

Grindon, Leger. 1998. 'Getting into Shape: Classic Conventions Make Their Move into the Boxing Film, 1937–1940.' *Journal of Sport & Social Issues* 22, no. 4 (November): 360–72.

———. 2012. 'Cycles and Clusters: The Shape of Film Genre History.' In Grant 2012, 42–59.

Hallam, Julia, and Margaret Marshment. 2000. *Realism and Popular Cinema*. Manchester: Manchester University Press.

Hampton, Mark. 2011. 'Early Hong Kong Television, 1950s–1970s: Commercialisation, Public Service and Britishness.' *Media History* 17 (3): 305–22.

Harper, Ralph. 1969. *The World of the Thriller*. Cleveland: Press of Case Western Reserve University.

Ho Manlung 何文 . 1990. 'Zetai faatfai dik "Deiha tungdou"' 借 揮 '地下 ' (*Underground Express*'s Opportunistic Use of a Hot Topic). *Film Biweekly*, no. 294 (July 5): 62.

Ho, Sam. 1996. 'Licensed to Kick Men: The Jane Bond Films.' In *The Restless Breed: Cantonese Stars of the Sixties*, edited by Law Kar, 40–6. Hong Kong: Urban Council.

Ho, Sam 何思 , and Ernest Chan 志 , eds. 2013. *Zicaa, hungjing, siusiman: Lei Tit dik dinjing ngaiseot* , 兇影, 小市 : 李 影 (Purple Hairpin, Murderous Shadows, Urbanites: The Film Art of Lee Tit). Hong Kong: Hong Kong Film Archive.

Hong Kong Film Archive. 2007. *Hoenggong jingpin daaicyun dai luk gyun (1965–1969)* 影 大全 六卷 (1965–1969) (Hong Kong Filmography Volume VI (1965–1969)). Edited by Ching-ling Kwok. Hong Kong: Hong Kong Film Archive.

———. 2014. *Hoenggong jingpin daaicyun dai baat gyun (1975–1979)* 影 大全 八卷 (1975–1979) (Hong Kong Filmography Volume VIII (1975–1979)). Edited by Kwok Ching-ling. Hong Kong: Hong Kong Film Archive.

Hong Kong Government Information Services. 1980. *Address by H.E. The Governor Sir Murray MacLehose, G.B.E., K.C.M.G., K.C.V.O., at the Opening Session of the Legislative Council 1st October, 1980*. Hong Kong: Hong Kong Government Information Services.

Hong Kong Movie News. 1973a. 'Cing Gong faatgwat faanzeoi taicoi dongnin gwangdung Hoenggong dik jat gin bongpiu laksok pongon ginggwo saam long ngon bunsoeng nganmok' 剛掘 材当年 动 一件 勒 案 三 案搬上 幕 (Cheng Kang Explores the Topic of Crime, Documents the Process of Solving a Kidnapping and Blackmail Case that Shook Hong Kong at the Time: The Three Wolves Case Is Turned into a Movie). *Hong Kong Movie News* 85 (January): 30–1.

Hong Kong Movie News. 1973b. '*Fannou cingnin* miuseot cingnin faanzeoi jyunjan' 憤怒 年描 年 原因 (*The Delinquent* Depicts the Reasons for Youth Crime). *Hong Kong Movie News*, no. 85 (January): 32–3.

Hunt, Leon. 2003. *Kung Fu Cult Masters: From Bruce Lee to Crouching Tiger*. London: Wallflower Press.

Jacobs, Lea. 1997. *The Wages of Sin: Censorship and the Fallen Woman Film, 1928–1942*. Berkeley: University of California Press.

Jenner, W. J. F. 1996. 'Tough Guys, Mateship and Honour: Another Chinese Tradition.' *East Asian History*, no. 12 (December): 1–34.

Jiao, Allan Y. 2007. *The Police in Hong Kong: A Contemporary View*. Lanham: University Press of America.

Jik Zing 亦晶. 1978. 'Hoenggong dinjing sanlongciu: hoeng cyuntung tiuzin gaakmingze?' 影新 ：向傳 挑戰 命 (The Hong Kong Cinematic New Wave: Revolutionaries Who Challenge Tradition?). *Close-Up*, no. 63 (August 18): 3–4.

Jing Bongzyu 帮主. 1984. '"Saang Gong keibing" cungpo cungcung zonaau' ' 奇兵' 撓 (*Long Arm of the Law* Breaks Through Various Barriers). *Film Biweekly*, no. 140 (July 5): 7.

Jones, Carol, and Jon Vagg. 2007. *Criminal Justice in Hong Kong*. London: Routledge-Cavendish.

Kaminsky, Stuart M. 1985. *American Film Genres*. 2nd ed. Chicago: Nelson-Hall.

Kinkley, Jeffrey C. 2000. *Chinese Justice, the Fiction: Law and Literature in Modern China*. Stanford: Stanford University Press.

Kitses, Jim. 1969. *Horizons West – Anthony Mann, Budd Boetticher, Sam Peckinpah: Studies in Authorship within the Western*. London: Thames & Hudson.

Klein, Amanda Ann. 2011. *American Film Cycles: Reframing Genres, Screening Social Problems, Defining Subcultures*. Austin: University of Texas Press.

Kong Chi-nam 之南. 1973. *Jan zoi gongwu* 人在 (The Heroic Deeds of a Villain). Hong Kong: Manngai syunguk.

Ku, Agnes S. 2004. 'Immigration Policies, Discourses, and the Politics of Local Belonging in Hong Kong (1950–1980).' *Modern China* 30, no. 3 (July): 326–60.

Kuhn, Annette. 1988. *Cinema, Censorship and Sexuality, 1909–1925*. London: Routledge.

Kung, James, and Yue'ai Zhang. 2002. 'Hong Kong Cinema and Television in the 1970s: A Perspective.' In *A Study of Hong Kong Cinema in the 1970s*, 14–17. 8th Hong Kong International Film Festival. Rev. ed. Hong Kong: Urban Council.

Laan Si . 1976. 'Waa Saan doujin sanzok gongwu zidai' 山導 新作子弟 (Hua Shan's New Film *Brotherhood*). *Southern Screen*, no. 216 (February): 34–5.

Lai, Lawrence W. C., and Mark Hansley Chua. 2018. 'The History of Planning for Kowloon City.' *Planning Perspectives* 33 (1): 97–112.

Landy, Marcia. 1991. *British Genres: Cinema and Society, 1930–1960*. Princeton: Princeton University Press.

Lau Shing-hon 劉成 . 1979. '"Hangkwai" zeoi ceotsik dik gingcaat mantai pin' ' '最出 察問 (*The System*, the Most Outstanding Police Problem Film). *Film Biweekly*, no. 24 (December 6): 14.

Law Kar 卡. 1969. 'Ping *Feineoi zingcyun*: gim leon Lung Gong' 女正傳：兼 剛 (Evaluating *Teddy Girls* and Discussing Patrick Lung). *Chinese Student Weekly*, no. 872 (April): 11.

———. 1986. 'Archetypes and Variations: Observation on Six Cantonese Films.' In *Cantonese Melodrama, 1950–1969*, edited by Cheuk-to Li, 15–20. Hong Kong: Urban Council.

———. 1996. 'Stars in a Landscape: A Glance at Cantonese Movies of the Sixties.' In *The Restless Breed: Cantonese Stars of the Sixties*, 53–8. 20th Hong Kong International Film Festival. Hong Kong: Urban Council.

———. 1999. 'Hong Kong New Wave: Modernization amid Global/Local Counter Cultures.' In *Hong Kong New Wave: Twenty Years After*, 44–50. 23rd Hong Kong International Film Festival. Hong Kong: Provisional Urban Council.

———. 2000. 'Crisis and Opportunity: Crossing Borders in Hong Kong Cinema, its Development from the 40s to the 70s.' *Hong Kong Cinema Retrospective: Border Crossings in Hong Kong Cinema*. 24th Hong Kong International Film Festival. Hong Kong: Leisure and Cultural Services Dept. 116–22.

———. 2001. 'An Overview of Hong Kong's New Wave Cinema.' In *At Full Speed: Hong Kong Cinema in a Borderless World*, edited by Esther C. M. Yau, 31–52. Minneapolis: University of Minnesota Press.

———. 2005. 'A Wizard in Crossing Disciplines: Yam Wu-fa.' In *The Hong Kong – Guangdong Film Connection*, edited by Ain-ling Wong, 152–69. Hong Kong: Hong Kong Film Archive.

―――. 2006a. *Hoenggong dinjing dim jyu sin* 影 (Dots and Lines in Hong Kong Cinema). Hong Kong: International Association of Theatre Critics (Hong Kong).

―――. 2006b. 'Rules and Exceptions: Cantonese Productions by Kong Ngee and Shaws.' In Wong 2006a, 110–21.

―――. 2010. 'Lung Gong bunsik' 剛本 (The True Colours of Lung Kong). In *Lung Gong* 剛 (Director Lung Kong), edited by Angel Shing and Yam Lau, 92–6. Oral History Series 6. Hong Kong: Hong Kong Film Archive.

―――. 2017. 'Black and Red: Post-War Hong Kong Noir and Its Interrelation with Progressive Cinema, 1947–1957.' In *Hong Kong Neo-Noir*, edited by Esther C. M. Yau and Tony Williams, 30–50. Edinburgh: Edinburgh University Press.

―――. 2018. 'Changes and Social Influences in Hong Kong Cinema Post-1967: A Comparison with Hong Kong Television.' Translated by Rachel Ng. In May Ng 2018a, 40–57.

Law, Kar, and Frank Bren. 2004. *Hong Kong Cinema: A Cross-Cultural View*. Lanham: Scarecrow Press.

Law Kar 卡, Ho Ng 吳昊, and Pak-tong Cheuk 卓伯棠. 1997. *Hoenggong dinjing leoijing leon* 影型 (On Hong Kong Film Genres). Hong Kong: Oxford University Press.

Law Wai-ming 明. 1979. 'Pincapsat bougou: zoi caakloeng "dinying" fonghoeng' 室報告：再 ' 影方向 (Report from the editors' room: Reviewing the direction of *Film Biweekly*). *Film Biweekly*, no. 20 (October 11): 2–4.

Law, Wing-sang. 2006. 'The Violence of Time and Memory Undercover: Hong Kong's *Infernal Affairs*.' *Inter-Asia Cultural Studies* 7 (3): 383–402.

―――. 2008. 'Hong Kong Undercover: An Approach to "Collaborative Colonialism"'. *Inter-Asia Cultural Studies* 9 (4): 522–42.

Lee, Vivian P. Y. 2020. *The Other Side of Glamour: The Left-wing Studio Network in Hong Kong Cinema in the Cold War Era and Beyond*. Edinburgh: Edinburgh University Press.

Lee, Yi-chong. 1999. 'Artist Provocateur – On Tsui Hark's Artistic Character.' In *Hong Kong New Wave: Twenty Years After*, 77–82. 23rd Hong Kong International Film Festival. Hong Kong: Provisional Urban Council of Hong Kong.

Lee, Zardas Shuk-man. 2013. 'From Cold War Politics to Moral Regulation: Film Censorship in Colonial Hong Kong.' MPhil diss., Hong Kong University.

―――. 2017. 'From Cold War Warrior to Moral Guardian: Film Censorship in British Hong Kong.' In *From a British to a Chinese Colony? Hong Kong before and after the 1997 Handover*, edited by Gary Chi-hung Luk, 143–65. Berkeley: Institute of East Asian Studies, University of California.

Leitch, Thomas. 2002a. *Crime Films*. Cambridge: Cambridge University Press.

———. 2002b. 'Twice-Told Tales: Disavowal and the Rhetoric of the Remake.' In Forrest and Koos 2002a, 37–62.

Lemire, Elise. 2000. 'Voyeurism and the Postwar Crisis of Masculinity in *Rear Window*.' In Belton 2000a, 57–90.

Lent, John. 1990. *The Asian Film Industry*. London: Christopher Helm.

Lethbridge, Henry J. 1985. *Hard Graft in Hong Kong: Scandal, Corruption, the ICAC*. Hong Kong: Oxford University Press.

Li Cheuk-to 李 桃, comp. (1981) 'Cungsan gimtou "san dinjing"' 新檢 '新影' (To Critique the 'New Cinema' Afresh). *Film Biweekly*, no. 63 (June 25): 13–15.

———. 1984. '"Deoi jansing citdai satmong!" Mak Donghung taam "Saang Gong keibing"' '對人性徹底失望!' ' 旗兵' ('Completely disillusioned with human nature!' Johnny Mak talks about *Long Arm of the Law*). *Film Biweekly*, no. 140 (July 5): 8–11.

———. 1994. 'The Return of the Father: Hong Kong New Wave and Its Chinese Context in the 1980s.' In Browne et al. 1994, 160–79. Cambridge: Cambridge University Press.

Lin Man-on 安, and Kwai-lung Ng 吳 . 2017. *Jinghung bunsik: Ng luk sap nindoi Jyutjyupin jinjyun zinjing* 本 ：五六十年代 員剪影 (The Essence of Heroes: Sketches of Actors in 1950s and 1960s Cantonese Cinema). Hong Kong: Chung Hwa Book Company.

Liu Wing-leung 廖 亮. 1981. '"Binjyunjan": Bun longmaan gojan beikek?' ' 人': 半 個人悲劇? (*Man on the Brink*: Semi-Romanticized Personal Tragedy?). *Film Biweekly*, no. 52 (January 22): 24.

Lo, Kwai-cheung. 2007. 'A Borderline Case: Ethnic Politics and Gangster Films in Post-1997 Hong Kong.' *Postcolonial Studies* 10 (4): 431–46.

Lo Wai-luk 偉力. 2019. *Hoenggong Jyutjyupin ngaiseot leonzaap* (Collected Writings on the Art of Hong Kong's Cantonese Cinema). Hong Kong: Chung Hwa Book Company.

Loock, Kathleen, and Constantine Verevis. 2012. 'Introduction: Remake/Remodel.' In *Film Remakes, Adaptations and Fan Productions: Remake/Remodel*, edited by Kathleen Loock and Constantine Verevis, 1–15. London: Palgrave Macmillan.

Louie, Kam. 2002. *Theorising Chinese Masculinity: Society and Gender in China*. Cambridge: Cambridge University Press.

Maa Tin . 1979. 'Jyu Jantaai cung "Tiufui zukzaap" dou "Coengleoi coengngoi"' 于仁 從" "到" 外" (Ronny Yu from *Jumping Ash: The Sequel* to *The Servants*). *Film Biweekly*, no. 6 (March 29): 15–17.

Magnan-Park, Aaron Han Joon. 2011. 'Restoring the Transnational from the Abyss of Ethnonational Film Historiography: The Case of Chung Chang Wha.' *Journal of Korean Studies* 16, no. 2 (Fall): 249–83.

Mak, Grace Yan Yan. 2006. 'Intimate Partners: Chun Kim and Chan Man.' In Wong 2006a, 82–95.

Maltby, Richard. 1983. *Harmless Entertainment: Hollywood and the Ideology of Consensus*. Metuchen: Scarecrow Press.

———. 1993. 'The Production Code and the Hays Office.' In *Grand Design: Hollywood as a Modern Business Enterprise, 1930–1939*, edited by Tino Balio, 37–72. New York: Charles Scribner's Sons.

Man, Glenn. 2000. 'Ideology and Genre in the *Godfather* Films.' In *Francis Ford Coppola's* The Godfather Trilogy, edited by Nick Browne, 109–32. Cambridge: Cambridge University Press.

Man Syun 文. 1980. 'Gingfeipin waan howai maa?' 匪 可 嗎? (Are Cops-and-Robbers Films Still Viable?). *Film Biweekly*, no. 42 (August 28): 11.

Marchetti, Gina. 2012. 'The Hong Kong New Wave.' In *A Companion to Chinese Cinema*, edited by Yingjin Zhang, 95–117. Malden: Wiley-Blackwell.

Marris, Paul. 2001. 'Northern Realism: An Exhausted Tradition?' *Cinéaste* 26, no. 4 (Fall): 47–50.

Mayer, Geoff. 2012. *Historical Dictionary of Crime Films*. Lanham: Scarecrow Press.

McArthur, Colin. 1972. *Underworld U.S.A*. London: Secker & Warburg.

Mittell, Jason. 2004. *Genre and Television: From Cop Shows to Cartoons in American Culture*. New York: Routledge.

Mok, Florence. 2021. 'Chinese Illicit Immigration into Colonial Hong Kong, c. 1970–1980.' *Journal of Imperial and Commonwealth History* 49 (2): 339–67.

Morgan, W. P. 1960. *Triad Societies in Hong Kong*. Hong Kong: Government Printer.

Morris, Meaghan, Siu Leung Li and Stephen Ching-kiu Chan, eds. 2005. *Hong Kong Connections: Transnational Imagination in Action Cinema*. Durham: Duke University Press.

Morton, Lisa. 2001. *The Cinema of Tsui Hark*. Jefferson: McFarland.

Moss, Peter. 2006. *No Babylon: A Hong Kong Scrapbook*. New York: iUniverse.

Mulvey, Laura. 1975. 'Visual Pleasure and Narrative Cinema.' *Screen* 16, no. 3 (Autumn): 6–18.

Munby, Jonathan. 1999. *Public Enemies, Public Heroes: Screening the Gangster from Little Caesar to Touch of Evil*. Chicago: University of Chicago Press.

Murray, Dian. 2002. 'Mutual Aid, Migration and the Development of the Tiandihui in China and Singapore.' In *Chinese Triads: Perspectives on Histories, Identities, and Spheres of Impact*, edited by Irene Lim, 5–17. Singapore: Singapore History Museum.

Naremore, James. 1998. *More than Night: Film Noir in Its Contexts*. Berkeley: University of California Press.

———. 2000. 'Introduction: Film and the Reign of Adaptation.' In *Film Adaptation*, edited by James Naremore, 1–18. New Brunswick: Rutgers University Press.

Naylor, Alexandra Mary Patricia. 2007. 'Discourses of Affect in the 1930s Hollywood Horror Film Cycle and in Its Aftermath to 1943.' PhD diss., University College London.

Neale, Steve. 2000. *Genre and Hollywood*. London: Routledge.

Newman, David. 2013. 'British Colonial Censorship Regimes: Hong Kong, Straits Settlements, and Shanghai International Settlement, 1916–1941.' In *Silencing Cinema: Film Censorship around the World*, edited by Daniel Biltereyst and Roel Vande Winkel, 167–90. Basingstoke: Palgrave Macmillan.

Ng, Grace, and Ching-ling Kwok, eds. 2006. *Director Chor Yuen*. Oral History Series 3. Hong Kong: Hong Kong Film Archive.

Ng, Ho 吳昊. 1980. 'When the Legends Die: A Survey of the Tradition of the Southern Shaolin Monastery.' In *A Study of the Hong Kong Martial Arts Film*, edited by Shing-hon Lau, 56–70. Hong Kong: Urban Council.

———. 1999. 'The Confessions of a Film Anarchist.' In *Hong Kong New Wave: Twenty Years After*, 55–9. 23rd Hong Kong International Film Festival. Hong Kong: Provisional Urban Council of Hong Kong.

———, ed. 2005. *Dai saam leoijing dinjing* 三 型 影 (The Alternative: Cult Films). Hong Kong: Joint Publishing.

———. 2008. *Gusing gei: Leon Hoenggong dinjing kap zuk manhok* 孤城 ：影及俗文學 (Notes from the Orphan City: On Hong Kong Cinema and Popular Culture). Hong Kong: Subculture.

Ng, Kenny K. K. 吳國坤. 2008. 'Inhibition vs. Exhibition: Political Censorship of Chinese and Foreign Cinemas in Postwar Hong Kong.' *Journal of Chinese Cinemas* 2 (1): 23–35.

———. 2009. 'Laangzin sikei Hoenggong dinjing dik zingzi samcaa' 冷战时期 影 政 审查 (The Political Censorship of Hong Kong Films during the Cold War). In *Laangzin jyu Hoenggong dinjing* 冷戰 影 (The Cold War and Hong Kong Cinema), edited by Ain-ling Wong and Pui Tak Lee, 53–69. Hong Kong: Hong Kong Film Archive.

———. 2020. 'Screening without China: Transregional Cinematic Smuggling between Cold War Taiwan and Colonial Hong Kong.' *Journal of the European Association for Chinese Studies* 1: 161–88.

———. 2021. *Zoktin gamtin mingtin: Noidei jyu Hoenggong dinjing dik zingzi ngaiseot jyu cyuntung* 昨天今天明天: 內地 影 政 ， 傳 (Yesterday, Today, Tomorrow: Hong Kong Cinema with Sino-links in Politics, Art, and Tradition). Hong Kong: Chunghwa Bookstore.

———. 2022. '"Gwokngonfaat" jamjinghaa dik Hoenggong dinjing' '國安 ' 影 下 影 (Hong Kong Cinema under the Shadow of the National Security Law). *Film Appreciation Journal*, no. 191: 76–7.

Ng, May, ed. 2018a. *When the Wind Was Blowing Wild: Hong Kong Cinema of the 1970s*. Oral History Series 7. Hong Kong: Hong Kong Film Archive.

———. 2018b. 'Foreword.' Translated by Piera Chen and Elbe Lau. In May Ng 2018a, 4–7.

Ng, May, and Ha-pak Wong, eds. 2016. *The Essence of Entertainment: Cinema City's Glory Days*. Hong Kong: Hong Kong Film Archive.

Ng, Michael. 2017. 'When Silence Speaks: Press Censorship and Rule of Law in British Hong Kong, 1850s–1940s.' *Law & Literature* 29 (3): 425–56.

———. 2022. *Political Censorship in British Hong Kong: Freedom of Expression and the Law (1842–1997)*. Cambridge: Cambridge University Press.

Ngaan Naamcoeng 南 . 1976. 'Syun Zung dik cungging' 孫仲 勁 (Sun Chung's Pioneering Spirit). *Hong Kong Movie News* 132 (December): 41–2.

———. 1978. 'Jat gau cat cat nin si Gwokjyupin fungsaunin' 一九七七年是國 收年 (1977 Was a Bumper Year for Mandarin Cinema). *Hong Kong Movie News* 145 (January): 28–9.

Nip, Miu-fong, and Mini Lam. 1985. 'Twenty Years of Cantonese Comedy: Five Interviews – Wu Hui.' In *The Traditions of Hong Kong Comedy*, 31–3. 9th Hong Kong International Film Festival. Hong Kong: Urban Council.

Niu Ge 哥. 2007. *Dougwok sausing* 國仇城 (Feuds in a Gambling City). Taipei: Toiwaan soengmou jansyugun.

Nochimson, Martha P. 2007. *Dying to Belong: Gangster Movies in Hollywood and Hong Kong*. Malden: Blackwell Publishing.

Odham Stokes, Lisa, and Michael Hoover. 1999. *City on Fire: Hong Kong Cinema*. London: Verso.

Ownby, David. 1993. 'Introduction: Secret Societies Reconsidered.' In *"Secret Societies" Reconsidered: Perspectives on the Social History of Modern South China and Southeast Asia*, edited by David Ownby and Mary Somers Heidhues, 3–33. Armonk: M. E. Sharpe.

———. 1996. *Brotherhoods and Secret Societies in Early and Mid-Qing China: The Formation of a Tradition*. Stanford: Stanford University Press.

Palmer, Jerry. 1979. *Thrillers: Genesis and Structure of a Popular Genre*. New York: St. Martin's Press.

Pang, Laikwan. 2002. *Building a New China in Cinema: The Chinese Left-wing Cinema Movement, 1932–1937*. Lanham: Rowman & Littlefield Publishers.

Peirse, Alison. 2013. *After Dracula: The 1930s Horror Film*. London: I. B. Tauris.

Po Fung. 2013a. 'Lei Tit dik zingtaam daksik dinjing' 李   偵探   影 (Lee Tit's Films with Detective Characteristics). In Ho and Chan 2013, 89–94.

———. 2013b. 'The Organisational Structure and Developmental History of Golden Harvest.' Translated by Johnny Ko. In *Golden Harvest: Leading Change in Changing Times*, edited by Po Fung, 8–25. Hong Kong: Hong Kong Film Archive, 2013.

———, ed. 2014a. *Always in the Dark: A Study of Hong Kong Gangster Films*. Hong Kong: Hong Kong Film Archive.

———. 2014b. 'The Origins of Hong Kong Gangster Films.' In Po 2014a, 6–17.

———. 2018. 'From Detective to "Ah Sir": The Birth of Hong Kong Cop Films in the 1970s.' In May Ng 2018a, 74–85.

Pomerance, Murray. 2013. *The Eyes Have It: Cinema and the Reality Effect*. New Brunswick: Rutgers University Press.

Poon, Erica Ka-yan. 2020. 'Crafting a World-Class Brand: Shaw Brothers' Appropriation of Foreign Models.' *Media Industries* 7 (1): 127–43.

Pribram, E. Deirdre. 2011. *Emotions, Genre, Justice in Film and Television: Detecting Feeling*. New York: Taylor & Francis.

Qin, Xiqing. 2013. 'Pearl White and the New Female Image in Chinese Early Silent Cinema.' In *Researching Women in Silent Cinema: New Findings and Perspectives*, edited by Monica Dall'Asta, Victoria Duckett and Lucia Tralli, 246–62. Bologna: University of Bologna.

Rafter, Nicole. 2000. *Shots in the Mirror: Crime Films and Society*. Oxford: Oxford University Press.

Ren, Rex 任俠, Ngon Naa 安娜, Crystal Chow 周   and Daniel Chan   力. 2022. 'Hoenggong zijau dinjing syunjin'   影宣 (Manifesto for a Free Hong Kong Cinema). *Film Appreciation Journal*, no. 191: 104–5.

Rodriguez, Hector. 2001. 'The Emergence of the Hong Kong New Wave.' In E. Yau 2001, 53–72.

Roffman, Peter, and Jim Purdy. 1981. *The Hollywood Social Problem Film: Madness, Despair and Politics from the Depression to the Fifties*. Bloomington: Indiana University Press.

Rubin, Martin. 1999. *Thrillers*. Cambridge: Cambridge University Press.

Schatz, Thomas. 1981. *Hollywood Genres: Formulas, Filmmaking, and the Studio System*. Boston: McGraw Hill.

Scott, James C. 1985. *Weapons of the Weak: Everyday Forms of Peasant Resistance*. New Haven: Yale University Press.

Sek, Kei. 1988. 'The Social Psychology of Hong Kong Cinema.' In *Changes in Hong Kong Society through Cinema*, 15–20. 12th Hong Kong International Film Festival. Hong Kong: Urban Council.

———. 1992. 'Advancement and Crisis: Hong Kong Cinema in the '80s.' In *Hong Kong Cinema in the Eighties*, 54–63. 15th Hong Kong International Film Festival. Rev. ed. Hong Kong: Urban Council.

———. 2005. *Hoenggong dinjing sanlongciu* 影新 (Hong Kong Cinema's New Wave). Shanghai: Fukdaan daaihok ceotbaanse.

———. 2018. 'Creating a Uniquely Hong Kong 1970s.' In May Ng 2018a, 58–73.

———. 2022. *Hoenggong keingon daai sampun: "Zingji wuilong" han haksik* 奇案大審判"正 廊"很 (Great Trial of a Hong Kong Case: *The Sparring Partner* Is Very Noir). Facebook, October 16. https://www.facebook.com/影-960817010662872.

Shahar, Meir. 2001. 'Ming-Period Evidence of Shaolin Martial Practice.' *Harvard Journal of Asiatic Studies* 61, no. 2 (December): 359–413.

———. 2008. *The Shaolin Monastery*. Honolulu: University of Hawai'i Press.

Shin, Chi-Yun, and Mark Gallagher, eds. 2015. *East Asian Film Noir: Transnational Encounters and Intercultural Dialogue*. London: I. B. Tauris.

Shu Kei. 1979. 'Dang Gwongwing sai haksewui bindak GLAMOUROUS' 光榮使 會 得GLAMOUROUS (Alan Tang Makes the Triads Become Glamourous). *Film Biweekly*, no. 5 (March 15): 13–14.

———. 1990. 'Saang Gong keibing dai saam zaap' 奇兵 三 (*Long Arm of the Law, Part III*). In *The China Factor in Hong Kong Cinema*, 147. 14th Hong Kong International Film Festival. Hong Kong: Urban Council, 1990.

Simonet, Thomas. 1987. 'Conglomerates and Content: Remakes, Sequels, and Series in the New Hollywood.' In *Current Research in Film: Audiences, Economics, and Law*, Vol. 3, edited by Bruce A. Austin, 154–62. Norwood: Ablex.

Sinclair, Kevin. 1983. *Asia's Finest: An Illustrated Account of the Royal Hong Kong Police*. Hong Kong: Unicorn.

Smart, Josephine. 1983. 'Dog King, Triads and Hawkers: Spatial Monopoly among the Street Hawkers in Hong Kong.' *Canadian Journal of Development Studies* 4 (1): 158–63.

———. 1986. 'The Impact of Government Policy on Hawkers: A Study of the Effects of Establishing a Hawker Permitted Place.' *Asian Journal of Public Administration* 8 (2): 260–79.

Soenggun Gwanbou 上官君宝. 1980. '"Jece" bei "Zinsi" waan zeonbou' '夜 ' 比'戰士' 步 (*The Happenings* Is Even More Progressive than *The Warriors*). *Film Biweekly*, no. 31 (March 27): 3–4.

Sorrento, Matthew. 2012. *The New American Crime Film*. Jefferson: McFarland.

Suo Yabin 亚斌. 2010. *Hoenggong dungzokpin meihok funggaak* 动作 学 格 (An Aesthetical Study on Hong Kong Action Movie). Beijing: Zunggwok cyunmui daaihok ceotbaanse.

Szeto, Mirana M., and Yun-Chung Chen. 2012. 'Mainlandization or Sinophone Translocality? Challenges for Hong Kong SAR New Wave Cinema.' *Journal of Chinese Cinemas* 6 (2): 115–34.

Takacs, Jeff. 2003. 'A Case of Contagious Legitimacy: Kinship, Ritual and Manipulation in Chinese Martial Arts Societies.' *Modern Asian Studies* 37, no. 4 (October): 885–917.

Tan, See Kam. 1996. 'Ban(g)! Ban(g)! *Dangerous Encounter – 1st Kind*: Writing with Censorship.' *Asian Cinema* 8, no. 1 (Spring): 83–108.

———. 2015. 'Shaw Brothers' *Bangpian*: Global Bondmania, Cosmopolitan Dreaming and Cultural Nationalism.' *Screen* 56, no. 2 (Summer): 195–213.

———. 2021. *Hong Kong Cinema and Sinophone Transnationalisms*. Edinburgh: Edinburgh University Press.

Television and Films Division. 1973. *Film Censorship Standards: A Note of Guidance*. Hong Kong: Government Printer.

Teo, Stephen. 1997. *Hong Kong Cinema: The Extra Dimensions*. London: BFI Pub.

———. 1999. 'Hong Kong's New Wave in Retrospect.' In *Hong Kong New Wave: Twenty Years After*, 17–23. 23rd Hong Kong International Film Festival. Hong Kong: Provisional Urban Council of Hong Kong.

———. 2009. *Chinese Martial Arts Cinema: The Wuxia Tradition*. Edinburgh: Edinburgh University Press.

———. 2014. 'Black Gangs, Black Path, and Black Film.' In Po 2014a, 31–46. Hong Kong: Hong Kong Film Archive.

Ter Haar, Barend J. 1998. *Ritual and Mythology of the Chinese Triads: Creating an Identity*. Leiden: Brill.

Thompson, Kirsten Moana. 2007. *Crime Films: Investigating the Scene*. London: Wallflower.

Thompson, Kristin, and David Bordwell. 1994. *Film History: An Introduction*. New York: McGraw-Hill.

Todorov, Tzvetan. 1975. *The Fantastic: A Structural Approach to a Literary Genre*. Translated by Richard Howard. New York: Cornell University Press.

Tsai Kuo Jung 國榮. 1985. *Zunggwok gandoi manngai dinjing jingau* 中國 代

文影 (A Study of Modern Chinese *Wenyi* Films). Taibei: Zungwaa mangwok dinjing tousyugun.

Tsang Siu Wang 曾 弘. 2013. 'Lei Tit jyu Zunglyun dinjing' 李 中 影 (Lee Tit and the Union Films). In Ho and Chan 2013, 31–44.

Tsang, Steve. 2004. *A Modern History of Hong Kong*. London: I. B. Tauris.

Vagg, Jon. 1997. 'Robbery, Death, and Irony: How an Armed Robbery Wave in Hong Kong Led to the Abolition of the Death Penalty.' *Howard Journal of Criminal Justice* 36, no. 4 (November): 393–405.

Van den Troost, Kristof. 2014. 'Born in an Age of Turbulence: Emergence of the Modern Hong Kong Crime Film.' In Po 2014a, 48–68.

———. 2017. 'Under Western Eyes? Colonial Bureaucracy, Surveillance and the Birth of the Hong Kong Crime Film.' In *Surveillance in Asian Cinema: Under Eastern Eyes*, edited by Karen Fang, 89–112. London: Routledge.

———. 2020. 'Genre and Censorship: The Crime Film in Late Colonial Hong Kong.' In *Renegotiating Film Genres in East Asian Cinemas and Beyond*, edited by Lin Feng and James Aston, 191–216. Cham: Springer International Publishing.

Vasey, Ruth. 1997. *The World According to Hollywood, 1918–1939*. Madison: University of Wisconsin Press.

Wan, Marco. 2021. *Film and Constitutional Controversy: Visualizing Hong Kong Identity in the Age of "One Country, Two Systems"*. Cambridge: Cambridge University Press.

Wang, Yiman. 2013. *Remaking Chinese Cinema: Through the Prism of Shanghai, Hong Kong, and Hollywood*. Honolulu: University of Hawai'i Press.

Wei Yan . 2016. Noeihap jingzoeng dik laubin: ji 'Neoi feicaak Wong Ang' jyu 'Neoihakhap Muk Laanfaa' kap kei jingsi goipin wai lai 女俠形 ：以"女 " "女 俠木 " 及其影 改 例 (Transforming the Image of Female Chivalry: Taking 'Wong Ang, the Female Cat Burglar' Series and 'The Dark Heroine Mulan Hua' Series as Examples). *Journal of Modern Literature in Chinese* 13, no. 1 (Summer): 131–55.

White, Luke. 2015. 'A "Narrow World, Strewn with Prohibitions": Chang Cheh's *The Assassin* and the 1967 Riots.' *Asian Cinema* 26, no. 1 (April): 79–98.

Williams, Linda. 1984. '"Something Else Besides a Mother": "Stella Dallas" and the Maternal Melodrama.' *Cinema Journal* 24, no. 1 (Autumn): 2–27.

———. 1998. 'Melodrama Revised.' In Browne 1998, 42–88.

Wilson, Christopher P. 2000. *Cop Knowledge: Police Power and Cultural Narrative in Twentieth-Century America*. Chicago: University of Chicago Press.

Wong, Ain-ling, ed. 2006a. *The Glorious Modernity of Kong Ngee*. Hong Kong: Hong Kong Film Archive.

———. 2006b. 'Preface.' In Wong 2006a, 16–21.
Wong Bakfei 北. 1978. 'Sesat doujin Waa Saan' 寫實導山 (Realist Director Hua Shan). *Hong Kong Movie News*, no. 146 (February): 50–1.
Wong Chung-ming 仲. 2014. 'Kongzinhau dik Jyutjyu siusyut' 抗戰後小 (Cantonese Fiction in Postwar Hong Kong). In *Jyutjyu dik zingzi: Hoenggong Jyutjyu dik jizat jyu dojyun* 政：多元 (The Politics of the Cantonese Language in Hong Kong), edited by Eva Man Kit-wah, 43–63. Hong Kong: Chinese University of Hong Kong Press.
Wong Jing. 2002. 'Lauhang manfaa wonggwok: Waankau ceotbaanse' 文化 國— 出 (Popular Culture Kingdom: Universal Publisher). In *Qicai duhui xinchao: Wu, liushi niandai liuxing wenhua yu Xianggang dianying* 七彩 會新：五, 六十年代 文化 影 (New Style of the Colourful Metropolis: Popular Culture and Hong Kong Cinema in the 1950s and 1960s), 15–17. Hong Kong: Hong Kong Film Archive.
Wood, Robin. 1989. *Hitchcock's Films Revisited*. London: Faber & Faber.
Xu Guangping 廣平. 2000. *Sapnin kwaisau gung gaanngai: Heoi Gwongping jik Lou Seon* 十年攜手共 危：廣平憶 (Ten Years of Sharing Difficulties and Dangers Together: Xu Guangping Remembers Lu Xun). Shijiazhuang: Hobak gaaujuk ceotbaanse.
Yau, Esther C. M. 1994. 'Border Crossing: Mainland China's Presence in Hong Kong Cinema.' In Browne et al. 1994, 180–201.
———, ed. 2001. *At Full Speed: Hong Kong Cinema in a Borderless World*. Minneapolis: University of Minnesota Press.
Yau, Esther C. M., and Tony Williams, eds. 2017. *Hong Kong Neo-Noir*. Edinburgh: Edinburgh University Press.
Yau, Herman Lai To. 2015. 'The Progression of Political Censorship: Hong Kong Cinema from Colonial Rule to Chinese-Style Socialist Hegemony.' PhD Diss., Lingnan University.
Yau, Kinnia Shuk-ting. 2005. 'Interactions between Japanese and Hong Kong Action Cinemas.' In Morris, Li and Chan 2005, 35–48.
———. 2009. *Japanese and Hong Kong Film Industries: Understanding the Origins of East Asian Film Networks*. New York: Routledge.
Yeh, Emilie Yueh-Yu. 2013. 'A Small History of *Wenyi*.' In *The Oxford Handbook of Chinese Cinemas*, edited by Carlos Rojas and Eileen Cheng-Yin Chow, 225–49. Oxford: Oxford University Press.
———, ed. 2018. *Early Film Culture in Hong Kong, Taiwan, and Republican China: Kaleidoscopic Histories*. Ann Arbor: University of Michigan Press.
Yip, Man-fung. 2017. *Martial Arts Cinema and Hong Kong Modernity: Aesthetic, Representation, Circulation*. Hong Kong: Hong Kong University Press.

Yung, Sai-shing 容世. 2003. 'The Joy of Youth, Made in Hong Kong: Patricia Lam Fung and Shaws' Cantonese Films.' In *The Shaw Screen: A Preliminary Study*, edited by Ain-ling Wong, 221–35. Hong Kong: Hong Kong Film Archive.

———. 2007. 'Cung zingtaam zaapzi dou moudaa dinjing: "Waankau ceotbaanse" jyu "Neoi feicaak Wong Ang"' (1946–1962) 從偵探 到武打 影: ' 出 ' '女 ' (1946–1962) ('From Detective Magazines to Martial Arts Movies: "Universal Publisher" and "Female Flying Thief Yellow Oriole"' (1946–1962)). In *Dousi manfaa zung dik jindoi Zunggwok* 市文化中 代中國 (Popular Culture of the Modern Metropolis), edited by Jiang Jin, 323–44. Shanghai: Waadung sifaan daaihok ceotbaanse.

Yung, Sai-shing, and Christopher Rea. 2014. 'One Chicken, Three Dishes: The Cultural Enterprises of Law Bun.' In *The Business of Culture: Cultural Entrepreneurs in China and Southeast Asia, 1900–1965*, edited by Christopher Rea and Nicolai Volland, 150–77. Vancouver: UBC Press.

Zhang, Yingjin. 1994. 'Engendering Chinese Filmic Discourse of the 1930s: Configurations of Modern Women in Shanghai in Three Silent Films.' *positions* 2, no. 3 (Winter): 603–28.

———. 2004. *Chinese National Cinema*. New York: Routledge.

Zhang, Zhen. 2005. *An Amorous History of the Silver Screen: Shanghai Cinema, 1896–1937*. Chicago: University of Chicago Press.

———. 2012. 'Transplanting Melodrama: Observations on the Emergence of Early Chinese Narrative Film.' In *A Companion to Chinese Cinema*, edited by Yingjin Zhang, 23–41. Malden: Wiley-Blackwell.

Ziu Lik 力. 1980. 'Gingcaat dinjing zoi haauleoi' 察 影再 慮 (Reconsidering the Police Film). *Film Biweekly*, no. 42 (August 28): 7–9.

Zoeng Tin 張 . 1976. 'San doujin hin zyu pin' 新導 (Short Dispatch on New Directors). *Close-Up*, no. 20 (September 9): 32.

Index

Note: Word by word alphabetical order. Page numbers in **bold** refer to illustrations and those in *italic* denote tables.

Abbas, Ackbar, 171
Absolute Monarch, 148, 149
action films, 7
    action-adventure films, 33–8, **34**, 167
    action-crime films, 144
Adventure in Fishing Harbor, 35–6, 38, 128
All in the Family, 106
Anti-Corruption, 105, 137, 139, 140, 146
The Arch, 168
The Assassin, 127
auteurism, interplay with genre and ideology, 57–60

Back Street, 99–101, **100**
Backyard Adventures, 21, 56, 72, 74–81, **78**
Banana Cop, 145
Bank Busters, 154–5, **155**, 156, 181
Bat Girl, 45
The Battle of Hong Kong, 87
The Beasts, 172
A Better Tomorrow, 1–2, 24, 38, 44, 142, 165–6, 171, 172, 186, 188
Big Bad Sis, 147
The Big Boss, 98
Big Brother Cheng, 104, 132, 133, 139, 147, 153–4
The Big Holdup, 138
'Big Timer' films, 145, 146, 148–9, 157

The Black Dragon, 103, 109
The Black Hero and Lee Ching-mei, 64
Black Rose, 47, 52–3, **52**
Bloodshed on Wedding Day, 35, 37–8, 40, 128
The Bloody Paper Man, 58
The Bloody Sucker, 58
Board of Review, 88, 93–4, 96, 109–10
Boat People, 157
The Bodyguards, 99
The Boxer from Shantung, 98, 107, 127, 128–9
Boys and Girls, 123
Brotherhood, 145, 147, 150, 187
But Fu, 35
Buddha's Palm series, 65
Bullets or Ballots, 86
Bullitt, 151
Bus Money Wiped Out the Evils, 53–4

The Call Girls, 135, 139, 172
Capra, Frank, 57
A Chase of the Murderer at the Canidrome, 65
castration, 78–9
To Catch a Thief, 73
censorship, 2, 10, 12–13, 20, 22, 28, 32, 34, 74, 82–110, 113, 118, 132, 139, 146–7, 151–2, 153, 170, 174
    appeals, 96, 103, 106–7, 109–10, 135

complications of, 106–10
Directive for Film Censors 1950, 91–2
Film Censorship Guidelines for Censors, 192–3
Film Censorship Ordinance 1988, 160–1, 192
Film Censorship Regulations, 87–8, 90, 105
Film Censorship Standards: A Note of Guidance, 101–2, 107, 108
film classification, 107–8
and film distributors/theatre owners, 107–8
and film genre, 84–6
General Principles for Guidance of Film Censors and the Film Censorship Board of Review, 92–3, 94, 96–7, 101
Hong Kong censorship apparatus, history of, 86–91, **89**
localisation, 86, 90–1, 110
moral censorship, 83–4, 91–2, 96
policy and the modern Hong Kong crime film, 97–105
policy and the 'New Wuxia Century', 91–7
policy changes, 83
political censorship, 13, 22, 83, 87n, 91, 92, 93, 191–2
pressure from mainland authorities, 155–6, 162
problem youth films, 175–8
public opinion and the media, 108–9
special treatment to big companies, 106–7
Chan, Charlie, 61–3, **62**
Chan, Connie, 47, 49, 50, 53
Chan, Daniel, 195
Chan, Jackie, 19, 117, 171, 179
Chan King-sam, 75
Chan Man, 69, 70–1
Chan, Michael, 99, 187, 188
Chan Pei, 74
Chan, Philip, 140, 160, 179
Chan Wan, 53, 123
Chang Cheh, 48–9, 97, 98, 101, 114, 117, 126–32, 151, 179, 186, 187
Chang, Paul, 51
chaos theory, 3–4
Cheng Kang, 135, 136
Cheng Xiaoqing, 63

Cheng Yuet-ying, 146
Cheuk Pak-tong, 164, 170
Cheung, Alex, 164, 182–6
Cheung, Irene, 105
Cheung, Mabel, 171
Cheung Sum, 126
Cheung Ying, 74
Cheung Ying-choi, 50
Chiang Wai-kwong, 52, 123
China Behind, 155–6
The Chinese Boxer, 97
Chinese Godfather, 103
Chor Yuen, 117, 122–4, 126, 138, 168
Chow, Doven, 107
Chow Yun-fat, 19, 152, 158
Chu Kea, 74
Chu Mu, 130
Chu Yingchi, 30
Chu Yiu Kong, 15
Chui San-yuen, 62, **62**
Chun Kim, 69
Chung Chang-hwa, 51
Chung, Cherie, 158
Chung Kwok-yan, 140, 148
Cinema City, 167
City on Fire, 160, 185
civil unrest, 51–2, 114–16
class, 80
Cleopatra Jones and the Casino of Gold, 151
Close-Up, 168, 169
The Club, 164, 187–8
clusters, 4–5
Cold War, 13, 22, 28, 49, 83–4, 87, 91
Coming Back to Life in a Dead Body, 64
Coolie Killer, 187, 188
cop/police films, 7–8, 101, 129–30, **131**, 132, 139–40, 141–2, 144–5
growing dominance, 146–53, **149**
police populism, 151–2
police thrillers, 165, 178–86, **180**, **183**
and traditional values, 145
undercover cops, 10, 49–50, 148, 160, 184–7
Cops and Robbers, 164, 179, 181, 182–4
corruption, 16, 20, 116, 121, 137, 147
Cream Soda and Milk, 173
crime cinema, 5–8, 97
and censorship policy, 97–105
and Hong Kong identity, 143–6

crime cinema (*cont.*)
    and melodrama, 38–9
    and society, 8–10
    values and concepts in Hong Kong crime films, 18–20
crime problems, 84, 98, 98–9, 102, 113, 115–16, 118, 142
    youth crime, 121–2, 166–7, 172
criminal realism, 9, 10, 11–13, 20, 28n, 56, 84, 113–40, 143, 146, 165, 170, 171–2
    and Chang Cheh and Kuei Chih-hung, 126–35, **129**, **131**, **134**
    concept, 2
    dominance, ending of, 186–9
    new form of, 118–21
    and problem youth films, 121–6, **123**, **125**
    true crime productions, 135–40
    uncertain present and future of, 190–7
The Criminals, 118, 139, 141
Curtiz, Michael, 60
cycles, 4–5

The Dancing Voice of Youth, 193
Dangerous Encounter of the First Kind, 23, 174, 175–8, **176**, 196
The Dead and the Deadly, 167
Dead End, 127
Deane, Walter Meredith, 16
death penalty, 135–6, 152
Death Valley, 94–5, **95**, 96
Death Wish, 133
The Delinquent, 101, 129, **129**
Delon, Alain, 41–2
detective films, 21, 55–6, 58
    genre and star, 61–7, **62**, **66**
Dial 999 for 24-Hour Murder Case, 71, 73
Dial M for Murder, 73
Dirty Harry, 12, 102, 113, 151, 181
The Discharged, 148–9
Discharged Prisoners Aid Society (DPAS), 43
Don't Kill Me, Brother, 157
Dragnet, 69–70, **70**, 71
Drifting, 194
The Drug Connection, 147
The Drug Queen, 139, 146–7, 150, 152
Drug War, 145
The Duel, 98, 127–8, 133
Duel of Fists, 98

Easy Rider, 88
Election, 14, 145
Encounter of the Spooky Kind, 167
Family, 81
fanzuipian, 8
Far From Home, 193
The Fascinating Messenger, 47
Father and Son, 32, 81
Father is Back, 40–1, 57
Film Biweekly, 162, 169, 170
film classification, 107–8
film genre, 2–5
    and censorship, 84–6
    and stars, 61–7
    and studio, 67–72
The Five Tiger Heroes, 35

Forbidden Tales of Two Cities, 106
Four Ways Out, 38, 60
The French Connection, 12, 102, 151
Friends, 127
Fung Fung, 122n
Furukawa Takumi, 51

'G' Men, 86
Games Gamblers Play, 104
Gangs, 173–4
gangster films, 8, 20–1, 127–8
    censorship, 86
    guerrilla gangsters, 10, 33–8, **34**
    immigrant gangsters, 23, 142–3, 153–63, 178
    reformed gangsters, 38–44, **40**
    and traditional values, 145, 147
gender, 77, 80
    gender discrimination, 173
Generation Gap, 127
generic landscape, 4, 5, 29, 30–3, 56, 60, 74
genre studies, 5, 8, 85
    interplay with auteurism and ideology, 57–60
Ghost Chasers, 68
The Ghost That Was Not, 41, 73
The Ghost That Was Not in the Moon-Light, 68
The Ghostly Murderer, 68
Girl Detective, 50
The Girl on the Bus, 53–4
The Girl with Long Hair, 53

A Glorious Festival, 93
Godber, Peter, 116, 137
The Godfather, 12, 102–3, 103, 113, 133, 150
Golden Butterfly, The Lady Thief, 53
Golden Harvest, 106, 117, 147, 167
Goldfinger, 47–8
The Green Swan Nightclub, 35
Guan Yu, 19
The Guangzhou Adventure of the Fearless, 33, 34

haohan, 19, 21, 33, 34, 35, 66n
The Happenings, 174–5, 178
Heath, Henry W. E., 14
heibangpian, 8
heishehuipian, 8
Her Fatal Ways, 145
Hero of Our Time, 62–3
Hill, Walter, 174
Hitchcock, Alfred, 10, 21, 172
 Hong Kong remakes, 60, 61, 72–81, *73*, **78**
 horror films, 68
Ho Cheuk-tin, 194
Ho Meng-hua, 101
Hong Kong New Wave *see* New Wave cinema
Hong Kong Police Force, 10, 14, 16–18, 50, 92, 114, 132, 142, 160, 175, 184
 affinities with triads, 19, 121
 and corruption, 116, 121, 137, 147
 reputation, 116
Hong Kong University Press, 171
horror films, 68, 85, 167
Hot Blood, 152
Hot-Tempered Leung's Adventure in Hong Kong, 33–4, **34**, 64
House No. 13, 65
House Number Sixty-Six, 27, 38, 119–20
The House of 72 Tenants, 104, 117
How Wong Ang the Heroine Caught the Murderer, 47
How Wong Ang the Heroine Solved the Case of the Three Bodies, **46**, 47
Hua Mulan, 45
Hua Shan, 127, 139, 140, 147
Hui, Ann, 157–8, 163, 164, 172
Hui Tak, 64
Hung, William, 96, 97, 107

identity, 10, 12, 24, 28, 114, 118–19
 and crime films, 143–6
 growing dominance of triad and cop/police films, 146–53
 illegal immigrants as self and other, 153–63
ideology, interplay with genre and auteurism, 57–60
immigration, 153–63
Independent Commission Against Corruption (ICAC), 16, 116, 121, 137, 139, 147, 152, 180
Infernal Affairs, 185
Information Services Department (ISD), 88–9
Inside the Red Brick Wall, 193
In the Face of Demolition, 32, 81
Ironside 426, 148
It's a Wonderful Life, 57

James Bond, 21, 45, 47–8, 51, 65
Jane Bond, 21, 45, 47, 48, 49, 51
jiafa, 147, 150
jianghu, 16, 18, 19–20, 128, 147
jiating lunlipian, 56, 67–8, 70, 71, 74
jingfeipian, 7–8
To, Johnnie, 14, 145, 171
The Joys and Sorrows of Youth, 122–4, **123**
Jumping Ash, 138, 140, 151, 152, 178, 179, 181
Jun Lee, 194
Between Justice and Love, 42, 57–8, 60
justice genres, 7, 20–1; *see also* unofficial justice fighters

Kangxi Emperor, 13
The Kid, 122n
Kidnap, 135–6
The Killer, 188
Kiss of Death, 101
Kong Chi-nam, 147
Kong Ngee film studio, 56, 67, 80
Kuei Chih-hung, 101, 103, 114, 132–5, 137, 139, 140, 153–4, 168, 191
kung fu films, 97–8, 103–4, 114, 117
Kwan Man-ching, 28
Kwan, Stanley, 171
Kwan Tak-hing, 34

Lady Black Cat, 53
Lai, David, 172
Lam Kwok-cheung, 148
Lam, Ringo, 160, 171, 172, 178
Lam Sum, 194–6
Lau, Lawrence, 171, 173–4
Lau Shing-hon, 170, 182
Lau, Stephen, 105
Law Bun, 35
Law, Clara, 171
Law Don, 148, 149–50, **149**
Law, John, 99, 126
Law Kar, 188
Leblanc, Maurice, 63
Lebrun, Pierre, 89, 90, 110, 156
Lee, Bruce, 19, 98
Lee Choi-fat, 148–9
Lee, Danny, 171
Lee Pang-fei, 69, 71
Lee Tit, 21, 27, 32, 38–9, 40–1, 42, 43, 56, 57–61, **59**, 69, 71, 81, 119–20, 138
Leftist Riots 1967, 51–2
Leong Po-chih, 138, 151, 178
Li Han-hsiang, 117
Li Pingqian, 34–5
Liangyou Film Company, 75
liberal (de)colonisation, 22, 84, 110
Lifeline, 87
Lion-Hearted Warriors, 34
Litton, Henry, 88
Lo Duen, 53–4
loengzi, 196
Lo Wei, 51
localisation, 23
  of censorship, 86, 90–1, 110
  of cinema, 114, 127, 163, 167–8, 169
location-shooting, 2, 51, 118, 120, 129, **129**, 143, 168, 182
Lonely Fifteen, 172, 173, 174
Long Arm of the Law III, 161, **162**
Long Arm of the Law series, 143, 153, 154, 159–63, 179
Lost Souls, 157
Love and Hate in Jianghu, 37
Love Massacre, 172
Lu Ping, 63
Luddington, Donald C. C., 101, 106
Lung, Patrick, 42, 43–4, 72, 121, 125–6, **125**, 133, 135, 168, 172, 186, 187, 191, 196
lunlipian, 29, 31–3, 32, 120
  and realist tradition, 38–44, **40**, 55, 56, 69, 113

Ma brothers, 149, 150
Mak, Johnny, 153, 159–60, 161, 163
The Man from Hong Kong, 151
Man Killer of China series, 33n, 34, 64
Man on the Brink, 164, 183, 184–7, **187**
The Mandarin, 103
Mandarin cinema, 28–9, 30, 50–1, 116–17
Manifesto for a Free Hong Kong Cinema, 195–6, 197
maopian, 105
March of the Guerrillas, 87
Marnie, 77
martial arts films, 82–3, 94–5, **95**, 96, 97, 117
masculinity, 16, 18–19
Matsuo Akinori, 51
May You Stay Forever Young, 24, 194–7, **195**
media crossover, 35
melodrama, 11, 21, 29, 31–3, 136, 187
  and crime cinema, 38–9
  melodramatic-redemption cycle, 39–40
  and suspense thrillers, 67–8
Mildred Pierce, 60
Million Dollars Snatch, 138–9, 140, 146, 151–2, 154, 155
Mobfix Patrol, 157
Mok Hong-si, 53
Money, Money, Money, 106
Mong Wan, 64
morality, 67, 91–2
Morgan, W. P., 14
Motion Picture & General Investment Company (MP&GI), 29, 30, 50n, 69
Mou Tun-fei, 127, 139, 154–5, 157, 191
Murayama Mitsuo, 51
Murder on the Beach, 70–1
Murderer in Town, 21, 56, 57–61, **59**
misogyny, 150, 174
The Mystery of the Human Head, **66**

Nakahira Koh, 51
National Security Law 2020, 191–2

The Net of Divine Retribution, 62, **62**
New Hong Kong Cinema, 23, 167–71
New Wave cinema, 2, 12, 23, 163, 164–89
  ambiguous cop thrillers, 178–86, **180**, **183**
  crime, importance of, 164–5
  criminal realism's dominance, ending of, 186–9
  film cultural field, 168–9
  and New Hong Kong Cinema, 167–71
  and normative realism, 169–70
  problem youth films, 171–8, **176**
Ng Cho-fan, 41, 58–9, **59**, 64
Ng See-yuen, 137, 138–9, 146, 154, 172
Ng Sik-ho, 146
Ng Wui, 32, 68, 69, 71, 72, 74–5, 81
The Night the Spirit Returns, 73, 80
999 Grotesque Corpse, 71–2
999 series, 56, **70**
Niu Ge, 37

Once a Thief, 41–2, 60, 188
One-Armed Swordsman, 48–9, 95–6, 97, 117, 127
One by One, 103
Outlaw Genes, 24, 187, 188–9

Pak Yan, 53
Pao Hsueh-li, 128
Payment in Blood, 101, **102**, 103, 132
Places of Public Entertainment Ordinance 1919, 86, 108n
police, 8, 23–4, 42
  attitudes to, 39, 193
  depictions of, 43, 57–61, 71–2, 92, 93, 103, 125–6, 129–30, **131**, 132, 137, 139–40, 144–5, 151–2, 160–1, 175, 178–86, **180**
  see also Hong Kong Police Force
Police Force, 101, 129–30, **131**, 132, 139–40, 151, 152, 179
Police Story, 179
Police Woman, 130
Port of Call, 194
premodern codes, 145
Prison on Fire, 172
problem youth films, 9, 22, 24, 114, 121–6, **123**, **125**, 165, 166–7, 171–8, **176**
The Prodigal, 123
Production Code Administration (PCA), 85

Psycho, 68, 72
Public Relations Office (PRO), 87, 88
pulp fiction-derived films, 11, 21, 29, 48, 55, 113

qiqing, 119–21, 181

Radio Television Hong Kong (RTHK), 108–9
The Rascal Billionaire, 148–9
realism, 2, 11–12, 22, 31–2, 97, 113, 118, 139, 140, 172–3
  normative realism, 169–70
  realist *lunlipian* tradition, 38–44, **40**, 55, 56, 69, 113
  social reality, 2, 11, 39, 82, 140, 170, 182
  subjective realism, 12
  see also criminal realism
Rear Window, 21, 56, 74–81
Rebecca, 74
The Red Detachment of Women, 93
reflectionism, 170
reforming-mentor narrative, 40
remakes, 60–1
  of Hitchcock films, 60, 61, 72–81, *73*, **78**
Ren, Rex, 194–6
Return of the Black Hero, 64
Righting a Wrong with Earthenware Dish, 27
Rock N' Roll Cop, 145
Rope, 72
The Rouge Tigress, 69, 80

Sammo Hung, 117, 167
The Saviour, 181–2
School on Fire, 178
Scorsese, Martin, 109, 151
The Secret, 164, 172
secret agents, 45–6, 49–50, 51
The Servants, 179–81, **180**
set construction, 75
sexual politics, 78–9
Shadow of a Doubt, 57, 72
Shaolin monastery, 13, 16
Shaw Brothers, 11, 12, 22, 29, 30, 49, 50–1, 94–5, 104, 106, 107, 114, 116–17, 118, 127, 139, 140, 141, 147, 168–9
shehui lunlipian, 71
shehui qiqingpian, 22, 113–14, 119, 120–1
Shek Kin, 53

Sherlock Holmes, 63, 71
Shiu, Stephen, 161
Shu Kei, 188
Siao, Josephine, 138, 151, 178
Sima Fu, 63–4
Sima Fu's Encounter with the Honey Gang, 64
Sisters in Crime, 60, 71
Siu, Stanley, 148, 187
Social Characters, 123, 126
social justice warriors, 51–2, **52**
society
  and crime film, 8–10
  social awareness, 43
Southern Film Corporation, 93
The Sparring Partner, 194
Spy with My Face, 47
Star Ferry Riots, 114–15
Stealing a Roasted Duck, 27
Story of a Discharged Prisoner, 38, 41, 42–4, 124, 126, 187, 188
The Story of Woo Viet, 157–8, **158**, 161, 163
The Stowaways, 156
Studio Relations Committee (SRC), 85
Suet Nei, 49
Sun Chung, 127, 139, 140, 147
Sun Liaohong, 45, 63
Superman, 182, **183**
suspense thrillers, 6–7, 10, 21, 55–6
  definition, 67
  genre and studio, 67–72
  and horror films, 68
  and melodrama, 67–8
synthetic criticism, 57
The System, 181, 182, **183**

Tam, Patrick, 172
Tang, Alan, 105, 140, 145, 148, **149**, 150, 157
Tang Ching, 51
Tang Huang, 36, 37
Tang Shu-shuen, 155–6, 168
Taxi Driver, 109–10, 151
The Teahouse, 104, 127, 132–3, 147, 153–4
Teddy Girls, 43, 125–6, **125**, 133, 172, 173, 196
Television and Entertainment Licensing Authority (TELA), 90
The Tenants of Talkative Street, 104

Theatres Regulation Ordinance 1908, 86
Tong, Terry, 187, 188
Tradition, 35, 36–7, 38, 128, 145
Treasure Hunt, 42
triad films, 8, 22–3, 132–3, 141, 142, 144, 144–5, 173–4, 178, 188
  growing dominance, 146–53, **149**
  numbers films, 148
  and traditional values, 147, 150, 173
triads, 10, 144
  affinities with police, 19
  mythology and history, 13–16
  and recruitment of young people, 173–4, 178
true crime films, 119, 135–40, 146, 159, 194
Tsai Yang-ming, 129, 151
Tsang, Kenneth, 50
Tse, Patrick, 43, 50, 66–7
Tso Kea, 69, 71
Tso Tat-wah, 21, 56, 64–6, **66**, 69
Tsui Hark, 167, 174, 175–8, 191, 196

Umetsugu, Inoue, 51
Underground Express, 161–2
Union Film Enterprises, 41, 59, 69
  unofficial justice fighters, 44–54, **46**, **52**, 61, 62–3
The Unwritten Law, 172

Vertigo, 73, 74, 77, 80, 172
victims, 31, 32, 38–9, 67
vigilantes, 44, 133
voyeurism, 77–8

Wang, Jimmy, 97
Wang Yin, 37
Wang Yuan-long, 36
The Warriors, 174
Watt, Nigel J. V., 88–91, **89**, 96, 104, 105, 108, 109–10
The Way of the Dragon, 98
The Way We Keep Dancing, 194
Wayne, John, 66
We Want to Live, 38–9, 40, **40**, 43, 57, 58, 59–60, 138
wen-wu dyad, 18–19
We're Going to Eat You, 177
White-Dappled Snake, 47

The Window, 43, 124
Wing-Scope, 148–50
women, 35, 36–7, 45, 47–8, 51, 53–4, 150
Wong, Adam, 194
Wong Chung, 132, 157
Wong, Kirk, 164, 187–8
Wong Yiu, 42
Woo, John, 2, 24, 41, 43, 142, 145, 165–6, 171, 186, 188
Wu Lai-chu, 28, 47
wu masculinity, 16, 18–19
Wu Song, 19

Xiao Ping, 46
xieshipian, 29, 31–3; *see also* realism

Yam Pang-nin, 27–8
Yam Wu-fa, 33, 48, 64

Yan Ruisheng, 27, 28
Yau, Herman, 87, 155–6
Yee Chau-shui, 74
Yellow Giant, 47
Yellow Oriole, 45–7, 61, 65
Yeung Kuen, 146, 152
yi/yiqi, 18, 133, 134
Yim Ho, 174–5
yingxiong, 19
Young People, 127
Yu, Dennis, 172
Yu, Ronny, 179, 181
Yu So-chau, 47, 65
Yu Tsong, 106–7
Yung, Peter, 182
Yung, Philip, 194

Zen, Rachel, 173

EU representative:
Easy Access System Europe
Mustamäe tee 50, 10621 Tallinn, Estonia
Gpsr.requests@easproject.com

www.ingramcontent.com/pod-product-compliance
Lightning Source LLC
Chambersburg PA
CBHW051120160426
43195CB00014B/2279